PULPIT IN PARLIAMENT

Pulpit in Parliament

Puritanism during the
English Civil Wars
1640-1648

BY JOHN F. WILSON

Princeton
University Press
Princeton, N.J.
1969

For

Ursula and Reinhold Niebuhr

PREFACE

WHILE IN London during the academic year 1958-1959, I attempted to study Puritanism in the early Stuart period, concentrating especially on the two decades following 1630. As a consequence, "puritan studies" increasingly became a source of disillusionment to me. Far from proving to be a subject which might be illuminated through interdisciplinary approaches, it began to seem as though no common material was involved and that four or five rather unrelated families of disciplines were represented. Some scholars were interested in social history, others in "classical" political history; each construed subject matter and approach in vastly different ways. Students of literature understood Puritanism to be something scarcely recognizable to denominationally oriented church historians—Anglican or free church. Questions raised by those concerned with political theory seemed to bear no connection, at least in significant ways, to any of the foregoing groupings. There are obvious exceptions to this lamentable situation, for some studies do exhibit extraordinary sensitivity to many dimensions of the phenomenon. In general, however, the multiplicity of approaches and the diverse definitions of the subject which have come to characterize "puritan studies" seem to have more confused than clarified our perception of Puritanism.

In a central respect these interdisciplinary interests have constituted a movement directly at odds with the goal intended, and the development of "puritan studies" has issued in an ironic outcome. The essential claim made by the puritans was that their faith rendered intelligible *all* of their experience, even those aspects not manifestly religious. Through their procedures, however, students and interpreters have sought to understand especially individual puritans, but also by extension Puritanism itself, precisely in terms of external relationships and usually without remainder. Thus, regularly, scholars have failed to give attention to the character and claims of the subject. In this way the most distinctive element of Puritanism, that which defined it as a movement for those who participated in and were identified with it, has been systematically excluded from much serious study of the subject. It has become increasingly difficult to identify Puritanism or to define it in any widely acceptable sense—this, despite the assertion by puritans that their common faith provided them with their "identities." The proliferating approaches to the puritans, intrinsically valuable as they may have been, in this manner have worked toward a nominalistic conclusion, namely, that, although individuals might properly be denominated "puritans," Puritanism as such was not a fruitful topic for study. This position may have appeal for antiquarians, but it would seem to be untenable for historians concerned with generalization and interpretation.[1]

During the course of that year devoted to research at the British Museum and Dr. Williams's Library, I became intrigued with a series of sermons originally preached by invitation to members of the Long Parliament at periodic fasts and occasional thanksgivings. For some reason this series had never been extensively analyzed, yet it seemed to represent precisely the sort of subject which ought to be. Turning it to account would make possible a review of Puritanism during the civil war period which would avoid the nominalism described above while also demonstrating the need for interrelationships among historical, literary, religious, and political approaches to puritan studies. In a subsequent dissertation entitled "Studies in Puritan Millenarianism under the Early Stuarts,"[2] I made use of materials from the early years of the preaching program. A full-length analysis of the phenomenon, however, required much more attention than could there be paid to it.

The present work, which expands and refines my earlier effort, is an attempt to provide that analysis. Chapter II

[1] For a recent discussion of attempts to define Puritanism, see Basil Hall, "Puritanism: the Problem of Definition," in *Studies in Church History*, II, ed. G. J. Cuming (London, 1965), 283-296. Also useful is a monograph by John F.H. New, *Anglican and Puritan* (Stanford, 1964).

[2] (Th.D. diss., Union Theological Seminary, New York, 1962.)

supplies the needed review of background and sources, while the third chapter undertakes a narrative study of the institution during the 1640's. Next follows an impressionistic discussion of the sponsors sitting in the parliament, together with a fuller scrutiny of the preachers in this pulpit. Chapter V looks at the published sermons as part of a distinctive literary tradition of religious exhortations and takes up the scriptural texts on which they were based. The following chapter exploits the "plain style" in order to analyze the "doctrine" (that is, formal teaching) which was collectively present in the sermons to the Long Parliament. Chapter VII, the last, seeks to reveal what the preaching indicates about the development of Puritanism during this decade of civil war.

Pulpit in Parliament thus fails to fit exclusively into any of the genres mentioned above. It does place emphasis on religious questions—but fundamentally because that seems to be required by the subject. The puritans maintained that their theological conceptions made the world intelligible for them, and their sermons represented a distinctive tradition of religious literature. At the same time, the issues of the civil wars were centrally present as the context for these exhortations. About "denominational" matters very little will be said, although attention is focused on the breakdown of the puritan brotherhood during this decade. In sum, I should like to think that some justice has been done to the rich and suggestive phenomenon which is present in the humiliations and thanksgivings undertaken by the Long Parliament and which is available for historical study in the numerous published sermons.

A Fulbright grant, together with a traveling fellowship provided by Union Theological Seminary, made possible the original year of study in England. Subsequently support from Princeton University (as well as several leaves) enabled me to return for further research. In the United States the McAlpin Collection at Union Theological Seminary was my chief resource, although the holdings of the Firestone Library, Princeton University, and the Speer Library,

Preface

Princeton Theological Seminary, have both proved invaluable to me. Personally I am much indebted to Dr. R. W. Greaves of Bedford College, London, who has graciously assisted more than one Fulbright student, and to Dr. G. F. Nuttall of New College, London, who extended frequent and much-valued assistance to a younger scholar. Professor Robert T. Handy of Union Theological Seminary was unfailingly a wise and patient counselor at early stages, and more recently I have benefited from the puritan learning of my senior colleague, Professor Horton M. Davies. In the preparation of this study Mr. Daniel A. Kiger helped me at a critical stage, and Mrs. Marthe Cella, Mrs. Denise Landry, and Mrs. Julie Lentze typed long sections. Mr. Sanford Thatcher of Princeton University Press, who served as editor of my manuscript, knows how indebted I am to him. Of course, none of the above, or others, are responsible for errors or mistakes. Finally, my wife and our four children have been long suffering with a husband and father preoccupied with these and other matters.

John F. Wilson

Princeton, New Jersey
January 1, 1969

CONTENTS

Preface   vii

I. Preaching in the Long Parliament   3

II. The Genesis of the Commons Preaching
       Program   22

III. The Program of Humiliations and
       Thanksgivings   60

IV. Parliamentary Sponsors and the
       Puritan Preachers   98

V. The Plain Style and Puritan Texts   137

VI. Puritan Piety for a Covenanted Nation   166

VII. Puritanism in the Time of Civil War   197

Appendix One: Calendar and Checklist of
       Humiliations, Thanksgivings, and Preachers in
       the Long Parliament   237

Appendix Two: Calendar of Printed Sermons
       Preached to Members of the Long
       Parliament   255

Appendix Three: Sermons Preached to Sundry of
       the House of Commons, 1641   275

Index   281

PULPIT IN PARLIAMENT

"Because the Lord who is just, is also Mercifull, and
in his infinite Mercy hath left the excellent
and successfull remedy of Repentance to Nations
brought neer to the Gates of Destruction and despaire,
O let not England be negligent in the
application of it."

—*An Ordinance of the Lords and Commons . . .*[1]

I

Preaching in the Long Parliament

IN *BEHEMOTH* Thomas Hobbes proposed that the decades between 1640 and 1660 might be taken as the "highest of time" in which was concentrated all manner of social disorder. To survey it was like being set upon a veritable "Devils Mountain" from which there was available "a Prospect of all kinds of Injustice, and of all kinds of Folly that the World could afford."[2] Accordingly, his review of the "causes" of the English civil wars became a study in the subversion of, and eventual return to, established order. Hobbes's point of departure was a basic question: how had it been possible for a stable country to be reduced to virtual chaos when it boasted a six hundred-year-old monarchy secured by enough trained soldiers to constitute an army numbering sixty thousand (which was equipped with "divers Magazines of Ammunition in places fortified")?[3] He concluded that only the corruption and seduction of the people could explain this utter breakdown of authority and power. Clearly seducers of "divers sorts" had been at work; chief among them, in Hobbes's estimation, were "Ministers (as they call'd themselves) of Christ."[4] The theme of "presbyterian" perfidy runs throughout the extended

[1] *An Ordinance of the Lords and Commons Assembled in Parliament, Exhorting all his Majesties good subjects in the Kingdome of England, and Dominion of Wales, to the duty of Repentance, (as the onely remedy for their present Calamities) with an earnest Confession, and deepe Humiliation for all particular and Nationall Sins, that so at length we may obtaine a firme and happy Peace both with God and Man. Die Mercurii,* Feb. 15, 1642 (London, 1642), A₂ *recto.*

[2] *Behemoth, The History of the Causes of the Civil-Wars of England,* in *Tracts of Mr. Thomas Hobbs of Malmsbury* (London, 1682), 1f.

[3] *Ibid.,* 3.

[4] *Ibid.,* 4.

dialogue. At various points he termed the ministers "seditious," specifically accusing them of preaching rebellion from their pulpits. He also viewed them as endowed with a "histrionique faculty" and directly linked them with "Ambitious Ignorant Orators."[5] That such men should have been permitted to exercise great influence within the body politic was manifestly, in Hobbes's opinion, one of the basic "causes" of the turmoil England had suffered.

The argument Hobbes advanced, that puritan ministers had been instrumental in the subversion of the realm, combined at least two judgments. In the first place, he estimated the degree of influence which they exercised within the realm. It had been, he asserted, so significant as to have constituted a chief cause of the civil wars. His other judgment concerned the manner or effective mode through which their influence was exerted. He believed that the puritans were primarily distinguished by their activity as preachers, that is, as propagandists. Hobbes's argument, of course, was based upon a conjunction of these "observations." During the last thirty years of the present century, major studies of puritan materials have offered related arguments, interpreted, however, within markedly different contexts.

Several generations of students interested in Puritanism have been instructed by the writings of William Haller. *The Rise of Puritanism* has been an extraordinarily influential study on both shores of the Atlantic, representing as it does the way in which clerical puritans were effective within Stuart England primarily as publicists and preachers. Its sequel has interpreted the "Puritan Revolution" as well from that point of view.[6] Contemporary with Haller's earlier study was a new edition of the important Army Debates (1647-1649), including an extended essay-introduction (together with supplementary documents) by A.S.P. Wood-

---

[5] See *ibid.*, 38ff., 65, 80-81, 104-105, 177, 237, 262.
[6] *The Rise of Puritanism* (New York, 1938); *Liberty and Reformation in the Puritan Revolution* (New York, 1955).

house.[7] By implication *Puritanism and Liberty* also stressed the importance of the sermon and the religious tract as critical to an understanding of the relationship between English Puritanism and the public realm of politics. These authors, and those who have followed them, have emphasized—though not narrowly—the direct and indirect contributions made by Puritanism to that "freedom" which is cherished within modern liberal society.

Within the last decade there has been renewed interest in the connection between religious Puritanism and revolutionary behavior during the period of civil war and the Interregnum. Christopher Hill, for instance, while arguing against designation of the era as the "Puritan Revolution," nevertheless has underscored the radical engagement of the religious movement with the developing English society.[8] Hugh R. Trevor-Roper, for his part, has pointed up the continuing clerical presence and participation in the political struggles of the epoch.[9] Another author, Michael Walzer, has undertaken to represent the puritans as ideologues of a "revolution of the saints."[10] No less than in William Haller's work, the significance of the puritan sermon and the religious tract is acknowledged in these studies. Preaching especially has been recognized as important in effecting the purposes of the reforming party within the Church of England. Although some of these authors might draw back from Hobbes's judgment that puritan propagandistic activity was a chief "cause" of the civil wars, all of them (and others as well) would seem to concur that

---

[7] *Puritanism and Liberty* (London, 1938).

[8] Thus in the course of his argument Hill asserts that "religion was the idiom in which the men of the seventeenth century thought." "Recent Interpretations of the Civil War," in *Puritanism and Revolution* (London, 1958), 3-31 (the quotation is from page 29). See also his subsequent *Society and Puritanism in Pre-Revolutionary England* (London, 1964).

[9] Especially relevant to the present study is "The Fast Sermons of the Long Parliament," in *The Crisis of the Seventeenth Century* (New York, 1968), 294-344—hereafter cited as "Fast Sermons."

[10] *The Revolution of the Saints* (Cambridge, Mass., 1965); see also "Puritanism as a Revolutionary Ideology," *History and Theory*, III/1 (1963), 59-90.

preaching had a crucial impact and was without question one dominant mode of puritan influence, particularly during the 1640's.

In view of this widespread agreement about the importance of the sermon as a vehicle for puritan influence, it is surprising that comparatively little attention has been directed to that literature as a *particular type of source* (insofar as it is accessible) specifically useful in study of the decade of civil war and valuable for interpretation of Puritanism as a religious movement. Consideration of this material is, of course, implicit in many of the studies already cited, as well as in others. Godfrey Davies, for example, apparently had this subject in mind when drafting the article he entitled "English Political Sermons, 1603-40."[11] Leo Solt recognized that the preaching of the chaplains in the New Model Army constituted a discrete body of material.[12] There have been no critical surveys of the preaching of the Civil War period, however, nor any major systematic attempts to study puritan preaching more generally in relationship to the public realm.[13]

Putting aside the vexing question of the precise degree to which the clerics exerted influence, the present monograph directs attention to the second aspect of Hobbes's argument, specifically his judgment about the character and content of puritan political preaching during the civil wars. The intention underlying this investigation is to offer reasonably secure generalizations about the terms in which puritans, as members of a relatively coherent religious movement, understood the revolutionary political epoch which has taken their name. As a result, we may gain

[11] *The Huntington Library Quarterly*, III/1 (Oct. 1939), 1-22.

[12] *Saints in Arms* (Stanford, 1959). In this study the author argues that "authoritarian" as well as "democratic" strains were present in Puritanism.

[13] On puritan preaching in general, see J. Brown, *Puritan Preaching in England* (New York, 1900), Chs. III and IV (67-128); also H. Davies, *The Worship of the English Puritans* (Westminster, 1948), Ch. XI (182-203). For useful background, see C. F. Richardson, *English Preachers and Preaching: 1640-1670* (New York, 1928).

some insight into their conception(s) of the relationship between the movement to which they belonged and the political events of the period. The specific subject matter to be considered is the preaching of puritan divines (mainly members of the Westminster Assembly) to the Long Parliament (primarily the House of Commons). In all there are available a series of approximately two hundred and forty published sermons dating from the decade of the 1640's in which the chief clerical members of the puritan movement, at the invitation of the houses of parliament, preached to the latter largely in the context of formal fasts of humiliation and thanksgiving celebrations for the common cause. These provide a unique opportunity to examine how the constitutive members of the puritan movement conceived of the social crisis and advocated responses to it. Thus the sermons give access not only to individual interpretations of events within the period but, more important, to a collective and (to some degree) officially authorized construction of the "times."

Collectively the formal preaching before members of the Long Parliament was extensive in scope and internally diverse. At one level this study simply attempts to chronicle the development of the preaching institution. Beyond this, however, considerable attention will be given to the content of the sermons which actually reached print. The latter constitute separate classes which reflect different types of occasions on which sermons were delivered. A brief review of these classes will indicate both the scope of the institution and the dimensions of the literature under analysis.

MINOR CLASSES. A small proportion of the parliamentary sermons reaching print originated under certain definite sets of circumstances. Five minor groups, which include some twenty published exhortations, may be identified.

1. *Opening sermons.* A few sermons were authorized at the beginning of the Long Parliament, essentially as a continuation of practices established in previous parliaments. Under James and Charles preaching to parliament had

been related to the administration of the sacrament as a test of loyalty. This development is traced in the following chapter, for in many respects it anticipated and probably made possible the remarkable program of authorized fast and thanksgiving preaching which became prominent within the Long Parliament.

2. *Sermons to sundry members.* Another group of printed sermons originated at occasions which appear to have been organized by some members of the Long Parliament during the spring of 1641 and which were probably confined to a three-month period of that year. This class, unlike the others under consideration, was not officially sponsored by either one or both of the houses. In at least certain cases, however, the publication of these exhortations was permitted by a committee of Commons, and the circumstance of their delivery to "sundry of the House of Commons" was frankly advertised.

3. *Powder Plot sermons.* Annual sermons commemorating Guy Fawkes Day or the "Powder Plot" were a regular feature of the Long Parliament. These occasions were used by the preachers to rehearse the alleged threats from "Rome," a theme generally accented throughout the preaching before parliament.

4. *Covenanting sermons.* The parliamentary agreement to the Solemn League and Covenant with Scotland, and subscription to it on the part of individual members, provided several occasions for preaching during the late summer and early fall of 1643. The Covenant itself (as well as the sermons at the ceremonies for its solemnization) was closely related to the overall program.

5. *State funerals.* A very few published sermons were originally delivered at state funerals for prominent or commanding figures in the parliamentary cause, especially Pym and Essex. This class merges into funeral orations for individuals of lesser stature.

MAJOR CLASSES. The published sermons which constitute the preceding five classes will be considered, when appropriate, in the course of the succeeding chapters. The basic material under discussion in this monograph, however, falls into three additional classes, each of which is numerically far larger than the minor groups taken singly or together. The existence of these major classes of printed exhortations provides the *raison d'être* for this study.

1. *Monthly Commons fast sermons.* The basic and most extensive series of sermons was delivered to the formal and regular monthly fasts which were instituted by the House of Commons early in 1642 (N.S.) explicitly as a response to the aggravated Irish crisis. Charles initially authorized the establishment of these fasts, and their celebration was, nominally at least, extended to the realm at large. One hundred and twenty-nine published sermons are included in this, the predominant class.

2. *Monthly Lords fast sermons.* Although it appears that from the first the Lords may have observed the monthly fasts, at least informally, their practice was rendered explicit and thus fully parallel to that of the lower house only in October 1644. Thereafter publication of these sermons was also invited, though marked by a response less regular than that which greeted those delivered to Commons. Thus the class of sermons originating from the Lords regular fasts appears to have been, fundamentally, a duplication of the Commons program. Thirty-six published exhortations represent this group.

3. *Exhortations to occasional fasts and thanksgivings.* Throughout the decade special humiliations and thanksgiving celebrations were authorized in response to the particular fortunes of the parliamentary cause. During the major military campaigns toward the climax of the first civil war, these fasts and feasts became remarkably frequent. Often the Lords joined the lower house in these affairs if the upper house did not sponsor its own. At times other appropriate authorities participated—the Westminster Assembly and the Lord Mayor of London, for example. On some few occasions one house appears to have organized a separate humiliation or thanksgiving. Fifty-three printed sermons belong to this class.

Preaching to parliament at formal fasts continued into the 1650's; indeed, the practice may be traced to the Restoration, although by then it was taking place on an irregular basis and at a greatly reduced rate. But 1648 was the last year during which a significant number of the sermons delivered actually reached print. In critical respects the death of Charles in January 1648-9 represents the most useful terminus for intensive study of the institution. At about the same time the House of Lords was abolished and Commons purged. Coincidentally a pronounced shift had occurred in the identities of those who did preach, and a striking decrease in the frequency of printing may be noted. Shortly thereafter the regular fast institution was entirely suppressed, and an effort was made to control political preaching. These several related and contemporary developments render less fruitful comparative study of the preaching beyond that point.

By way of summary it will be helpful to compare briefly the extent of the various groups of sermons which have been identified. The critical determination is the total number of sermons in the several classes, including those not published as well as—and this seems unlikely—any which may have been lost. The minor classes, excluding the series of informal fast sermons from 1641, comprise twelve printed sermons, in addition to which—according to evidence in the *Journals of the House of Commons*—several more were actually delivered, although apparently not printed. Besides the one hundred and twenty-nine printed sermons from the regular monthly Commons fast days, *at least* thirty-nine more which appear not to have been published are referred to in the *Journals*. *At least* eighty-six (possibly as many as one hundred and four) exhortations were originally delivered to the upper house at regular fasts between October 1644 and January 31, 1648-9 (the last ones preached). Of these, thirty-six are presently available in print. The formal extraordinary fasts and feasts are represented by fifty-three sermons out of *at least* eighty-seven (and probably more) originally delivered.

Excluding the informal fast sermons (regarding which there are no means available to estimate the size of the class), approximately sixty-five percent—and probably no less than sixty percent—of the sermons delivered during the fast program appear to have been printed. The percentage for the numerically dominant monthly Commons humiliations is remarkably higher—above seventy-five percent. This is evidence of how important the monthly exhortations to the House of Commons are for any study such as this one.

Insofar as attention is directed to published sermons, then, preaching before Commons (especially in the monthly fast sermons) stands out as particularly prominent. It should be emphasized that this importance follows from both the nature of the institution and the available published materials. The Lords did sit for exhortations, at least occasionally, prior to the fall of 1644.[14] Not until that time did they finally move to adopt the regular fast day practices already developed by the House of Commons (including formal designation of the preachers with the expectation that they would be invited to publish their efforts). For this reason the published sermons which had originally been preached to Commons constitute a far more extensive sequence than those which had first been delivered to the Lords. Furthermore, in general the same individuals, chiefly members of the Westminster Assembly, preached before both houses. Thus the program, when actually adopted by the Lords, and the corps of participating preachers as well were basically common to the parliament as a whole. Frequently, too, as has been indicated, the extraordinary fasts or feasts were joint affairs, usually initiated by the lower house. In addition to these points, the primacy of the preaching program to Commons reflects a general and increasing reduction in the influence of the Lords, as well as a centering of strategic considerations in the other house. The analysis of the content of preaching before the Long Parliament undertaken in subsequent chap-

14 See, e.g., *Thomas Cheshire, A Sermon Preached at . . . Westminster . . . before the Lords, and Judges . . .* (London, 1642).

ters, therefore, will necessarily place emphasis upon the fast sermons to Commons. This concentration might appear disproportionate were the above circumstances not pointed out beforehand.

The following chapters examine in considerable detail the institution of formal preaching before the houses of parliament at stated fasts and feasts during the civil wars. The genesis and development of parliamentary preaching will be discussed, and the course and characteristics of the program in the Long Parliament will be reviewed. Attention will be given to the participants. The literary form and the manifest teaching of the sermons will also be considered. Finally, the sermons will be surveyed for the purpose of determining their significance for the interpretation of Puritanism. What must be stressed in this introduction is that the formal preaching institution analyzed in this study did not constitute the only, and probably not the most direct and effective, means through which clerical puritan influence played upon the representatives of England sitting at Westminster.

Above all, it is clear that individual clergymen were frequent companions and close advisers to men in authority or persons holding power. Passing mention will be made of puritan preachers who came to London as chaplains to members of parliament. Clarendon, for example, unequivocally registered the effectiveness of Cornelius Burges and Stephen Marshall. His protest serves as a reminder that puritan clergymen represented an everyday presence at Westminster and played significant roles in the course of events:

[The] reformation [of the Bishops' prerogatives on the grounds that "their intermeddling with temporal affairs was inconsistent with, and destructive to, the exercise of their spiritual function"] . . . was driven on by no men so much as those of the clergy who were their instruments; as, without doubt, the archbishop of Canterbury had never so great an influence upon the counsels at

Court as Dr. Burgess and Mr. Marshall had then upon the Houses. . . .[15]

Other clerics clearly gained in influence with well-placed persons through service with the parliamentary forces.[16]

It is also evident that a remarkable volume of puritan preaching was directed to the members of the houses. A few of the published sermons in particular help one to imagine the immense number of exhortations which must have been delivered in and around Westminster during the decade, sermons aimed more or less exclusively at England's representatives in the Long Parliament. One example reaching print was originally a "Sunday sermon" preached at St. Margaret's, Westminster, by John Marston on February 6, 1641-2, "before many of the worthy members of the Honourable House of Commons in this Present Parliament." It was advertised as "printed upon the importunity of many auditors." The preacher compared his times with those of Judea reported in Joel 2:12-13a. He concluded that turning to God would settle the kingdom.[17] Another example is *A Sermon Preached at Westminster before Sundry of the House of Commons*[18] by Sidrach Simpson, who also participated in the formal fasts. It was dedicated to John, Lord Roberts, with the date October 16, 1643. Taking as his text Proverbs 8:15-16, Simpson extolled the importance of religion for the state. Undoubtedly groups of members sitting in the Long Parliament were exhorted on innumerable occasions at different locations and under various circumstances. Some of these sermons may

15 Clarendon, *History of the Rebellion*, ed. W. D. McCray (Oxford, 1888), IV, 34 (I, 401). See also Trevor-Roper, "Fast Sermons," *passim*, for references to the role taken by these and other puritan preachers.

16 Leo Solt's study, *Saints in Arms*, cited above, bears on this phenomenon.

17 *A Sermon Preached* . . . (London, 1642), 43.

18 (London, 1643). If this sermon is the one referred to by Alexander Gordon in the *Dictionary of National Biography* (London, Oxford, 1882-) —hereafter cited as *DNB*—it is difficult to accept his conclusion that it was originally preached in 1642, particularly since he gives no grounds for this conclusion.

have been published, but the vast majority certainly were not. Since it is difficult even to estimate the dimensions of this phenomenon, comment about these kinds of preaching to parliament could be only trivial, and any conclusions reached would be basically hypothetical.

Notice has been taken of the informal exhortations which were preached to "sundry members of the House of Commons" prior to the establishment of periodic fasts in February 1641-2. In certain respects this suggests that edification, probably radical in temper, was readily available early in the parliament, possibly on a regular basis.

The most significant and influential preaching was certainly that which in some fashion Commons immediately sponsored; it seems to have been a remarkable feature of the Long Parliament. On certain occasions the lower house directly authorized the delivery of specific sermons. One example is revealed through an incident related in the *Verney Papers,* which may also be traced in the *Journals of the House of Commons.*[19] On August 7, 1641, Commons resolved to meet at 6 a.m. on the following day (Sunday) in St. Margaret's, and it was also determined that Edmund Calamy would preach to them. Pressing business absorbed their time, so that on the afternoon of the eighth the following minute was recorded: "Mr. Venn is desired, in regard the House cannot, by reason of their many Occasions, hear a Sermon at this time, to thank the Minister for his Patience, and to discharge him."[20] An apology was then subscribed for sitting in session on the Lord's Day. This procedure illustrates the manner in which the house arranged to be exhorted on an *ad hoc* basis—and could presume the willing cooperation of the puritan clergymen congregated around London.

---

[19] John Bruce (ed.), *The Verney Papers* (Camden Society, 1845), 112-115; *Journals of the House of Commons,* II, 244ff.—hereafter cited as *CJ.*

[20] *CJ,* 246. Apparently on the basis of a reference in *Diurnal Occurrences,* S. R. Gardiner erroneously assumed that Calamy preached on August 8 as scheduled. *The History of England, 1603-1642* (London, 1884), IX, 415.

Preaching in the Long Parliament

A more dramatic illustration of the same kind has been noted by H. R. Trevor-Roper. Apparently a special fast was hurriedly arranged for December 8, 1648, immediately following Pride's Purge and the seizure of the King. Stephen Marshall, Joseph Caryl, and Hugh Peter were the preachers. These sermons, unfortunately, appear not to have been printed—understandably, since it is evident that they must have been immediately relevant to the internal discipline of Commons.[21] Thus one concludes that instant fasts, no less than instant exhortations, were important features of the Long Parliament.

An example of a slightly different sort is William Bray's *A Sermon of the Blessed Sacrament of the Lord's Supper,* published in 1641. David Clark has pointed out that it was identified on the title page of at least one version as "preached by order of Parliament at St. Margaret's, April 11, 1641, in order to renounce the licensing of Pocklington's books." Subsequently it was "Printed by order of Parliament." Clark interprets this sermon in the context of the continuing "Altar Controversy" and detects Bishop John Williams's influence in it.[22]

These *ad hoc* sermons and fasts seem to represent obvious cases of that "tuning" of the parliamentary pulpit which has intrigued Trevor-Roper.[23] Whether the purpose served was that of enunciating political policies, rallying party support during critical episodes, or resolving controversies such as that regarding the altar, the utility of the preaching to the Long Parliament is evident. It is not so clear, however, as this monograph will attempt to demonstrate, that this single perspective either adequately brings into focus the fast and feast institution or reveals the significance of the parliamentary pulpit for the interpretation of Stuart Puritanism in its relationship to the public realm. Puritan rhetoric may have directly served political

---

21 Trevor-Roper, "Fast Sermons," 331f.
22 "The Altar Controversy in Early Stuart England" (Th.D. diss., Harvard Divinity School, Cambridge, Mass., 1967), 537ff.
23 "Fast Sermons," *passim.*

purposes, but to view it simply in terms of its immediate political consequences is to ignore the more interesting questions about what kind of intelligibility it brought to political events for those who used it. In short, such a procedure entails a consistent failure to perceive the role of religious language as a bearer of meaning through symbolism, even when its immediate political function is explicitly acknowledged under a conception of "ideology."[24]

By contrast to these specific exhortations, Commons also authorized at least several sets of scheduled sermons which made the puritan pulpit prominent in the common life of the parliament. During the fall of 1643, for example, a provision was made that regular preaching be available for members of Commons. The *Journals* reports that on October 25 the Recorder, Mr. Wheeler, and Mr. Bell were charged to obtain preachers for St. Margaret's on the afternoon of the "Lord's-days."[25] Apparently in implementation of this task, they were instructed on November 29 to bring in an ordinance which would sequester the profits from the vicarage of the parish church to provide for an able minister to preach there, presumably for the edification of the members.[26] In what seems to have been unrelated to this arrangement for Sunday-afternoon preaching, the minutes of February 28, 1643-4, report "That in the Place of the Service read every Day in the Abbey of Westminster, Mr. Marshall, Mr. Palmer, Mr. Hearle, Dr. Stanton, Mr. Nie, Mr. Whitacre, and Mr. Hill, be desired to keep an Exercise for half an Hour every Morning to end at Eight of the Clock."[27] Thomas Case may have been referring to a development out of this practice when, during a formal sermon on April 9, 1644, he alluded to a lecture at Westminster "every morning at six of the Clock."[28] A still further provision for regular preaching seems to have dated from June 1647 when Commons explicitly arranged

---

[24] Cf. Clifford Geertz, "Ideology as a Cultural System," in *Ideology and Discontent*, ed. David Apter (New York, 1964), 47-76.
[25] *CJ*, III, 288.   [26] *Ibid.*, 324.   [27] *Ibid.*, 410.
[28] *The Root of Apostacy* (London, 1644), 33.

for Wednesday exhortations. The house met officially after
the sermon (s), listened to prayer, and heard a recital of
the "heads of the sermon."[29]

It would be surprising if these different sets of provisions
actually represented all the kinds of ingeniously contrived
situations under which clerical puritans regularly preached
to members of the Long Parliament. Furthermore, it is unlikely that some of the latters' tastes for sermons (whatever
different uses they may have served) were wholly satisfied
by the above arrangements.

Obviously Commons did not unanimously support com-
pulsory edification. Members grew restive even under the
comparatively moderate discipline of the formal occasions
to be surveyed in this monograph. During December of
1643, to cite an example, some members of Commons were
charged with "dining and being in a Tavern, most Part of
the Time that the House was solemnizing the [Monthly]
Fast, this last Day of Humiliation."[30] By February the
house ordered "That all the Members . . . do, upon the
Days of publick Humiliation, join with the rest of the
Members, in observing that Day at St. Margaret's, Westminster."[31] Under these circumstances it is difficult to
imagine that the offenders took advantage of the provisions
discussed above for additional and informal opportunities
to hear puritan exhortations. It is manifest, however—and
this is the basic point—that, in studying the formal preaching at the fasts and feasts which reached print, it must be
set against a background of frequent and influential relationships between the puritan clerics and members of the
Long Parliament. These relationships ranged from counsel
and service, through a multitude of informal exhortations,
to the regular and formal preaching engagements here under
review.

It is critical to recognize, therefore, that the present study
is offered as an analysis of the program of preaching before
the members of parliament at formal humiliations and

[29] *CJ*, v, 200f., 203, 209.   [30] *Ibid.*, III, 353.   [31] *Ibid.*, 410.

thanksgivings which took place between 1640 and 1649. This did not represent, it ought to be clear, the full scope of preaching before the members. (The preceding paragraphs will have indicated the dimensions of that broader phenomenon, as well the difficulties entailed in securing evidence about it.) The formal subject of this inquiry, then, is not the clerical puritan influence in the councils of the Long Parliament, nor is it the actual effectiveness of that movement within the politics of the period, or the separate issue of its manifest and latent social roles or functions. The data examined here could not provide answers to such questions, and the frame of reference adopted could not register them. Still, though this study is restricted to the authorized pulpit and rigorously controlled by that principle, it is possible to offer other sorts of limited generalizations with some confidence.

In this perspective the present monograph is basically an inquiry into the common mind of the leading clerical puritans in their formal preaching to the Long Parliament. That preaching was their attempt to render intelligible for themselves and for the parliament the period of civil strife which they collectively experienced. Interest is directed especially toward the symbols by means of which the preachers construed their "times." Thus emphasis naturally falls upon certain characteristics of Puritanism: its biblicism and its utilization of corporate categories for interpretation of the social crisis. These themes will be woven as threads throughout the fabric of the present study.

As a movement for a Reformed Protestant Christian England, Puritanism was not really an impulse of one book, but rather of one *authoritative* book.[32] Puritan thought and action were thus not only informed by the Bible but molded by it also. The many approaches to Puritanism undertaken in recent years by students of the movement have exhibited the richness, diversity, and comprehensiveness that characterized it, in vivid contrast, for exam-

---

[32] Cf. Alan Simpson, *Puritanism in Old and New England* (Chicago, 1955), esp. Ch. 1: "The Puritan Thrust," 1-18.

ple, with later denominational Protestantism. In this regard the movement was medieval in the sense of "com-
prehensively traditional." The puritan had a breadth of
concern and interest which made him truly worldly. His
faith informed, actively, all facets of his individual and social life. But normative to the entire experience was one
authoritative book—the Bible.

Readers may despair at this last statement and protest
that much scholarly ink has been spilt to prove that the
puritans were not presuppositionless in reading the scriptures. Many assumed that a formal "covenant theology"
was implicit in the Old and New Testaments, a mode of
thinking perhaps better understood as related to social
changes of the later middle ages rather than as directly derived from the life of Israel in Palestine and the ancient
literature preserved by that people. Many more puritans
read sacred writ in terms of a formal logic far removed from
"Hebraic modes of thought." To be sure, this point is acknowledged by any intelligent student of puritan literature. It is equally important to recognize, however, that
these technical tools were the *means*—and, most important,
consciously chosen means—to the deeper and living end of
articulating the biblical premises and promises. The
scriptural corpus was presumed to be of divine creation.
Logic and theology were consciously appropriated for the
understanding of that corpus. Furthermore, the biblical materials were believed to possess a form of their own, which
made as deep an impression upon puritan thought as did
their scholastic disciplines. This form inherent in the
biblical books was what might be termed the historical
cast of Israel's life and thought. Each book of the Bible
had a role within the drama which moved from Creation to
Redemption. The Old Testament works could be construed
typologically in conjunction with the New Testament anti-
types. Particularly Revelation, but also Daniel, foretold the
course of events between the period of the early church
and the consummation of all things. These are the materials which the puritan imagination—particularly during

the 1640's—used in construing the "times." The scholastic disciplines were means chosen for comprehending and articulating what was understood to be a cosmic struggle manifested in Stuart England.

Associated with the historical character of the biblical materials was a pronounced emphasis upon corporate or collective realities. Puritanism in this era exhibited a striking quest for national piety and regeneration which will appear foreign to the twentieth-century reader—although there remain in both British and American cultures evidences for the earlier significance of the movement. In any case, this quest made Puritanism sufficiently "real" for the participants to legitimate historical study of it.

The puritans were English patriots who construed their nation's historical destiny in terms of the biblical drama. England had been the seat of the pure church and the great locus of resistance to Antichrist throughout Christian history. In turn they believed it would be the fountainhead of a purified Europe delivered from the Roman incarnation of Antichristian power. Englishmen generally cherished their native land and held it to be unique. This Reformed Protestant movement elaborated these strong sentiments in theological images which led to a vision of England as instrumental in the regeneration of the Christian world. These characteristics, of course, made Puritanism attractive to some and hideously repulsive to others.[33]

In this perspective we may appreciate the dynamic character of Puritanism which rendered it a significant ideological movement within the common life. The present period of scholarship, possibly "beyond" ideological struggles but certainly alert to them, seems prepared to recognize the ideological character of Puritanism, however divergent may be the estimates of its actual influence. This study of

[33] See the suggestive article in local ecclesiastical history which indicates that such an interpretation of Caroline Puritanism proves to be useful at that level: Claire Cross, "Achieving the Millennium: the Church in York during the Commonwealth," in *Studies in Church History*, IV, ed. G. J. Cuming (Leiden, 1967), 122-142.

formal puritan preaching before the Long Parliament is intended as a means of understanding the conceptual framework within which the puritans' political experiences were comprehended and by which their political activities were authorized. As an initial step the following chapter will trace the genesis and development of the preaching institution in the House of Commons, which ultimately proved to be precedential for the puritan pulpit in the Long Parliament.

II

The Genesis of the Commons
Preaching Program

A PROGRAM for parliamentary fast days was apparently first proposed in the middle years of Elizabeth's reign. The *Commons Journals* records that on Saturday, January 21, 1580, "a Motion [was] made for a public Fast, with Prayer and Preaching to be exercised by this House for the Assistance of God's Holy Spirit, to the Furtherance of his Glory, the Preservation of her Majesty, and the better Direction of the Actions of this House."[1] Some debate must have followed on the question of whether the fast should be celebrated individually and personally or publicly. By a narrow margin the ensuing division of the house determined that it should be public.[2] The Privy Council was instructed to nominate the preachers, "to the end they might be such as would keep convenient Proportion of Time, and meddle with no Matter of Innovation or Unquietness," and the time and place were agreed upon: "tomorrow [Sunday] sevennight" at 8 a.m. in the Temple Church.[3]

Reference to this proposed fast does not appear in the minutes recorded for Monday, January 23. By Tuesday the twenty-fourth, however, it is evident that the Queen had responded decisively and with dispatch when she learned of the plans. The Speaker of the house abjectly confessed his error in entertaining the original resolution for the fast and reported upon "her Majesty's great Misliking of the Proceeding of this House therein, . . . advising the House to a Submission in that Behalf. . . ." Commons was instructed to deal with proper and pertinent matters only,

[1] *CJ*, I, 118.
[2] The division was reported as 115-100.   [3] *CJ*, I, 118.

omitting "all superfluous and unnecessary Motions and Arguments."[4] To indicate her displeasure further, Elizabeth sent another message by the hand of the Vice Chamberlain. She was amazed at the rashness of the house "in committing such an apparent Contempt against her Majesty's express Commandment" regarding innovations. She noted the zeal, duty, and fidelity of Commons and construed the offense and contempt to be a "rash, unadvised, and inconsiderate Error," proceeding from the zeal of the members and not from "wilful or malicious Intent." She indicated that the brother of Peter Wentworth, the puritan, had first proposed the fast, and in this way she summarily condemned it through guilt by association. The Queen implied that submission of the house would be in order, and the responsive members of Commons immediately granted that wish.[5] On January 25 the Vice Chamberlain communicated Elizabeth's pardon to them. She hoped that they would "employ their best Endeavours and Travels more gravely and advisedly in the Service of her Majesty and the Realm, according to their special Vocations in this Service."[6] With this ignominious rebuff an Elizabethan puritan attempt to organize a parliamentary fast was squelched and its chief movers humiliated. When fast preaching before Commons was next proposed, it originated in a very different context.

In the second Jacobean Parliament (1614) a motion was offered on April 9 by Sir James Perrott "that all the Members may, before a certain Day, receive the Communion."[7] Three reasons were given for this proposal. First, the bond between King and Commons would thereby be strengthened. Second, it would free "those that shall take it, from unjust Suspicion." Third, it would "keep the Trojan Horse out of the House."[8] The motion was passed—no division was reported—and date, place, and time were arranged: Palm Sunday in the Abbey at 9 a.m. Thereafter "whosoever shall not then receive, shall not after be ad-

4 *Ibid.*
7 *Ibid.*, 457.
5 *Ibid.*, 118f.
8 *Ibid.*
6 *Ibid.*, 119.

mitted into the House, till he have received, whether he be now in Town, or no."[9]

The first "reason" or ground was formal and conventional; it serves to mask, rather than disclose, the significance of the motion. Strengthening of the bond would follow from achievement of the second and third aims. These "reasons" come into relief against the background of the Guy Fawkes Powder Plot and persistent recusant sentiment within England. Evidently this motion would enable the puritans, and other Protestants who were considered to be potential subversives, to demonstrate their loyalty. The test of the sacrament would clear them from suspicion. Romanists, on the other hand, would be forced to reveal their allegiance by disqualifying themselves, unless they were willing to engage in hypocrisy. That puritan sensibilities were to be respected was indicated on April 13 when the house voted that the communion would take place in St. Margaret's, the parish church of Westminster, rather than in the Abbey. "In the Abbey, [the *Journals* reported,] they administer not with common Bread, contrary [to the] 20th Canon, and the Book of Common Prayer."[10] Apparently the Speaker of the house arranged for a preacher, who is not identified. The "test" service took place on April 17. The next day distribution of monies collected at the service was delegated to the Speaker and several associates.[11]

In this way there originated occasional preaching services in St. Margaret's, Westminster, directly sponsored by the House of Commons. The practice would be developed as a prominent feature of a later parliament, a program the scope of which certainly was unimagined by either Jacobean or Elizabethan puritans. Until 1614, members of Commons had celebrated the sacrament with the House of Lords in Westminster Abbey, or they had attended the Temple with the lawyers in the lower house—a place in which the authority of the Church of England was secure, since the Master of the Temple was a Crown appointee.

---

[9] *Ibid.*   [10] *Ibid.*, 463.   [11] *Ibid.*, 466.

The pattern of separate services, apparently adopted in order to make it possible for the Protestants to demonstrate their loyalty to the Crown, was reaffirmed in the parliaments which followed in that decade. During the 1640's this same institution became elaborated into periodic fasts of national humiliation quite independent of any sacrament to test Protestant loyalties to the regime.[12]

A test communion was repeated in the parliament of 1620 (1621 N.S.). On the fifth of February it was voted that Dr. James Ussher, who had demonstrated skill in confuting recusants and who was in London on a visit from Dublin, should preach at the service.[13] Five days later February 18 was selected as the date.[14] On February 27 Commons thanked Ussher and began a long tradition of requesting the preacher to print his sermon.[15] This invitation would not have been considered unusual or inappropriate since to preach from prominent pulpits on noteworthy occasions often implied this prerogative. Very substantial numbers of the printed sermons from the sixteenth and seventeenth centuries were preached initially at Paul's Cross, or before his Majesty at Hampton Court, or at St. Mary's, Oxford. Indeed, the significant historiographical point is that relatively few printed sermons were *not* delivered under formal auspices—suggesting how pulpit and press served state ends. Commons's request may be understood, therefore, as an expression of the importance the

12 H. F. Westlake, *St. Margaret's, Westminster* (London, 1914), Ch. 7: "St. Margaret's Church and the House of Commons," 95-110. This study traces the development recounted above from the perspective of the increasingly close relationship between Commons and the parish church. Our present interest, of course, is with the other side of the story—how the association with St. Margaret's allowed the puritans to demonstrate their essential loyalty to the regime and, having done this, to develop an institution of puritan preaching before the House of Commons in the context of the national fasts of humiliation.

13 *CJ*, I, 508. Cf. R. B. Knox, *James Ussher: Archbishop of Armagh* (Cardiff, 1967), 27-28.

14 *CJ*, I, 516.

15 *Ibid.*, 529. It was also determined that the collection should go to the poor.

house attached to the occasion. Formal publication of the fast and feast sermons would also prove to be a prominent characteristic of the pulpit in the Long Parliament.

Ussher obliged Commons in its request and offered in print *The Substance Of That Which Was Delivered In A Sermon before the Commons House of Parliament, in St. Margaret's Church at Westminster, the 18. of February, 1620.*[16] In the "Dedicatory Epistle" he confessed: "The very words which then I uttered, I am not able to present unto you: the substance of the matter I have truly laid downe, though in some places (as it fell out) somewhat contracted, in others a little more inlarged."[17] His exhortation was clearly directed toward the test sacrament. The text was I Corinthians 10:17. Ussher stressed the special "cause" of the unity of Protestants and their disjunction from false (that is, popish) idolators. He portrayed the struggle between the parties as international in scope. The tone was generally irenic, a call for reconciliation with friends in spite of those real differences which might exist and divide. A final discourse on the sacraments as both signs and seals preceded, presumably, their administration.

With the following parliament the nature of the occasion began to change. On February 23, 1623-4, Sir Edward Cecil moved that Commons hold a fast, citing the like practice in the Low Countries.[18] It should be "general," that is, for the entire kingdom, and the King's consent should be solicited. A practical benefit might well be a relief fund which could be collected for the poor.[19] Although the sacrament was probably administered once again, the occasion was evidently construed not only as a religious test of loyalty applied to the members of parliament but also as an opportunity to bring the whole body under the discipline of preaching. The proposal was passed and encountered no royal objections.

[16] (London, 1621).
[17] *The Substance* . . ., A_3 *recto*—A_4 *recto*.
[18] *CJ*, I, 671 (715).
[19] Cecil pronounced it "Very bountiful to the Poor [in the Low Countries]."

"Dr. Bargrave" was selected to preach the sermon. At the time Isaac Bargrave was a chaplain to Prince Charles, and he also held an official appointment at St. Margaret's parish. He later became its "pastor," was made Dean of Canterbury in 1625, and subsequently held the living at Chartham (1628). Bargrave later proved to be a staunch supporter of Charles when the latter was King, and he was subjected to considerable abuse by parliamentary agents before his death in January 1642-3. During James's reign, however, he seems to have been in some measure of sympathy with the "puritan" faction and program. The sermon which he preached to Commons in 1623-4 appears to have earned him considerable disfavor at Court.[20]

The fast took place on the last day of February, and on Monday, March 1, thanks were voted to Bargrave and he was asked to "take further Pains, to put the same [sermon] in Print."[21] The text had been Psalm 26:6, and his conception of the occasion was clearly expressed. "The prime end of the Creature, is the glory of the Creator: this end cannot be attained without the preservation of the Creature: The common good of the whole world in generall; and of every part and Common-wealth in particular. Upon this ground . . . all understanding men have beene wont to Praeface all great Consultations for the common good, with some such religious Acts, as did best conduce to the glory of God."[22] The sermon was still very much directed toward the reception of the sacrament, so much so that the text was "divided" into what he termed Preface and Work, or Condition and Dutie. It might have been denominated Preparation and Communion.[23] Through the whole, however, ran a theme which was to become highly significant: the character of parliament as representative of England before God. Thus in "preparation"—which was chiefly repentance—as well as in the "communion" the members of the house stood as a collective representation of

---

20 On Isaac Bargrave, see *DNB*. 21 *CJ*, I, 675 (722).
22 I. Bargrave, *A Sermon Preached . . . 1623* (London, 1624), 1-2.
23 See *ibid.*, 6ff.

the commonwealth. "Yee now [re]present the whole body of the Land, and therefore now before you approach the *Altar*, Repent for the whole body of the Land."[24] As the altar was a pledge of God's love to England, it should be the seat of reconciliation among her divisions.[25] Probably this explicit conception of Commons as a corporate representation of England before the ultimate Majesty is what agitated the Stuart court when the sermon was preached.[26]

In this development from the test sacrament of 1614, accompanied by an exhortation, to the representative corporate repentance before God of the 1623-4 fast—which was, to be sure, sealed in the sacrament—we find the germ of the completed puritan program of preaching before the Long Parliament. It is important to recognize that during the later years of James's reign the puritans regrouped their forces and planned new thrusts within the existing political and social structures, thrusts which unashamedly were intended to convert the Stuart society and give to it a puritan complexion. Formation of the Massachusetts Bay Company and associated overseas ventures (which were turned to puritan ends, if not initially dedicated to them) should be noted in this regard. In addition, organization of the very important Feoffees scheme dates from this period (1625).[27] Both were roughly contemporaneous with the program of a fast in which Commons was to represent the entire realm before God. It would be surprising if these several schemes were not supported by much the same group of "puritans," both clerical and lay.

During the early years of Charles's reign Commons developed the practice of initiating "fasts" during each session

24 *Ibid.*, 17.

25 *Ibid.*, 34-36.

26 Cf. Louise F. Brown, "Ideas of Representation from Elizabeth to Charles II," *Journal of Modern History*, XI/1 (March 1939), 23-40.

27 The fullest account of the Feoffees program is I. M. Calder's *Activities of the Puritan Faction of the Church of England, 1625-33* (London, 1957). This study presents the proceedings of the Crown against the group and their legal defenses. It does not, however, analyze the broader implications of the scheme itself or the context in which it was developed.

so that they would become an established and secure parliamentary tradition. The lower house appears to have taken the lead in these matters, but the Lords cooperated with it and joined in the ceremonies. In the initial parliament of 1625, arrangements for a fast were proposed on June 21. After important deliberation about whether it should be "general," it was decided that the support of the upper house should be sought.[28] A petition went to the Lords two days later, and the next day (June 24) it went to the King, calling for a "General Fast throughout [the] whole Kingdom."[29] Finally it seems to have been determined that the fast would be celebrated at different times by different parts of the realm.[30] Thus the houses kept the fast on Saturday, July 2. On this day the upper house, possibly joined for the occasion by Charles, was exhorted by several bishops.[31] Commons chose its preachers with care, originally naming "Mr. (Josias) Shute" of Lombard Street, Dr. John Preston of Trinity, Cambridge, and Lincoln's Inn, and a Dr. Westfield.[32] A "Mr. Oldsworth" (Richard Holdsworth) replaced the last named (no explanation for the change being noted), and it was settled that they should preach in the following order: Shute, Holdsworth, and Preston.[33] There is no further record in the *Commons Journals* about this fast, except a note on August 2 that it had not been observed in "divers Places" because the bishops had failed to send the required books.[34] It is noteworthy both that several preachers were invited to exhort the members of Commons during the fast and that the event was extended throughout the realm. These became two common characteristics of the puritan fasts under the Long Parliament. It is also plausible to suspect that the bishops' failure to arrange the fast throughout the country was, in part at least, intentional.

John Preston's sermon at this fast of July 2, 1625, was

[28] *CJ*, I, 799.
[29] *Journals of the House of Lords*, III, 441—hereafter cited as *LJ*.
[30] *LJ*, III, 448. [31] *Ibid.*, 448, 454. [32] *CJ*, I, 799.
[33] *Ibid.*, 800. [34] *Ibid.*, 810.

printed by his editors (Sibs and Davenport) as an appendix to *The Saints Qualification*.[35] In it first appeared that theme which so clearly characterized many of the sermons in the fully developed fasts under the Long Parliament. This was a prophetic insistence upon repentance and return in order to placate divine wrath for sins general and specific. Conjointly a plea was entered for divine mercy to extend temporal as well as spiritual blessings. In this theme, as in many other features of civil war Puritanism, Preston appears to have charted paths to be followed by his colleagues and successors.[36]

At the time Preston preached this sermon to the house, a plague was sweeping the country. In a characteristically puritan way he treated the plague as indicative of a deeper sickness in the society. Before "opening" and "applying" the text, he presented a brief analysis of fasting as Humiliation, Reconciliation, and Reformation. Fasting he understood to be a turning from sin to faith, from the creature to God. After introducing his assumptions, Preston set forth his argument in five steps, representing the logic of God's dealings with his people: (1) God's anger brings all evil; (2) Sin is the cause of Divine Anger; (3) Zeal turns away that Anger; (4) Without zeal God's jealousy grows hotter; (5) God's jealousy leads to utter destruction.[37]

Clearly the plague was to be understood as a sign of God's anger. Zeal, if aroused and properly directed, could turn it away. Specifically, spiritual whoredom, idolatry, and

---

[35] (London, 1633), 246-305. Preston has had a recent biographer in I. Morgan, *Prince Charles's Puritan Chaplain* (London, 1657). In certain respects Morgan has done less than full justice to a man of exceptional talents and great stature. Probably the single most appreciative piece on Preston is an essay by Christopher Hill, "The Political Sermons of John Preston," in *Puritanism and Revolution* (London, 1958), 239-274. Perry Miller also called attention to Preston's intellectual contribution to the Federal Theology developed within Puritanism. He interpreted him as a great "rationalist" among the puritans. *The New England Mind: The Seventeenth Century* (Cambridge, Mass., 1954), esp. Book Two: "Cosmology," 111-235.

[36] Cf. Hill, *ibid.*, and Miller, *ibid.*

[37] *The Saints Qualification*, 253ff.

injustice were to be identified and punished. It was necessary that faith be contended for and a preaching ministry established as a means to that end. If God's anger was not turned away, the plague would be but the earnest of God's forthcoming destruction. "If you will be with the Lord, the Lord shall be with you, and if you forsake the Lord, he will reject you."[38]

This dramatic interpretation of history and construction of contemporary events as indices of God's pleasure were staples of "puritan" preaching, although generally they had been applied to the life of the individual person more than to the health of corporate society.[39] What is especially noteworthy about this sermon of Preston's was its delivery to the House of Commons in the context of the fast for the entire kingdom. Another Commons had already been instructed of its corporate representation of the nation before God in its weal or woe, its salvation or sin. With Preston's sermon the chief marks of the later sermons before the Long Parliament were already present, except for the necessary regularity.

It is significant as well as symbolic that, of the three sermons which were to be delivered before Commons that day, Preston's is apparently the only one which we now possess—and probably the only one which reached print. He was the most illustrious and eminent of the puritans, having both court and university connections. Preston possessed an immunity denied to others. But, at the same time, he did not fail to declare himself fully and freely. His words

---

[38] *Ibid.*, 304.

[39] This statement may be open to a great deal of misinterpretation. It is only important to note here that Preston himself represents the high-water mark of puritan influence in government councils until the period of the civil wars. Thus it would be legitimate to argue, as I would, that the *circumstances* of the puritan place within Tudor and early Stuart society necessarily led to comparatively less direct emphasis upon the corporate character of society in relationship to divine agency, whereas these convictions came to full expression quite naturally in the Stuart Interregnum. Puritanism changed less than its position within society, the consequent opportunities open to it, and therefore the conceptualization of its goals.

were undoubtedly the most eloquent of the day and also the most independent. The sermon he delivered anticipated in specifics as well as in its general spirit the developed program of preaching to parliament during the 1640's.

Whether or not it was intended as a direct response to Preston, another sermon delivered within days of it reflects the tensions developing within the realm under the new King. William Laud, Bishop of St. David's, apparently preached at Whitehall before the King at his personal celebration of the same fast on July 5. Laud's rendering of the text, Psalm 74:22, faithfully depicts the character of the sermon: "Arise, O God (plead or) maintaine thine own Cause: Rémember how the foolish man (reprocheth or) blasphemeth thee daily."[40]

Parliament was called again within the year (February 6, 1625-6). On that day William Laud preached at its opening in the Abbey, developing at some length the necessity for interdependence between church and state.[41] For his text he used Psalm 122:3-5: "Jerusalem is builded as a city," etc. He proposed that religion is necessary for the state; the church, therefore, must preserve true religion: "The *Commonwealth* cannot flourish without the *Church*. For where the Church is not to teach true Religion, States are enforced, out of necessitie of some, to imbrace a false [religion]."[42] Laud went on to raise the spectre of ecclesiastical radicals becoming political revolutionaries: "They, whoever they bee, that would overthrow *Sedes Ecclesiae*, the Seates of Ecclesiasticall Government, will not spare (if ever they get power) to have a plucke at the *Throne* of *David*."[43] Although on February 9 the lower house moved directly to

[40] *A Sermon Preached Before His Majestie . . . at White-Hall* (London, 1626).

[41] Reference to this sermon has been made by S. R. Gardiner in his *History of England, 1603-1642* (London, 1884) VI, 63-64, and by G. Davies in *The Early Stuarts, 1603-1660* (Oxford, 1937, 1952), 34. Cf. P. Heylyn, *Cyprianus Anglicus* (London, 1671), 139-140.

[42] *A Sermon Preached on Munday, the sixt of February, at Westminster: At the opening of the Parliament* (London, 1625), 4.

[43] *Ibid.*, 40.

arrange a test communion, the *Commons Journals* is strangely silent on the subject of a fast during this parliament. The tenor of Laud's sermon at least suggests that Charles was working to suppress the practice. Such an interpretation is supported by the course of events at the opening of the next parliament.

Laud, by this time Bishop of Bath and Wells, again preached on the first day (March 17, 1627-8).[44] For this occasion his text and his tone appear to have been less strident and more irenic. Preaching on Ephesians 4:3 ("Endeavouring to keepe the Unitie of the Spirit, in the bond of peace"), he emphasized unity of spirit throughout. "The State, whether Pagan or Christian, hath ever smarted more or lesse, as the Church hath crumbled into Divisions."[45] On March 20, the initial working day for Commons, a test communion was scheduled for early April, and, independently of it, a proposal for a "general Fast" was forthcoming. The Lords concurred in this request to Charles.[46] He agreed on the twenty-fourth, although probably out of political necessity.[47] April 5 was arranged as the day. The Lords settled on bishops, while for Commons were proposed several preachers, including Jeremiah Dyke of Epping, Essex, "R(obert) Harrys" of Hanwell, Oxford, and Walter Balcanquhall, Dean of Rochester.[48] Apparently the lower house chose to have Dyke and Balcanquhall exhort them.[49] The Lord Mayor of London was requested to have the shops in the City closed for the day. On April 3 it was determined that there should be a collection at both the communion and the fast.[50] The care and atten-

---

[44] *CJ*, I, 872.

[45] *A Sermon Preached on Munday, the Seaventeenth of March, At Westminster: At the opening of the Parliament* (London, 1628), 4.

[46] *CJ*, I, 873-874; *LJ*, III, 693.

[47] *CJ*, I, 875; *LJ*, III, 695. Peter Heylyn's comments on this occasion, in retrospect to be sure, at least suggest that agreement to the fast proposal was in the nature of a political bargain. He reported: "No sooner had they obtained their Fast (without which nothing could be done) . . . ." *Op.cit.*, 169.

[48] *LJ*, III, 698; *CJ*, I, 875.

[49] *CJ*, I, 878.   [50] *Ibid.*, cf. *LJ*, III, 711.

tion given to the arrangement of this event indicate how far the concept of the "fast" had developed independently of a "test communion." In this respect it clearly served essentially puritan purposes. Finally, on the sixteenth of April, eleven days after the celebration of the fast by the houses, it was recorded that £80 plus change had been collected. Plate was to be given in payment to the preachers, "Dr. Burgesse" and Mr. Dyke. This instruction indicates that Cornelius Burges, who was to become a favorite preacher with the Long Parliament in its early years, had probably replaced the Dean of Rochester.[51]

Dyke's sermon was published in the same year. Like Preston's earlier effort, it anticipated the puritan sermons which were to become frequent, if not commonplace, during the Long Parliament. His text was Hebrews 11:7, where Noah's faith is extolled as exemplary. The preacher listed the series of warnings God gives of impending Wrath and Judgment. They included extraordinary and immediate revelations, signs and wonders, the prophetic ministry of the Word, instances of God's dealings with others, divine acts against a corporate society, and, finally, his gradual departure from a nation and church as evidenced in the introduction of idolatries, the corruption of churchmen, and the failing of strength.[52] Noah was the great exemplar of faith because he recognized God's warnings and wisely prepared the Ark.[53] Dyke tactfully refrained from describing the specific details of the "ark" he propounded for England, but he did note the general steps which would have to be taken. All persons in a nation and a church should engage in humiliation and abasement. Personal reformation and amendment of ways might prove to be effective. In particular, the great "Senate" of the land was responsible

[51] *CJ*, I, 883-884; cf. James F. Maclear, "The Influence of the Puritan Clergy on the House of Commons: 1625-1629," *Church History*, XIV/4 (1945), 274-275. Laud's role in this period is discussed by H. R. Trevor-Roper, *Archbishop Laud, 1573-1645* (London, 1940), 71-96.

[52] J. Dyke, *A Sermon Preached* . . . (London, 1628), 7ff. There is no indication that Burges's sermon was published.

[53] *Ibid.*, 27ff.

for selecting sturdy materials to be used in the Ark and also for building it well.[54] Dyke reiterated the by now familiar puritan demands for "choice members" in the churches and for a "godly and learned preaching ministry."

Another fast was scheduled in the second session of the same parliament. On January 26 and 27, 1628-9, a petition for a "general Fast" was called for and presented.[55] This request was granted on the thirtieth of the month,[56] and on February 5 the dates were settled: London and Westminster should celebrate the fast on the eighteenth of the same month and the rest of England on March 20.[57] On the next day the house designated the preachers of its choice: a Mr. Harrys of St. Margaret's itself, Robert Harrys of Hanwell, Oxford, and a Mr. Fitz-Jeoffrey. Although the *Journals* provides no direct mention of the fact, it may be assumed that the Commons fast took place as planned.[58] Apparently none of the sermons was printed. A request for their publication might well have been forthcoming had the session not ended on March 2. In some sense, the fast must have failed in its purpose.

The next parliament was, of course, the "Short Parliament," which met in 1640, called only reluctantly by Charles. It is important to note that Commons moved immediately to propose a fast. Apparently the precedents governing such occasions were by this time considered secure, and obviously fasts were thought to serve a useful purpose, at least within the politics of Westminster. On April 18 a committee proposed joining with the Lords in a request to the King.[59] The Lords reported its willingness on April

---

[54] *Ibid.*, 32ff, esp. 35ff.

[55] *CJ*, I, 922; *LJ*, IV, 13-14.

[56] *CJ*, I, 924. The *Lords Journals* indicates that there was reluctance on Charles's part lest a "Precedent for frequent Fasts" be established. *LJ*, IV, 15.

[57] *CJ*, I, 926; *LJ*, IV, 20, 24.

[58] This conclusion seems warranted because on the day before the fast a committee was appointed to take the names of those in attendance. Thus any cancellation of the service would have occurred at the very last moment. See *CJ*, I, 931. The Lords did thank its bishops and "Ordered them to print their said sermons." See *LJ*, IV, 34.

[59] *CJ*, II, 6.

21 and recommended that the date be determined by the King at his pleasure.[60] Charles quickly assented, and on April 23 the fast was scheduled for "Saturday come sevennight," or May 2.[61] "Dr. Olseworth" (Holdsworth) and "Mr. (Stephen) Marshall" were selected to preach. The sacrament—undoubtedly construed as a test communion—would be celebrated the following day, also in St. Margaret's, with Dr. Brounrick preaching on that occasion. By this action the separation of the fast from the test sacrament was reaffirmed. To distinguish these events was of more importance to the puritans than to any other group. This independence of the two religious events served puritan purposes in a significant way. If the fast and the communion were yoked together, only one fast would be appropriate during each session of parliament. Severed from the test ritual, however, there was no theoretical limit to the number of occasions on which Commons could be subjected to preaching. Perhaps it is more important that these plans were carefully laid in the Short Parliament than that the events never actually came to pass during the abbreviated session. On May 1 it was voted that the communion should be postponed "till it be further declared by the House, after the Time for the Fast shall be settled."[62] The parliament was dissolved on May 5.[63]

When the Long Parliament assembled in November of 1640, the first order of actual business in the first session of Commons—not surprisingly—was a motion for a fast.[64]

---

[60] *Ibid.*, 8; *LJ*, IV, 61.

[61] *CJ*, II, 9; cf. *LJ*, IV, 63-65.

[62] Trevor-Roper assumes that this fast, scheduled for the Short Parliament, did take place. "Fast Sermons," 297. The reference he gives to the *State Papers (Domestic)* actually concerns observations—irrelevant to the fast—about the election in Essex which were reported by "Mr. Nevill, of Cressing Temple." In that document there is mention of pre-election activity on the part of "Mr. Marshall and others," who "preached often out of their own parishes before the election." *Calendar of State Papers (Domestic) 1639-40*, 608-609. The notation in the *Commons Journals*, from which one may infer that the fast was postponed at a late moment and never held, is not open to Trevor-Roper's construction of the matter. *CJ*, II, 17.

[63] *CJ*, II, 19; *LJ*, IV, 80-81.   [64] *CJ*, II, 20.

On the following day, the seventh, a report was brought in from the committee which had been appointed, and it was resolved that, if the Lords was willing, they jointly propose a fast for the whole kingdom.[65] This decision was carried out on the ninth, a Monday. At the same time, it was settled that the "particular Fast" involving both houses of parliament and the City of London would take place on "Tuesday come sevennight"—the seventeenth—no doubt considered a fitting celebration of "Queen Elizabeth's day." The general fast for the entire kingdom would be scheduled for a month from the immediate Tuesday.[66] At once Cornelius Burges and Stephen Marshall were selected to exhort Commons.[67] These clerics were to become pillars of the puritan preaching to the Long Parliament. The choice of these men to deliver the fast sermons did not mean, however, that *only* radical preachers would be heard by Commons—at least during the early months. Only on the point of specific insistence upon reform of the church was their preaching distinguished significantly from that heard by many of the continuing members from the former parliaments when, apparently, Burges had actually preached along with Preston, Dyke, and others.

Marshall's sermon, which may have followed Burges's, was the less innovative of the two and did not depart greatly from the "Dedicatory Epistle" shared by both:

> The God of Heaven steere all Your weighty consultations by his own Counsell, to his owne Glory; cover You still under his own Wing, and make You the most accomplisht, best united, & most successfull & glorious house of Commons that ever sate in that High Court; but chiefly in the effectuall endeavouring of a further Sanction of, and stronger Guard about our true Palladium, the true Religion, already established among us; in the perfecting of the Reformation of it; in the erecting, main-

---

[65] *Ibid.*, 22; *LJ*, IV, 84-85.

[66] *CJ*, II, 23f. Cf. J. E. Neale, "November 17th," in *Essays in Elizabethan History* (London, 1958), 9-20.

[67] *CJ*, II, 24. Again the Lords chose bishops for its service. *LJ*, IV, 85f.

taining, protecting and incouraging of an able, godly, faithfull, zealous, profitable, Preaching Ministery, in every Parish Church and Chapell throughout England and Wales; and in the interceding to the Kings sacred Majesty for the setting up of a Faithfull, Judicious, and Zealous Magistracy, where yet the same is wanting, to bee ever at hand to back such a Ministery. . . .[68]

The introduction suggested, intentionally to be sure, that the preachers were prophetic messengers conveying the word of the Lord:

The speciall end of your meeting this day, is to afflict your souls before God, that so with Ezra, you might seeke a right way for your selves, and the weighty affaires of his Majesty, and the whole State: and the speciall errand I have to deliver from the Lord, is to assure you of the same truth, although in other words, which Ezra told the Persian Emperour, that the hand of God is upon them for good that seek him; but his power and wrath against all them that forsake him, viz. That God will be with you, while you be with him.[69]

Taking as his text II Chronicles 15:2, Marshall argued that God's presence was a condition for the happiness of the Jewish Church under Ezra's leadership. The first "doctrine" was that "The presence of God in his Covenant of Grace with any people, is the greatest glory, and happinesse that they can enjoy";[70] his "application" was that the worst traitors to the kingdom were those neither prepared nor willing to avail England of these resources.[71] The second "doctrine" was related: "God will bee with his people to bee their glory, their portion, prosperity, and protection, just as they are with him."[72] Marshall immediately hedged the proposition to protect himself from charges of exalting free will over free grace and of counsel-

[68] C. Burges, *The First Sermon* . . . (London, 1641) , "Dedicatory Epistle."
[69] S. Marshall, *A Sermon* . . . *November 17, 1640* (London, 1641) , 2.
[70] *Ibid.*, 5.   [71] *Ibid.*, 17.   [72] *Ibid.*, 22.

ing reliance on merit. This studied qualification on his part indicates that the preacher of a covenant theological scheme was alert to its potential abuses. In the sermon this "doctrine" served the "uses" of humiliation and exhortation.

It fell to Burges to be more bold, and in the preface his point was bluntly summarized. He observed that "prayer" and "humiliation" were the common "uses" of religious fasts. These should not be construed as ends in themselves, however, but should be fulfilled in a "religious and inviolable Covenant with their God," without which "all their labour will be utterly lost, their expectations frustrate[d], . . . [and] the eyes of his Glory [provoked] more against them, causing him infinitely to loath and abominate both their persons, and service. . . ."[73]

Burges's text was Jeremiah 50:5—really 50:1-5. He reminded the members of the house that the yoke of Babylon was placed on Judah's neck to humble her. Jeremiah had foretold the total and final destruction in order to encourage the Jews.[74] "This Northern Army [Medes and Persians] should be the confusion of Babylon, the confusion of Babylon should prove the restoring of the Church. And the restoring of the Church should produce a *Covenant* with God."[75] If it took little imagination to cast the Scots in the role of the "Northern Army," the reference to the "yoke of Babylon" was equally transparent. The main "doctrine" made clear Burges's insistent theme: "When God vouchsafes any deliverance to his Church, especially from Babylon, then it is most seasonable and most necessary to close with God by a more solemne, strict, and inviolable Covenant to be his, and only his for ever."[76] The preacher further argued the necessity of the covenant from other precedents in Jeremiah (24:5; 30:18, 31; 32:37) and also Nehemiah 10. As for implementation of it, in "matter" it was a binding to the Lord, in "forme" "nothing else but an agreement or bargaine between two or mo[r]e persons, and

---

73 C. Burgess, *The First Sermon* . . . , 2.
74 *Ibid.*, 3ff.   75 *Ibid.*, 6.   76 *Ibid.*, 8.

ratified (ordinarily) by some externall solemnitie, or rites
that may testifie and declare the agreement, and ratifie it,
whereby it becomes unalterable."[77]

By way of "explication" Burges framed three "uses."
The first was a reproof of those who "come not up" to the
covenant for one or another reason. The second was a request for "information," that is, "Why God hath not yet
given us so full a deliverance from Babylon; why there
have been so many ebbings and flowings in matters of Religion, yea, more ebbings than flowings. . . ."[78] The third
was a basis for exhortation: "My businesse is, meerly to
persuade you into a *Religious Covenant with God,* as himselfe hath prescribed and commanded; and, his people, in
the best times of Reformation, have readily admitted:
namely, every man to stirre up himself & to lift up his Soule
to take hold of God, to be glued and united to him, in all
faithfulnesse, sincerity, care, and diligence, to be onely his
for ever."[79] Burges introduced an interesting qualification
to this third use, namely, that explicit covenants are less
important than individual and implicit ones. With a final
exhortation to set up a preaching ministry, he concluded
a sermon which in print runs to nearly eighty pages.

> I beseech you therefore by all the mercies of God, by all
> the Bowels of Christ in shedding of his deerest bloud
> for those precious Soules, who now, even by thousands
> and millions miserably perish in their ignorance and
> sins, that you would carefully reforme, or cast out all
> idle, unsound, unprofitable, and scandalous Ministers;
> and provide a sound, godly, profitable and setled
> Preaching Ministry in every Congregation through the
> Land and the annexed Dominions; and, to take no lesse
> care for their diligent and constant performance of their
> dutie both in life and Doctrine, as also for their liberall
> maintenance, (that may be still capable of improvement,
> as the times grow harder, and commodities deerer)
> that both themselves who preach the Gospel, and all

[77] *Ibid.*, 26.   [78] *Ibid.*, 49.   [79] *Ibid.*, 57.

others also, may cheerfully and comfortably live of the Gospel. And let us once see *Sion built up*, by your industry, *in perfect beautie*.[80]

The following day, November 18, Commons thanked the two preachers, and, although no formal motion to that end was recorded, it was intended, apparently, that they should print their sermons.[81]

The next occasion for formal exhortation of the house was provided at submission to the test communion on the twenty-ninth of the month. According to the *Commons Journals*, "Mr. Gawdy" was to preach in the forenoon and "Mr. Morley" in the afternoon.[82] The latter was undoubtedly George Morley, who, though considered a Calvinist, was to be a royalist and eventually, at the Restoration, to become Bishop of Winchester.[83] Both preachers were thanked and invited to publish their efforts. Probably John Gauden alone did so, apparently with special urging.[84] The extended period between fast and test sacrament did not indicate, it should be noted, any less concern for effective exclusion of papists. A select committee was specifically appointed to "take some Course, to prevent Profanation and Rejection of the Sacrament; and for the Securing of this House, that no Papist sit here amongst them." The membership of this committee included, among others, Pym, St. John, Hampden, and Vane.[85]

---

[80] *Ibid.*, 78.

[81] *CJ*, II, 30. Cf. Burges's sermon. The Lords's further preparation for the fast is noted in *LJ*, IV, 92.

[82] *CJ*, II, 24.

[83] This identification is made by E. W. Kirby, "Sermons before the Commons, 1640-42," *American Historical Review*, XLIV/3 (April 1939), 533, as well as by Trevor-Roper, "Fast Sermons," 299. On Morley, see *DNB*.

[84] On the basis of a reference in Anthony Wood, *Athenae Oxonienses*, ed. P. Bliss (1813-1821), IV, 150, Trevor-Roper concludes that no request was extended to Morley to publish his sermon. "Fast Sermons," 299-300. As a matter of record, Commons voted both preachers thanks and invitations to print their exhortations. Additional pains were taken in the case of Gauden, however, Sir Thomas Barrington being specially charged with "moving" him to publish his sermon. *CJ*, II, 40.

[85] *CJ*, II, 24. Notice should also be taken of Commons's sensitivity

Later to become a high churchman and "divine right" royalist, John Gauden was at the time apparently a moderate anglican, probably with sympathies toward (and perhaps with important ties to) the "great contrivers" of the Long Parliament.[86] In any case, his exhortation had a very different cast from those presented by his puritan predecessors at the recent fast. It was entitled *The Love of Truth and Peace*,[87] and the text on which it was based was Zechariah 8:19. "Truth" was discussed in a philosophical fashion and virtually defined in terms of "participation." Peace was, consequently, a matter of harmony and proportion.[88] "Nothing (I say) nothing, will restore the Church and Churchmen to their Pristine honour, love and authority in mens hearts and minds, but a serious setting of themselves to the study, preaching and practizing of Truth and Peace in a holy life."[89] His specific proposal was that Comenius and Dury, whom he believed to be advocates of these ideals, should be invited to England to assist in the settlement of ecclesiastical affairs.[90] With reference to this suggestion Trevor-Roper views Gauden as a mouthpiece for the "parliamentary reformers." He styles Dury and Comenius, together with their London contact Samuel Hartlib, "the philosophers of the 'country party' " and construes this incident as a direct indication of the social program which would be advocated in the Long Parliament.[91]

---

toward the altar controversy. S. R. Gardiner's summary is useful: "[Commons] applied to Williams, who had recently been liberated at the demand of the Peers, and who was again acting as Dean of Westminster, to give permission for the removal of the communion-table at St. Margaret's to the middle of the church, at the time of the administration of the Communion. Williams not only gave his consent, but expressed his readiness to do as much for every parish in his diocese." *History of England, 1603-1642*, IX, 237-238.

86 *DNB*; Trevor-Roper, "Fast Sermons," 299-301.

87 (London, 1641).

88 *The Love of Truth and Peace*, 10ff.

89 *Ibid.*, 35.

90 *Ibid.*, 42-43.

91 "Fast Sermons," 299-301. See also Trevor-Roper's essay "Three Foreigners: The Philosophers of the Puritan Revolution," in *The Crisis of the Seventeenth Century* (New York, 1968), 237-293.

Genesis of the Commons Preaching Program

Although Gauden may have been serving as Pym's agent in this particular matter, the contrasts in temper, tone, and form between his sermon and the prior ones of Marshall and Burges must be noted. These fundamental differences witness to the nascent differentiation between "puritans" and "anglicans" who might have reformist goals in common. The foregoing sermons had been consciously construed in terms of biblical precedents, which were used to draw parallels between England's experience and Israel's. To implement this end, the techniques which constituted the "plain style" of puritan preaching were employed. "Doctrines" were framed, defended, and applied. No chance was lost to invoke the spirit as well as the letter of prophecy. Gauden's abstract, irenic discussion of "Truth" and "Peace" lacked both the audacity and the program of the puritan exhortations. Part of this audacity and program was, of course, to preach before the members of parliament whenever the opportunity presented itself and to make available that opportunity where none existed. In this setting we may properly appreciate the puritan energies which were directed toward exhortation of Commons during the spring of 1641.

In the course of the troubled spring months of 1641 (and possibly extending into the early summer) there appears to have been a concerted effort to sponsor preaching before members of the House of Commons. The basic evidence for this project is the existence of nine or ten published items which comprise a distinctive class of parliamentary sermons.[92] During this period Commons deliberated over organizing at least one formal fast, although it appears not to have been held.[93] The exhortations constituting this group were not, however, delivered on the official invitation of the house, even though members thereof certainly

[92] See Appendix Three, "Sermons preached to Sundry of the House of Commons, 1641." Some critical problems which arise in consideration and use of these documents are discussed in this appendix.

[93] *CJ,* II, 129-130. Trevor-Roper also notes this entry. "Fast Sermons," 303.

contrived at or arranged the occasions.[94] There is no indication that attendance on the part of the entire membership of the house was expected. Publication of the sermons was generally authorized by a committee, rather than at the request of the Commons.[95] Although technically these sermons "preached before sundry of the House of Commons" were not a part of the formal pulpit preaching in the Long Parliament, they must be viewed as contributing very directly to the development of the major program of humiliations and thanksgivings.[96]

A pair of sermons later reaching print was originally preached to members of Commons on April 4, a Sunday. Trevor-Roper emphasizes the immediate parliamentary setting, namely, Pym's resolve to push for Strafford's impeachment in light of the discovery both of the Army Plot and of the plan to rescue the prisoner from the Tower. Trevor-Roper proposes that Pym "used the pulpit to declare policy."[97] In this context Samuel Fairclough, whose patron, Sir Nathaniel Barnardiston, was a close associate of Pym's, preached his sanguinary sermon *The Troublers Troubled, Or Achan Condemned, and Executed.*[98] Achan's offences were clearly the source of Israel's troubles; remedy for her state had been provided by Joshua through dispatch of the offender. With the parallel so plain that little elaboration was required, Fairclough urged the "Joshuas" of the parliament to seek out the "Achans." "The divine policie and heavenly remedy," he declared, "is that those that have authority under God, doe totally abolish and extirpate all the cursed things whereby it was disturbed."[99]

94 This conclusion may often be inferred from dedicatory epistles. See S. Fairclough, *The Troublers Troubled* (London, 1641), and T. Case, *Two Sermons* (London, 1641).

95 Most frequently Dering's committee authorized publication.

96 Two of the articles on preaching to the Long Parliament, both already cited, interpret these sermons as integral to the developed program: E. W. Kirby, "Sermons before the Commons, 1640-42," *op.cit.*, 534-538, and Trevor-Roper, "Fast Sermons," 301-303.

97 "Fast Sermons," 302.

98 (London, 1641).

99 *The Troublers Troubled*, 24.

Extended exhortation to discharge the task followed. Trevor-Roper unequivocally concludes that "Fairclough's sermon was the means of [Pym's] declaring a new party line."[100]

In view of this interpretation the companion sermon of the day, which Trevor-Roper does not discuss, assumes significance. Thomas Wilson, another country parson, also preached before "sundry members of the House of Commons." His *David's Zeale For Zion*[101] was dedicated to Sir Edward Dering. Preaching on Psalm 69, Wilson argued that David's exertions were aimed at both purging Israel of that which offended God and promoting that which served God's glory.[102] In his argument that "Persons [should] bee removed, as enemies to Christ, men of false callings, not warranted of God, pretending divine right, which cannot bee demonstrated out of his Word," Wilson's exhortation seems to corroborate Trevor-Roper's judgment about the immediate uses to which the parliamentary pulpit was put.[103]

Upon further inspection of these sermons, however, it seems clear that neither of them can be interpreted adequately *only* in the perspective of Strafford's case. An Achan, a chief troubler of Israel, the prisoner may have been, but in the puritan economy of good and evil his sin lay not so much in particular offences as in general support for the "Babylonish Garments" in which "Church and Commonwealth" were wrapped. "Restauration" of them "according to the patterne in the Mount" was the true mission entrusted to the Joshuas.[104] In a similar fashion David's zeal on behalf of Zion was to be turned upon "corrupt doctrines" and "false, superstitious and idolatrous" worship, as much as against the "enemies of Christ" who sustained them.[105] In fact, Wilson's exhortation took

---

100 "Fast Sermons," 303.
101 (London, 1641).
102 See *David's Zeale For Zion*, 4ff., 10ff.
103 *Ibid.*, 4.
104 S. Fairclough, *The Troublers Troubled*, 29-30.
105 T. Wilson, *David's Zeale For Zion*, 4ff.

a positive turn in one section where he delineated at length the "good services for the house of the Lord" which were required of the Long Parliament. Thus, although direct, though passing, references throughout these sermons may seem to have heralded a new policy or party line toward the case of Strafford, the fundamental theme of both exhortations was directed toward agitation for wholesale reform of church and commonwealth. The theme provided, of course, an ideological justification for new tactics which Pym appears to have adopted toward the confined minister of the King. Each one of the additional published sermons in this class, though varying in particulars and emphases, contributed to this concert of petition and prayer for a renewed nation. In this sense, reform of the commonwealth was construed in religious terms and was considered more fundamental than the disposition of the King's agent. Indeed, given the coherence of puritan rhetoric, the latter made sense only in light of the former.

The sermons preached by Fairclough and Wilson echoed the long denial of puritan hopes for reformation. Another in the series, which may have been contemporary with those just considered, or possibly was delivered even earlier, exhibits the radical turn of expression, if not conviction, which had been adopted by some of Laud's victims. William Bridge exhorted members of Commons on Revelation 14:8, titling his effort *Babylons Downfall*.[106] Bridge had been driven to the Low Countries, probably in 1636; in explanation of his return from expatriation he cited the increasing openness toward Christ manifest in England: "As the fall of Babylon is much expected, so the rising of the churches is much desired."[107] The preacher specifically proposed that the fall of Babylon might be hastened by ferreting out those who were its supporters, by engaging in days of humiliation and fasting, and by blessing the

---

[106] (London, 1641). See Appendix Three (277) for discussion of the problem of dating this sermon.

[107] *Babylons Downfall*, A$_2$ recto.

churches with all the ordinances of Jesus Christ "in their native beauty."[108] Bridge rejected in particular both English (Episcopal) and Scottish (Presbyterian) patterns of church government, calling instead for "God's form."[109] As a dissenting brother in the Westminster Assembly and an acknowledged leader of Independency at a later date, he seems to have meant by the latter an essentially congregational policy.[110]

Two different sermons preached by Thomas Case must have fallen relatively early in this series, although the precise dates on which they were delivered are uncertain.[111] The first one took Ezekiel 20:25 as a text. Case's exhortation resembled those of Fairclough and Wilson more than Bridge's. Detailed parallels were drawn between England's sins and Israel's; divine grace alone had prevented appropriate judgments, possibly assisted by the work of pious Israelites.[112] Essentially Case called on the "Worthies of Israel" to reform: "Make such Statutes and Judgements as shall be wanting for the safety and beauty of this Church and Common-wealth; wherein let your care and commendation be that of Moses, to do all things according to the patterne."[113] The second sermon concerned the efficacy which might be expected from "covenanting." The text from Ezra (10:2-3) was put to use in arguing that both parliament and people ought to pursue reformation through national and personal covenants basically directed against popery. In advancing this theme, Case was self-consciously echoing the sermons which Marshall and Burges had addressed to the initial fast at the beginning of the parliament: "But this was solidly proved, and prudently

[108] *Ibid.*, 10-13.
[109] *Ibid.*, 13.
[110] G. F. Nuttall has summarized Bridge's career in the context of early Independency in *Visible Saints, The Congregational Way, 1640-1660* (Oxford, 1957).
[111] *Two Sermons Lately Preached at Westminster* (London, 1641). See the discussion in Appendix Three (278).
[112] *Ibid.*, 16ff. [113] *Ibid.*, 22.

limited, and lively pressed by those Reverend Divines, whom your wisdom selected for the late work of Humiliation."[114]

Another pair of sermons originated at services on May 30, 1641. It seems clear that complementarity was intended, and both preachers represented positions closer to that taken by Bridge than to the others discussed up to this point. Joseph Symonds delivered the morning exhortation. He had withdrawn to Rotterdam in 1639 and later became identified as an Independent. His colleague of the afternoon, Nathaniel Homes (or Holmes), also became allied with that party; indeed, toward the close of the Interregnum he received lodgings at Whitehall. Symonds discoursed upon the "new house of the reformed Church"; Homes described "the new world of the Church."[115] Symonds's effort especially seems to have been conceived as a supplement to the petitions flooding in upon Westminster, and he explicitly sought to interpret them.[116] For his part, Homes assured his audience that "the godly in all ages hope for new Heavens and a new Earth, of a righteous reformed Church, according to Gods promise."[117] In this elucidation of "Cosmographie" he explicitly repudiated, it should be noted, both "spiritual" and "millenarian" readings of the text (II Peter 3:13), preferring a "middle-path."[118]

Further comment on the ecclesiastical agitation engulfing Westminster during May and June was provided by a sermon on June 15. *Reformation Sure and Stedfast*[119] was the work of "T. F." and was "Published by order" of a committee of the house. The text was Zephaniah 1:1, and the preacher's intent was to suggest that, "though Josiah [the King] himselfe had a right spirit in way of Reforma-

---

114 *Ibid.*, 23 (second series of pages).
115 J. Symonds, *A Sermon* (London, 1641); N. Homes, *The New World* . . . (London, 1641).
116 *A Sermon*, C$_4$ recto ff.
117 *The New World* . . . , 9.
118 *Ibid.*, 7.
119 (London, 1641). See Appendix Three (276) for discussion of the author's identity.

tion, yet the spirits of the greatest part of the Nobles of Judah, and also of the Commons, inclined to their old superstitions in worship, and corruption in government."[120] "T. F." argued, in brief, that the hearts of the "People" must be prepared for reformation and that the settling of affairs must be directed conjointly by the magistrate and ministers in their respective spheres.[121] Especially the present reformers were in danger of making themselves "wiser then their Fathers, and [removing] things out of Church, and State, which their Predecessors found no fault with."[122] Thus the note of cautious reform, as well as support for Charles's authority, was struck by one of the preachers who appears to have participated in preaching to "sundry members" of Commons during this period.

Five days later, on June 20, parliament was summoned to take radical measures. Henry Burton, martyr turned demagogue, reminded his assembly that some four years previously "that very month" he had preached in "another kind of Pulpit, not far from this place."[123] *Englands Bondage and Hope of Deliverance* detailed the gravity of her predicament in stark contrast to the more optimistic vision of the previous preacher. Basically, Burton proclaimed the need for complete reform of the English Church, especially release from the kinds of bondage afflicting it: liturgy, ceremonies, discipline, hierarchy.[124] "So then for the patterne of Christ in the New Testament left for us, wee must goe by that which Christ hath set up in his word, and what is the summe of it, the very summe of the service of God. . . . Christ hath tyed the Church to no Ceremony, to shew, that all our service and worship of God, it must be in Spirit and Truth, . . . not . . . in shadowes and types, in imitation of the Jewes. . . ."[125] Burton looked to purge the universities

[120] *Reformation Sure and Stedfast*, 3.

[121] *Ibid.*, 13, 17.

[122] *Ibid.*, 23.

[123] *Englands Bondage and Hope of Deliverance* (London, 1641), 1. This work is severely mispaged.

[124] *Ibid.*, (21)-(24).

[125] *Ibid.*, (26) —second so numbered.

and schools that "the Church of God may be furnished with able Ministers, able to pray, and able to Preach. . . ."[126]

Burton represented an older generation than the preachers of the preceding sermons. Born in 1578, trained at Cambridge, he was a disappointed Clerk of the Closet to the Princes Henry and Charles. Rector of St. Matthew, Friday Street, with Prynne and Bastwick he had captured the imagination of English dissidents in 1637 when the three were banished. In the eyes of some they had become (upon their recent return authorized by parliament) eschatological figures—perhaps even the Three Witnesses of the Apocalypse, an interpretation which Burton himself favored at one time.[127] Others have principally emphasized that Burton preached before members of Commons—even if informally. Without doubt his appearance served at one level as a calculated repudiation of Laud's regime and also as a direct affront to the confined Archbishop. Yet it is perhaps equally significant, as the foregoing discussion indicates, that he essentially agreed with at least the more radical among the other puritan preachers heard at Westminster.[128] This sermon and other documents demonstrate, however, that in other particulars he departed from typical puritan positions. One obvious example is the sermon structure of the "plain style" preaching by which he does not appear to have been constrained. Thus, although Burton stood in continuity with the puritan brotherhood, his radical opinions suggest that some members of it were experiencing a considerable transmutation of their views.

One additional published sermon which may have originated from this period has been identified, although no external or internal evidence has been located to establish

---

[126] *Ibid.*, (29).

[127] For Burton, see W. Haller, *The Rise of Puritanism* (New York, 1938), 250-259. Burton's understanding of his own times is expressed in *The Sounding Of The Two Last Trumpets* (London, 1641); autobiographical materials are in *A Narration Of The Life Of Mr. Henry Burton* (London, 1643).

[128] His was not, as E. W. Kirby thought ("Sermons before the Commons, 1640-42," *op.cit.*, 536), the first "plea" for a "congregational" polity.

the point. *Scripture A Perfect Rule For Church-Government*[129] was "Delivered in a Sermon at Margarets Westminster, before sundry of the House of Commons." William Sedgwick, its author, later became known as "Doomsday." Not to be confused with Obadiah Sedgwick, consistently a more conservative puritan, William gained notoriety as an army preacher and carried his speculation about the impending new age to radical conclusions. At the time he delivered this sermon, possibly the late spring or early summer of 1641, his enthusiasm seems to have passed even beyond that of others in the brotherhood like Symonds and Homes, and possibly Burton too. In essence he argued for a "congregational" version of church order as scriptural. It would also be independent of the state and expressive of the overruling kingship of Christ.[130]

Taken either singly or collectively, there is no ready means by which to estimate the effect or influence of these sermons preached to "sundry of the House of Commons" during the agitation over the Root and Branch question. It seems necessary, however, to draw back from the basic implication in Trevor-Roper's assessment of Fairclough's sermon, namely, that the preaching functioned primarily to enunciate changes of parliamentary policy. In some measure it may have. Fundamentally, though, it served two more general purposes, one rather immediate and the other not fully anticipated at the time. In the short run this preaching to members of the Long Parliament amplified the broadly puritan demands for reform of church and commonwealth which were being bruited about Westminster through other means as well. Accordingly, the pulpit resonated to, and was a sounding board for, opinions in the public realm. The other function served was articulation of a common ideology (rendered in a religious idiom) which would sustain radical activity and contribute to its coherence through the various vicissitudes soon to be experienced by those who stood with parliament. In this sense,

---

129 (London, n.d. [1643?]) .
130 On the last point, see esp., 37-38.

there was continuity between these informal sermons dating from the spring months of 1641 and the fully developed program of humiliations and thanksgivings of the Long Parliament.

Apparently as early as the middle of May, Charles had begun to weigh the benefits which might accrue to him from a visit to his subjects north of the Tweed. Underlying the venture was his belief that reconciliation with the Scots and consequent support from them would be a means of reestablishing authority over his English subjects. After several delays Charles finally departed during the first days of August. At this point the attention of the House of Commons turned rather decisively from continuing agitation over ecclesiastical matters to the mundane problem of raising funds to pay off the armies so that the Scots, especially, might be returned home. In this connection a day of public thanksgiving was scheduled for September 7 to celebrate peace between the two kingdoms.[131] Stephen Marshall was asked to preach again before the house. His colleague this time was Jeremiah Burroughs.[132] Burroughs was another puritan who had been expatriated in the Low Countries, and, like William Bridge, he also became one of the "dissenting brothers" in the Assembly. The initial plan had been to hold this service in St. Margaret's, but actually it seems to have taken place at Lincoln's Inn.[133]

Both exhortations were published. Burroughs's was entitled *Sions Joy*[134] and was based upon a text in Isaiah (66:10). Its direct application was clear: "You Right Honorable, are *the anoynted of the Lord*, I meane, set a part from your Brethren, to the great worke of the Lord that He is doing in this latter age of the world."[135] The preacher paraphrased the scripture, declaring "Jerusalem" to be but a type of the true church and "Babylon" a type of the false.[136] Three doctrinal conclusions or observations formed

---

[131] *CJ*, II, 253.   [132] *Ibid.*, 276.

[133] *Ibid.*, 287. Two days after the occasion both men were thanked for their pains and asked to print their sermons.

[134] (London, 1641).   [135] *Sions Joy*, 2.   [136] *Ibid.*, 5-8.

the structure of the sermon. Throughout it, however, Burroughs equivocated about the responsibilities of parliament and deity. Ultimately this ambiguity was remedied in the assertion that God was the great disposer of human affairs: "When God *brings to the birth*, as he hath done in those great things he hath begun to doe for us, he will give strength to bring forth."[137] Marshall's sermon was published as *A Peace-Offering to God*.[138] His text was taken from Psalms (124:6-8), and in exegesis of it he presupposed an "Antecedent Doctrine," that "God, and God alone is on his peoples side to deliver them in all their most deadly and desperate dangers."[139] Marshall construed the sermon —and the text itself—as consequents or uses of this doctrine. Despite this high doctrine of divine agency, Marshall readily exhorted the members of the Long Parliament to look upon themselves as agents and not merely as pawns in the hand of the deity. "Now you have built your own house, and procured Civill Liberties, should you let Gods house lie waste, should you be . . . lesse zealous in Gods cause, then in your own."[140] For Burroughs, it had been a "great worke of the Lord" that "All things should be so carried, that Religion is maintained, Superstitious vanities removed, Praelaticall Tyranie banished, and all in a peaceable way."[141] He did advocate provision for triennial parliaments, as well as an oath and covenant against popery, but more basically he counseled that the members' attention should be given to further reform of religion.[142] Marshall, too, strenuously urged action on the matters of church and kingdom where good work had been started: "But beloved, there is yet much work to be done, yet the root of our evils is not taken away, yet the Ministery is not purged. . . ."[143]

Parliament went into recess, or interrupted its sitting, on September 9 as a result of the plague and fear of a small-

---

[137] *Ibid.*, 56-57. [138] (London, 1641).
[139] *A Peace-Offering to God*, 4-5.
[140] *Ibid.*, 50. [141] *Sions Joy*, 24. [142] *Ibid.*, 25-26, 32-33.
[143] *A Peace-Offering to God*, 50.

pox epidemic. Until October 20, therefore, business at Westminster was in the hands of committees. At that point the issue of religion was forcefully thrust upon the members by reports of massacres in Ireland. Commons seized the occasion to authorize the first of an annual series of public thanksgivings for the deliverance from the Gunpowder Treason.[144] November 5 provided an obvious opportunity for the puritan preachers to rehearse the perfidy of papists so dramatically displayed, they believed, in the Irish rebellion. Cornelius Burges was the sole preacher at this service.[145] His text was Psalm 76:10, which, freely rendered, provided his major "observation": "Let the rage of the wicked men be what it will, it shall onely raise that glory to God, and benefit to his people, which the wicked never intended; and ever fall short of that issue which they chiefly projected."[146] The original treason plot served to demonstrate "God's over-ruling and mastering the rage of man in times past."[147] Thus scripture confirmed the very recent experience of England. Burges declared that it ought to provide comfort to the godly while filling the ungodly with terror.[148]

Charles returned to London toward the end of November. Shortly thereafter suspicions were aroused by evidence that he had connived with the Irish Catholics. Reports of further massacres amplified unrest, as did the King's move to require attendance within the month of all members of Commons. The latter body undertook to print the Remonstrance at this point, thereby taking their case to the public. Soon afterward, on December 17, in response both to the continuing Irish agitation and these associated events, Commons authorized an extraordinary humiliation.[149] This was prior to inauguration of the full program of regular monthly fasts—itself a further response to that

144 *CJ*, II, 299.   145 *Ibid.*, 299, 306.
146 *Another Sermon* (London, 1641), 37.
147 *Ibid.*, 50.   148 *Ibid.*, 54ff.
149 *CJ*, II, 348. See S. R. Gardiner, *History of England, 1603-1642*, x, 83ff.

pathetic turmoil. December 22, 1641, was set aside for the exercise.[150]

In the exhortation of the morning Edmund Calamy delivered a classic analysis of God's ways with the kingdoms of men. The sermon was appropriately titled *Englands Looking-Glasse*.[151] A popular reception is indicated by the five editions through which it passed.[152] Calamy simply proposed the doctrine that "Sin ruins Kingdoms" and further assumed that, as the prophets were to the magistrates of Israel, so the preachers were in his time to the members of parliament.[153] His text, Jeremiah 18:7-10, was framed into four "doctrines," appropriately grounded in "reasons" and applied through "uses": (1) "That God hath an independent and illuminated Prerogative over all Kingdoms and Nations to build them, or destroy them as he pleaseth";[154] (2) "Though God hath this absolute power over Kingdoms and Nations, yet he seldome useth this power, but first he gives warning";[155] (3) "That Nationall turning from evil, will divert Nationall judgments, and procure Nationall blessings"[156] (repentance he construed as "Humiliation for sins past, Reformation for the time to come");[157] (4) "That when God begins to build and plant a Nation; if that Nation do evil in Gods sight, God will unbuild, pluck up, and repent of the good he intended to do unto it."[158] Thus Calamy articulated the

---

[150] Archbishop Ussher preached to the House of Lords as it sat for a corresponding fast at the Abbey. *LJ*, IV, 480, 485. Apparently there were note-takers present who arranged for publication of his sermon in their pirated edition as *Vox Hibernae* (sic) (London, 1642). Lords ordered this document suppressed in response to a petition from Ussher. Cf. *LJ*, IV, 576 (Feb. 10, 1641-2).

[151] (London, 1642).

[152] See Donald Wing, *Short-Title Catalogue of Books Printed in England, . . . 1641-1700* (New York, 1945), entries C 235-239.

[153] *Englands Looking-Glasse*, "Epistle."

[154] *Ibid.*, 3.

[155] *Ibid.*, 10.

[156] *Ibid.*, 22-23. Calamy—and the puritan parliamentary preachers in general—carefully protected their theological orthodoxy with such distinctions as "God doth sometimes *will a change*, but he never *changeth his will*." *Loc. cit.*

[157] *Ibid.*, 26.   [158] *Ibid.*, 52.

assumptions on which the program of fasts came to rest, especially the notion that the parliament, representative of the nation and hence its embodiment, in that capacity stood for the nation before God. Incumbent upon it, therefore, was the reformation of itself and also of the nation.

> If you that are the representative Body of this Nation, as you stand under this relation, be reformed, the Nation it self may be said to be reformed. For you are the Nation representatively, virtually, and eminently; you stand in the place of the whole Nation; and if you stand for Gods cause, the whole Nation doth it in you.

> The second way to reform a Nation, is when you that are the representative Body of the Nation do, as much as in you lieth, to reform the Nation you represent. This is a duty that God requires and expects from your hands.[159]

Among its other duties, Commons should "reforme the Reformation it selfe," that is, push beyond Edward to "perfect a Reformation according to the Word of God," preferably through a "free Nationall Synod."[160]

Marshall's exhortation at the afternoon service reworked the themes of the morning. It was, if anything, less universal in scope, but that very particularism undoubtedly lent a greater air of urgency to it. The text of *Reformation and Desolation*[161] was II Kings 23:26, on which he based his comment that even Josiah's excellencies did not cause the Lord to turn his wrath from Judah because of the enormity of Manasseh's provocations. The moral was that "sincere endeavours to doe God service is our whole work; but the successe of these endeavours is Gods work."[162] God's wrath, "a calme and quiet appointment of just punishment," was fearful and dreadful when "thoroughly kindled."[163] Indeed, there was no assurance that the reformation itself would avert God's vengeful desolation, even as in the instance of Judah.[164] Commons, as the "physitians" of England's

---

[159] *Ibid.*, 45. [160] *Ibid.*, 46-47. [161] (London, 1642).
[162] *Reformation and Desolation*, 6. [163] *Ibid.*, 8-9.
[164] *Ibid.*, 24-25.

health, as her Josiah, must labor to turn away the wrath even without presuming success.[165] Again Marshall articulated the proposal for a synod to legislate the health of the church: "if in your Wisdoms, you shall find it fitting that a grave Synod of Divines should be called to informe your Consciences what is to be done, I beseech you follow the direction of Gods Word in it."[166]

Two days later Commons initiated a request to the King which, when granted, was to authorize a structure of periodic fasts and regular preaching before that body. The motion of December 24, 1641, was to the effect that the Lords be asked to join with the lower house "to move his Majesty, that a monthly Fast may be kept and observed by both Houses of Parliament, and the whole Kingdom, while the Troubles continue in Ireland."[167] When the institution of regular fasts was created, the test sacrament, the original vehicle for the exhortation of parliament, was left entirely behind, except for its later resurrection as a required subscription to the Covenant. Thus developed the pattern of periodic humiliations supplemented irregularly with fasts or thanksgivings, depending upon the contingencies experienced by the emerging parliamentary (and puritan) cause.

The preceding story has been set forth in considerable detail. It discloses, in the first place, the profound differences between Elizabeth's recognition of the potential disruption embodied in unregulated preaching and the Stuart failure at least to deny the opportunity if the danger was perceived. The Queen had appreciated the potential power of the pulpit, and she jealously watched over it. She also feared an independent Commons and apparently realized that a conjunction of forces represented within these institutions would constitute a fundamental threat to the authority of the Crown. Her summary repudiation of the original proposal for a fast in Commons and her instant demand for fealty, indeed abasement, attest her decisive

---

[165] *Ibid.,* 51ff.   [166] *Ibid.,* 53.
[167] *CJ,* II, 356; *LJ,* IV, 488, 493.

eminence, as well as the Tudor intuition for which she was justly esteemed. What had been denied to the impulsive, almost clumsy "puritans" under Elizabeth, however, was slowly and carefully nurtured under the Stuarts. It is impossible, of course, to reconstruct the exact divisions on given issues. Still, it may be assumed that the 1614 test communion appealed to all members of the house who feared the power of Rome, an influence which appeared plausible, if not wholly real, after the Powder Plot and which subsequently seemed confirmed in Laud's program for the Church of England, as well as in Henrietta's apparent influence over her husband. That original proposal should not be construed as having been in any exclusive sense "puritan"; it was probably supported by any members who believed that the Protestant radicals constituted as grave a threat as the recusants. The significant point, however, is that the Stuarts were unable, in response to parliamentary initiative, to divide and separate the potential opposition. Perhaps more antipuritan in a dogmatic sense than Elizabeth, James and Charles failed to isolate the party and insulate it from the other sources of opposition to their reigns.

A second point, as important as the first, is the contrast between the shrewd procedures of the Stuart puritans (including sympathizers) and the blunt and forthright techniques of their predecessors. Careful planning and able execution were evident in the sophisticated Feoffees scheme and also in the colonial ventures, both of which have been more thoroughly studied. The painstaking and resourceful development of preaching to Commons in the context of fasts for the realm demonstrates the same characteristics of the seventeenth-century puritans. The pattern of fasts in parliament and throughout the kingdom had already been established by the time civil war broke out. The parliamentary fasts of humiliation had been separated from the test sacrament. The House of Commons had been explicitly construed as a body representative of the commonwealth before God. These were central presuppositions which would characterize the institution of fasts and thanksgivings as it was elaborated within the Long Parliament. Thus a program fully tuned to puritan ends was potentially present and required only Charles's sanction to be implemented on a regular basis. In the context of the Irish crisis his authorization was forthcoming.

III

The Program of Humiliations and Thanksgivings

THE PARLIAMENTARY petition of December elicited a formal response from Charles during the next weeks. On January 8, 1641-2, he issued a proclamation which was to become the charter for a program of monthly fasts or humiliations throughout the kingdom, including regular exhortation of the House of Commons. The "general, publick and solemn Fast . . . kept and holden, as well by abstinence from food, as by publick prayer, preaching and hearing of the word of God, and other sacred Duties in all Cathedral, Collegiate, and Parish Churches and Chapels within His Majesty's Kingdom of *England* and Dominion of *Wales*," already scheduled for the twentieth of January (except in London and Westminster), was confirmed. Thereafter similar fasts were to be held both in the parliament and throughout the realm "on the last *Wednesday* of every Month during the troubles of the said Kingdom of *Ireland*."[1]

It would be interesting to know how faithfully this proclamation was observed, at least initially, in the "Parish Churches and Chapels." Practice probably varied according to the loyalty and initiative of the local cleric, the temper of the congregation and parish, and the sympathy of diocesan authority insofar as it was effectively exercised. Such an assessment of the monthly fast institution at the parish or even cathedral levels has not been attempted in this study. A limited amount of circumstantial evidence might be accumulated, but it would be very difficult to complete a systematic evaluation of the practice as a local phe-

---

[1] J. Rushworth, *Historical Collections* (London, 1692), III, i, 494. Cf. *LJ*, IV, 497.

nomenon during the civil war period. To offer adequate generalizations about it would be hazardous indeed. The regular exercises of the Long Parliament, however, constitute another matter.

For the purposes of the clerical puritans, who aspired to a voice in the affairs of state, the royal proclamation represented a remarkable advance in their cause. The King had authorized fasts to be held on the last Wednesday of every month which would prominently include preaching before parliament. Obviously puritan preachers would continue to preach informally before the members of parliament under the less regular and less official circumstances discussed in Chapter I. Significant clerical energies were directly focused, however, by the opportunity which had been created by this mandate Charles had provided for the regular "humiliation" of the Long Parliament. Formally the provision was contingent upon the Irish crisis, and it was linked also to the more general fasting of the realm. Otherwise the institution was unencumbered. The program of periodic fasting and formal humiliation thus was a considerable development beyond those modest provisions in parliaments under James, in the early Caroline years, and during the preceding months of the Long Parliament which were discussed in Chapter II. "By agreeing to the system," Trevor-Roper observes, "Charles I had put into the hands of his enemies a means of co-ordination and propaganda to which he himself had no parallel."[2]

The system of monthly humiliations was most fully elaborated in the House of Commons. On the regular fast days business was usually omitted, and members of Commons were expected to attend the services at St. Margaret's, Westminster. The basic program included two exhortations, one in the morning and one in the afternoon. Conventionally the preachers were "thanked" for their efforts, and motions "desiring them" to print their sermons were passed, often on the fast day itself but sometimes after a lapse of several days. These sentiments were usually con-

2 "Fast Sermons," 306.

veyed by individuals specifically charged with the task. At the same time clerics were nominated to direct the next humiliation. As in the formal procedures for thanking the preachers, the invitations were extended personally, probably by that relative, patron, or acquaintance who had proposed him. As the routine continued through the years, it was often necessary, and increasingly so, to arrange for substitutes (for reasons too diverse, numerous, and insignificant to discuss at this point). Quite clearly Commons was asserting a "representative" role for itself, and the institution presumably embodied and reflected the practices which, on a lesser scale, the members expected would characterize fast celebrations throughout the kingdom. Supplementary humiliations and thanksgivings were also arranged during the decade as proper responses to the fortunes of the commonwealth.[3] In the House of Lords the pattern developed in the lower house was not adopted, at least formally, until the fall of 1644. Thereafter the peers generally met in Westminster Abbey (Henry VII's Chapel).

Primary emphasis within the present study falls upon the content of the exhortations at the fasts and feasts. In passing, however, it ought to be noted that the institution functioned also as a means of displaying the unity of the parliamentary cause and as a vehicle for rendering the cause coherent through symbolic political ceremonies which, theoretically at any rate, engaged the entire realm. The Solemn League and Covenant, when it was adopted and formal subscription to it was required, simply made manifest what, for the puritans in any case, had been implicit up to that point. In short, the "humiliations" at Westminster and throughout the land were a kind of ritual behavior, and the significance of the phenomenon was not exhausted by the particular circumstances during any month or by the specific content of the preaching—however much emphasis is placed upon those aspects of it in this study. The remainder of the present chapter will trace in skeletal form the course of development the fast institution underwent,

[3] *Ibid.*, 309.

especially as it was embodied in the exhortations to the House of Commons.

The first of the monthly fasts common to parliament and nation was held on February 23, 1641-2. Edmund Calamy and Stephen Marshall were the preachers, as they had been at the extraordinary fast of the previous December. In an epistle to the printed version of his sermon, Calamy did not fail to herald the advent of regular humiliations: "we are likely to be blessed by the providence of God, bringing good out of evill, with twelve Nationall, solemne, publike Fasts every yeare, which (if rightly kept) will be as the twelve Gates of the New Jerusalem, spoken of, Revel. 21. Every Fast will be as a Gate to let us in, into a part of the New Jerusalem of Mercy, and happinesse promised to the people of God, here upon the earth."[4] The immediate political context for this first regular fast was the impeachment of Digby and fresh suspicion of Charles's perfidy, the latter seemingly confirmed by the Queen's departure for the continent. Calamy preached an introduction to the religious significance of "humiliation": "Now my purpose is to lay the sins of England against God in one scale, and the mercies of God to England in the other scale, and to call upon you this day to be humbled, and ashamed, and broken in heart before the Lord, that ever you should sinne against such a God."[5] Stephen Marshall, his companion, elected to speak even more directly, inveighing against "neuters." In his *Meroz Cursed*[6] he proposed that "All people are cursed or blessed according as they doe or doe not joyne their strength and give their best assistance to the Lords people against their enemies."[7] Trevor-Roper notes that Marshall's *Meroz Cursed* was prototypical for a "long series of incendiary sermons."[8] Many of them explicitly elaborated Judges 5:23, a text which would again prove "fruitful" in the colonists' struggle for independence from London and Westminster more than a century

---

[4] *Gods Free Mercy to England* (London, 1642), "Epistle."
[5] *Ibid.*, 2.   [6] (London, 1641).   [7] *Meroz Cursed*, 9.
[8] "Fast Sermons," 308 (see also n. 1).

later.[9] Marshall's conclusion was ominous: "Gods blessing is upon them that come to helpe him: . . . Meroz, and with Meroz all others are cursed, who come not out to the help of the Lord against the mighty."[10] Within days, apparently, Hyde's active collaboration with Charles began. He became the King's agent at Westminster and, with his fellow royalist sympathizers, eventually fell subject to Marshall's curse, if not God's.[11]

During the month Charles withdrew northward, and his separation from both houses increased. Shortly before the March fast the "Kentish Petition" once again brought the matter of church reform to the attention of parliament.[12] The preachers at the fast on March 30 naturally took the opportunity to address themselves to these issues with the expectation of parliamentary action. Cornelius Burges had been without "an opportunity of finishing the Text" of his sermon until 1645, but his exhortation to repentance, when completed and published, still manifested that urgent pressure for reform which had been its original context. He made bold to suggest that the bloody rebellion in Ireland was divine punishment for failure to convene a "Synode or Assembly . . . the last Summer."[13] Simeon Ash echoed the need for an assembly to dismantle the "Prelaticall Government" which "hath . . . bin the root of all, or (at least) of almost all these oppressions," which he carefully detailed.[14] The sermons at the April fast were even less measured in their insistence upon purging the "leprosy" from the commonwealth and completing the unfinished "Temple."[15] As far as the pulpit in St. Margaret's was concerned, civil war had already begun.

[9] Alan Heimert, *Religion and the American Mind* (Cambridge, Mass., 1966), esp. Ch. IX: "The Curse of Meroz," 454-509.

[10] *Meroz Cursed*, 54.

[11] S. R. Gardiner, *The History of England 1603-42* (London, 1884), x, 169-170.

[12] *Ibid.*, 179-180.

[13] *Two Sermons* . . . (London, 1645), 46.

[14] *The Best Refuge* . . . (London, 1642), 61.

[15] The sermons were preached by Joseph Caryl and Thomas Goodwin.

The May 1642 fast was held as sides were clearly forming for the impending struggle. During these weeks
Charles's supporters were assembling with him at York. On
the morning of the twenty-fifth Robert Harris preached to
Commons, addressing his remarks to the apparent delay in
God's expected intervention on behalf of England. "If you
will wisely enquire into a reason of Gods proceedings," he
declared, "reflect upon your selves, and charge the slownesse
upon your owne soules."[16] In the afternoon Obadiah Sedgwick counseled reformation as the means to *England's
Preservation*[17] holding it forth as "the onely way to prevent destroying Judgments." At this point Commons,
which for some weeks had been about the business of nom-
inating divines for the projected assembly, placed a restriction on the fast day pulpit: "Ordered, that hereafter,
those of the Assembly shall be desired to preach, at the
Publick Fasts, before the House of Commons."[18] With the
flush of the later parliamentary victories, other clerics were
occasionally invited, at first only for the thanksgivings and
then subsequently for the regular humiliations as well.

The two fast sermons at the end of June clearly articulated what were to be the basic motifs of the puritan
propaganda delivered to the Long Parliament. William
Gouge, a patriarch of the brotherhood, held up Nehemiah
as an exemplar of true patriotism: "By this recollection of
the principall acts of this Patriot, you see what remarkable matters he did. . . . Hereby also you may further
see what becomes worthy Patriots to doe. . . ."[19] That afternoon "Doomsday" Sedgwick expatiated upon *Zions Deliverance And Her Friends Duty: Or The Grounds of Expecting, and Meanes of Procuring Jerusalems Restauration.*[20]
Patriotism and prophetism would continue to be chief
staples of the parliamentary diet throughout the decade.

---

[16] *A Sermon* (London, 1642), 42. [17] (London, 1642).
[18] *CJ*, II, 587 (March 25, 1642). Cf. W. A. Shaw, *A History of the
English Church . . . 1640-1660* (London, 1900), I, 124. It was actually
observed beginning with the July fast.
[19] *The Saints Support* (London, 1642), 29.
[20] (London, 1642).

The program of monthly humiliations, if it required justification as a religious ceremony for the kingdom, received it with the outbreak of the civil war. Introducing the published version of his sermon at the July fast, Thomas Hill proposed that "the stability of all our blessings must come by the True Religion."[21] Edward Reynolds, his colleague, made a plea for "more obedience and solemnitie" in observance of "these solemne dayes . . . of this whole Kingdome."[22] Early parliamentary reverses and fears, combined with overtures to the Scots, became in the hands of William Carter grounds for enjoining an explicit covenant upon the English "Israel" through analogy to the biblical period of the Judges.[23] The same theme was incidentally repeated two months later, on October 26, by Thomas Temple in his discussion of *Christ's Government In and over his People*,[24] a sermon which even more directly voiced the resolve to abolish episcopacy. (By this time there had been progress on a bill for establishing an assembly of divines.) Scripture proved no less a source for striking political symbolism in Thomas Wilson's *Jerichoes Down-fall*[25] and in Thomas Case's *Gods Rising, His Enemies Scattering*,[26] which graced the September and October fasts respectively. The printed version of the latter sermon indicates that during its delivery Lord Wharton passed Case a note which permitted the preacher to make a dramatic announcement of the divine intervention at Edgehill.[27]

The monthly pattern was first supplemented during November 1642 in celebration of "deliverance from the Gunpowder Treason." Matthew Newcomen preached on *The Craft and Cruelty of the Churches Adversaries*.[28] In the context of fitful negotiations between parliament and the King, Newcomen argued that God ordained deceit on the

21 *The Trade Of Truth Advanced* (London, 1642), "Epistle."
22 *Israels Petition* (London, 1642), 7.
23 *Israels Peace with God* (London, 1642), 28ff.
24 (London, 1642).   25 (London, 1643).
26 (London, 1644).   27 *Gods Rising . . .*, 49.
28 (London, 1643). His text was Nehemiah 4:11.

part of enemies for the trial and exercise of His people. The experience of deceit should serve as well to manifest His glory.[29] Turning his attention to King Charles, he boldly played upon the theme of a ruler's alienation from his people brought about by the craft and cruelty of his advisers: "As for our Sovereign, Thou O God in whose hands the hearts of Kings are, free his heart from the councels and ingagements of mischievous men and men of blood. Give him a true understanding of, and a due confidence in the loyall affections of his Protestant Subjects. Bring him backe among us, rather in the prayers and teares then in the blouds of his people."[30] Charles's tactics in pressing his military advantage during the following weeks while at the same time negotiating with parliament served to render suspect Newcomen's doctrine about the evil influence of advisers upon an innocent King.[31] The cautionary effect of the exhortation, however, may well have reflected the influence of Pym in his struggle with the "peace party."

The November humiliation was the work of Charles Herle and Richard Vines. The latter, in his discourse on *Calebs Integrity in Following the Lord Fully*,[32] espoused the conventional puritan criterion of faithfulness to a Hebraic God and inveighed against "murmuring and disaffected Israelites" who might, for example, begrudge financial support for the parliamentary forces.[33] The exhortation offered by Herle breathed a different spirit from that of Vines, as well as those which had preceded it. In a sober and reflective manner Herle proposed that "truth" and "peace" were a "Payre of Compasses" to guide church and state.[34] The exhortations at the December fast also revealed the popular currents which were working toward ac-

29 *The Craft and Cruelty* . . . , 12ff.
30 *Ibid.*, 38f.
31 S. R. Gardiner, *The History of the Great Civil War* (London, 1886) , I, 70.
32 (London, 1642) .
33 *Calebs Integrity* . . . , 20ff.
34 *A Payre of Compasses for Church and State* (London, 1642) .

commodation rather than war. Corbett presented a quasi-philosophical discourse on *Gods Providence*,[35] and Thomas Valentine described the graces of patience and hope which enabled the church to "endure the absence of Christ."[36]

The two exhortations which completed the first year of the monthly fasts were certainly less irenic than the December sermons. In the setting of impending negotiations between parliamentary Commissioners and Charles, the efforts of the preachers appear to have served directly the ends of the "war party." John Arrowsmith's sanguinary exercise exalted war and the sword as divine means of avenging covenant unfaithfulness. In detail he enumerated the "quarrell-breeding sword-avenged violations of the Covenant."[37] Jeremiah Whitaker's companion sermon glorified Christ as the "Settlement of Unsettled Times."[38] No less than Arrowsmith, however, he stressed the shaking of kingdoms and nations that alone would signify reform adequate to the desired goal. No hint of accommodation was present in these exercises, which clearly illustrate how the pulpit at St. Margaret's could have an immediate bearing on and effective role in the politics of Westminster.[39]

Trevor-Roper emphasizes Pym's manipulation of the fast preaching during the early months of 1643. Committed to negotiation with Charles but convinced of his bad faith, constrained by shifting sentiments at Westminster and without a secure military posture, this master of Commons still had one resource at his command: the influence he could exert over parliament. The regular humiliations were ideal instruments for this purpose. *Joabs Counsell, and King Davids Seasonable Hearing it*[40] was delivered by Walter Bridges at the February fast.[41] Preaching on II

[35] (London, 1642).   [36] *A Sermon* (London, 1643).

[37] *The Covenant-Avenging Sword Brandished* (London, 1643), 18ff.

[38] *Ejrenopojos, Christ the Settlement of Unsettled Times* (London, 1642).

[39] Cf. Trevor-Roper, "Fast Sermons," 310ff.

[40] (London, 1643).

[41] Trevor-Roper makes William Bridge, later dissenting brother, the mouthpiece for Pym. "Fast Sermons," 311-312. More likely it was

Samuel 19, Bridges found perspective upon the civil war of his time in the Old Testament histories of Israel's kingship. As Joab had spoken plainly to David about permitting his love for Absalom to supplant his love for his people, so parliament should not hesitate to remind Charles of his duties. "In sad times, and times of imminent danger, the greatest of men ought to suffer themselves to be very plainly dealt withall."[42] Bridges went on to insist that "retractions of publique persons, as Kings, &c. are exceeding attractive. . . ."[43] Equally explicit was his heralding of the attack on Henrietta, now returned to Charles, as an obstacle to settlement of the kingdom.[44]

Two additional fire-eating sermons, plainly supporting the now radical tactics of Pym, were preached at the April fast. John Ley titled his disquisition *The Fury of Warre*.[45] But, after admitting war's evil character, he insisted that perpetual tyranny and slavery were worse. He concluded that error was wickedness, and sin folly. His colleague's sermon might be taken as an application of these principles. William Greenhill, choosing his text from Matthew, exhorted Commons to lay "the Axe at the Root" as fit response to the divine judgments (Axe) England was experiencing.[46] Since the kingdom was being punished for the sin of some, their removal would ensure divine favor. Judicious care with the pruning knife would forestall blunt use of the axe. The link between this exhortation and the subsequent hewing down of Cheapside Cross (on May 2) seems clear. Before the month was out, the attack on

---

Walter Bridges. "W. Bridges" (title page of sermon) is identified as "Preacher of the Gospell at Dunstans in the East, London." In two other publications during the same year, William Bridge was identified as "Preacher of God's Word at Yarmouth." See *Catalogue of the McAlpin Collection*, II, 190. "Walter Bridges" was sanctioned as lecturer at Olave's, Hart Street, London, in January, 1642-3. Cf. *CJ*, II, 933; W. A. Shaw, *op.cit.*, II, 305.

42 *Joabs Counsell* . . . , 18.
43 *Ibid.*, 22-23.
44 Trevor-Roper, "Fast Sermons," 312.
45 (London, 1643).
46 *The Axe at the Root* (London, 1643).

the Queen was under way, and efforts were being made to resume the impeachment of Laud.[47]

The preaching on May 31 was less inflammatory. It concerned the preservation of Sion and the dependence of the church upon God.[48] During the humiliation Pym received a message informing him, ostensibly for the first time, of "Waller's Plot" (as it came to be known). "Mr. Pimm, . . . with some of the most active members rise from their seats, and after a little whispering together remove out of the church: this could not but exceedingly affect those who stayed behind."[49] This revelation of Charles's duplicity served Pym's immediate purposes since it directly undercut the peace party and enabled him to propose methods of discipline within the Lords as well as Commons.[50] This was the occasion for the first of many "thanksgivings," which were celebrated with preaching no less than were the "humiliations."

Each house set aside June 15 for the puritan preachers. Calamy and Herle did the honors for the Lords. Calamy's "doctrine" tells all: "It is the duty of all men, but especially of such as are Joshuah's, such as are Rulers and Nobles, to ingage themselves and their Families to serve God resolutely, speedily and publikely. . . ."[51] Herle was also unequivocal: "There is no man so great, but he is greater, by thrusting himselfe into the throng of such as sing unto the Lord and hartily rejoyce in the strength of their salvation."[52] These shameless pleas to the peers for their support in the reform of church and commonwealth contrast vividly with the method of the Commons preachers.

[47] Trevor-Roper, "Fast Sermons," 313-314.

[48] F. Cheynell, *Sions Momento, and Gods Alarum* (London, 1643); A. Perne, *Gospell Courage* (London, 1643).

[49] Clarendon, *History of the Rebellion*, ed. W. D. McCray (Oxford, 1888), VII, 62 (III, 44). Trevor-Roper points out that Thomas May, in *The History of the Parliament* (London, 1645, 1647), also reported this event. "Fast Sermons," 314, n. 1.

[50] S. R. Gardiner, *The History of the Great Civil War*, I, 173-174: "After this revelation everything was possible for Pym."

[51] *The Noble-Mans Patterne* (London, 1643), 5.

[52] *Davids Song of Three Parts* (London, 1643), 5f.

Stephen Marshall rhapsodized over the important "discovery of [this] dangerous, desparate, and bloudy Designe," clearly full of portent. For him it was to be interpreted as a work of Christ in pouring out the "vials of wrath" upon the Antichrist (Revelation).[53] Obadiah Sedgwick construed it as another Haman's plot (Esther), counseling that God would not forsake the righteous in England either.[54]

Following the regular fast on June 28, 1643, two extraordinary occasions supplemented the monthly routine at Westminster. On July 7 the now convened Assembly of Divines joined with the Lords and Commons in a fast at the Abbey dedicated to settlement of the English church.[55] Oliver Bowles sought to quicken "Zeale for Gods House."[56] Matthew Newcomen, apparently a last-minute replacement, defined the role of the clergy as "Jerusalems Watch-Men, the Lords Remembrancers."[57] A fortnight later, on July 21, the Lords and Commons joined in a fast for the "reformation of sundry and divers sins and enormities in the Church." Three exhortations graced this occasion, of which only two were published. Thomas Hill turned to the vein of apocalyptic imagery in the scripture to discourse on "the Militant Church, Triumphant over the Dragon and His Angels."[58] "In the Churches conflicts they prove victorious souldiers, who love not their lives so dearly, as they love Christ and his cause."[59] William Spurstowe assessed the monthly fast program and concluded that it had not been sufficiently effective, perhaps owing to its involuntary character, its failure to produce a passionate (rather than merely rational) sorrow, and its inability to make constant the hu-

---

[53] *The Song of Moses* (London, 1643), 3ff.

[54] *Haman's Vanity* (London, 1643).

[55] W. A. Shaw recounts the parliamentary background to the calling of the Assembly, *op.cit.*, I, 122ff.

[56] *Zeale for Gods House Quickened* (London, 1643).

[57] *Jerusalems Watch-Men, the Lords Remembrancers* (London, 1643).

[58] *The Militant Church, Triumphant Over The Dragon And His Angels* (London, 1643).

[59] *Ibid.*, 24.

miliation it intended to inculcate.[60] Thenceforward the monthly sequence was more frequently supplemented with humiliations and thanksgivings, as seemed appropriate to the "times."

The stated humiliations for July and August apparently reflected the labors engaging the Assembly, which had been set to work upon the Thirty-Nine Articles, charged with clearing their doctrine "from all Aspersions and false Interpretations."[61] Concurrently, however, another chain of events—parliamentary negotiations with the Scots—was fast closing in upon Westminster.[62] The English Commissioners to the Conference at Leith were effectively led by Vane, who was directly assisted by Stephen Marshall and Philip Nye representing the Assembly. The Solemn League and Covenant, ratified on August 17 by the Convention of Estates, bound England and Scotland to close political cooperation and, more ambiguously, to similar Reformed ecclesiastical polities. Both parliament and the Assembly directed their attention to the agreement as soon as it was received.[63] As revised by the Assembly and Commons, the Covenant was accepted by the Lords and returned for subscription.

September 25 was set apart for this event. On that day Philip Nye was joined as preacher by Alexander Henderson, one of the Scottish Commissioners to the Assembly. The occasion was fully reported as *The Covenant: with a Narrative of the Proceedings*.[64] Meeting in St. Margaret's on a Monday, members of Commons and the Assembly, in addition to the preaching, heard prayers by John White and William Gouge, listened to a reading of the text of the Solemn League and Covenant, and then

[60] *Englands Patterne and Duty In It's Monthly Fasts* (London, 1643), 16ff.

[61] W. A. Shaw, *op.cit.*, I, 145ff. Cf. *CJ*, III, 156. Among the sermons were S. Simpson's *Reformation's Preservation* (London, 1643) and A. Tuckney's *The Balme of Gilead* (London, 1643).

[62] Shaw, I, 125ff.

[63] Roughly from August 28 until September 15. Shaw, I, 153.

[64] (London, 1643).

individually took the oath.[65] Nye proclaimed that "The effect of that Oath you shall find to be this, that the kingdoms of the world become the kingdomes of the Lord and his Christ, and he shall reigne for ever, *Rev.* 11."[66] Henderson's expectations, if expansive, were less eschatological. He opined that "through the weight of the Covenant" divine providence would "cast the ballance, and make Religion and Righteousnesse to prevaile, to the glory of God, the honour of our King, the confusion of our common Enemies, and the comfort and safety of the people of God."[67]

Four days later, on September 29, another opportunity was offered for entering into the Covenant. The *Commons Journals* indicates that a total of four hundred and forty-five individuals took the oath at this time, including members of the nobility, knights, and gentry, as well as officers and soldiers, Scotsmen in London, and additional divines.[68] Thomas Coleman preached on Jeremiah 30:21b, which provided him with a means of directly exhorting those who were assembled on the subject of engagement of the heart to God.[69]

Still another convention for taking the Covenant was held on October 6. Joseph Caryl chose Nehemiah 9:38 as his text, grounding on it, appropriately, a rather full analysis entitled *The Nature, Solemnity, Grounds, Property, and Benefits, Of a Sacred Covenant.*[70] Thereafter Commons began the practice of excluding from the house those who would not take the oath.[71] During February 1643-4 subscription was enforced by ordinance.[72] As late as December 1646 the Covenant continued to be taken, and subscription duly recorded.[73]

---

[65] *The Covenant . . .* , 10. Cf. S. R. Gardiner, *The History of the Great Civil War,* I, 276.
[66] *The Covenant . . .* , 15.   [67] *Ibid.,* 34.
[68] *CJ,* III, 259.
[69] *The Hearts Ingagement* (London, 1643).
[70] (London, 1643).
[71] See *CJ,* III, 271, 275, 297, 299, 302.
[72] *Ibid.,* 389.   [73] See *CJ,* V, 33.

Interesting parallels might be drawn between the development of this Covenant subscription as an instrument of control within the Long Parliament and the use of the test sacraments adopted in earlier parliaments. However it may have been construed personally by Pym, who seems to have been relatively indifferent to strictly theological distinctions, the Covenant did serve to exclude the waverers while it bound together those who remained in, or loyal to, parliament. One major difference was that, whereas the test sacrament had exacted allegiance to the established ecclesiastical order, thereby excluding those who dissented from it, the Solemn League and Covenant required at least acquiesence in, if not active support for, a programmatic reform of the English church. In the technical sense, it stipulated as the common goal the completion of ecclesiastical revolution. In this way it may be viewed as an attempt to marshal the religious energies which had been vented during the preceding years and to direct them toward social reconstruction. It also represented, of course, the "conditions" under which Scottish assistance would be forthcoming.

The program of monthly fasts continued during the fall of 1643. On September 27, Humphrey Chambers offered *A Divine Ballance To Weigh Religious Fasts In*.[74] He pressed on to the conclusion that the Lord would "despise, and reject those solemn fasts, wherein men fast unto themselves, and not unto him."[75] The rest of the exhortations at these humiliations seem to reflect the tortuous path being taken toward the settlement of a government upon the church in England, a topic directly under discussion from about the middle of October.[76] Paired with Chambers in September, Anthony Burges tackled the problem in *The Difficulty of, And Encouragements to A Reformation*.[77] At the next fast Arthur Salwey condemned "neuters" or "Waverers" in religion: "Honourable, and Beloved, in matters civill we have sometimes a latitude, and libertie of

[74] (London, 1643) .
[76] W. A. Shaw, *op.cit.*, I, 154ff.
[75] *Ibid.*, 39.
[77] (London, 1643) .

suspension: but in Religion there is a necessitie of determination, and resolution."[78] On the same occasion Henry Wilkinson explored the application of apocalyptic imagery to the turmoil of the time.[79] During the course of the next month the deliberations in the Assembly revealed the great obstacles to accommodation between the parties represented. William Bridge, formerly an expatriate and now a dissenting brother in the Assembly, called bluntly for "exactnesse of reformation."[80] He referred implicitly to the ambiguous formulation of the Solemn League and Covenant and threw down this challenge: "You know what other Reformed Churches have done, the Reformation of all other Churches are round about you, you have their writings before you, their books, their practices, their examples, and this for many yeeres; can you think that God hath set us now for an hundred yeeres upon their shoulders, to see no farther into Reformation then they have done?"[81] Following Bridge's candid remarks the pulpit in parliament clearly became, in one of its roles, a sounding board for amplifying and making available to the public the discussions taking place within the Assembly behind the walls of the Jerusalem Chamber in the Abbey.

On December 8, John Pym, whose health had been poor throughout the fall, died. In tribute to his leadership the two houses and the Assembly paid respects with a funeral in the Abbey. Predictably Marshall was the preacher. His exhortation underscored the loss: Pym could ill be spared, and lament was the appropriate response.[82] The funeral oration which followed, published as an addendum to the sermon, portrayed "King" Pym as an exemplary Christian and an exemplary servant of the commonwealth. The

[78] *Halting Stigmatiz'd* . . . (London, 1644), 8.
[79] *Babylons Ruine, Jerusalems Rising* (London, 1643).
[80] *A Sermon Preached* . . . *Novemb. 29. 1643* (London, 1643), "Epistle."
[81] *Ibid.*, 24.
[82] *Threnodia, The Churches Lamentation* . . . (London, 1644), 1-21. Because of circumstance and content his "lamentation" should be viewed as closely related to the fast and thanksgiving sermons preached to the Long Parliament.

preacher also took great pains to lay to rest rumors that Pym's death had been unnatural.[83]

Convention rendered fitting—if conviction would not have required—invitations for the Scottish Commissioners to participate in the work of English humiliation. At the fasts during each of the following four months a Commissioner delivered one of the sermons. Alexander Henderson led off in December, followed in turn by Rutherford, Baillie, and Gillespie. Henderson summarized the counsel of the Scots and disclosed the attitude taken by the delegation with his blunt observation that "it is a speciall wisdom in these that have place and power, to prevent or turn away the wrath of God from the present and future generation by establishing true Religion, and ordering the house of God aright."[84] By the time his turn had arrived, at the fast on February 28, Robert Baillie had become wholly exasperated with "these extraordinary and unexpected delays of setting up the Government of God in his House."[85] The dour Scotsman was certain he detected the hand of Satan in the deliberate course pursued by parliament and its creature, the Assembly.[86] At the March fast George Gillespie pointedly declared that "Reformation ends not in contemplation, but in action."[87]

On each of these stated fast days the Commissioners were paired with clerical members of the Assembly. Although it would be too pat to discover explicit disavowal or repudiation of the Scottish sense of urgency at every point in these companion sermons, it was certainly present in several of them. At the December fast, for example, John Strickland argued that "It is not without some reference to the good of his people, that God suffereth so long, and visits not presently their wicked enemies."[88] In February,

[83] *Ibid.*, 21ff.
[84] *A Sermon . . . December 27. 1643* (London, 1644), 32.
[85] *Satan The Leader in Chief* (London, 1643), "Epistle."
[86] *Ibid.*, 33ff.
[87] *A Sermon Preached . . . March 27. 1644* (London, 1644), 39. On the role of the Scottish Commissioners in the fast institution, see H. R. Trevor-Roper, "Fast Sermons," 314-323.
[88] *Gods Work of Mercy In Sions Misery* (London, 1644), 3.

Thomas Young, in proposing that God's people were patient under affliction, directly controverted the Commissioners' position.[89] The parliamentary mood was probably best captured by an expansive Stephen Marshall in *A Sacred Panegyrick*,[90] which he preached at a special thanksgiving on January 18, 1643-4. In it he exulted over concurrence within so much of the realm of England.[91] As for the Assembly itself, Daniel Cawdrey's sermon[92] at the January fast might be construed as a negative response to the Independent manifesto, *The Apologeticall Narration*, which was probably issued at that very time.[93] That tract could only be interpreted as an appeal some members of the Assembly voiced to parliament and, for that matter, to the kingdom at large. John Bond, apparently inclined to Independency, suggested the dimensions of the confusion present in the English political and ecclesiastical scene by the attempt he made to resolve everything into a divine mystery.[94]

During the month of April 1644 astonishing time, energy, and attention were lavished on the preaching to Commons, which can only have proved distracting. Waller's victory over Hopton's Army provided the occasion for a day of thanksgiving on the ninth. Thomas Case reminded Commons that extensive preaching to the army had made a not inconsiderable contribution to the parliamentary cause.[95] "Will you give me leave, to speak a word in plain English, I know you will; If you do not purge your Armies, as well as recrute them, you may recrute them, to your own and the Kingdoms confusion." "Your armies are reforming Armies, let it bee your care to make them reformed Armies, and you may humbly expect that God will go out with

---

[89] *Hopes Incouragement Pointed At* (London, 1644), 4.

[90] (London, 1644).

[91] See *A Sacred Panegyrick*, 3.

[92] *The Good Man a Publick Good* (London, 1643).

[93] *The Apologeticall Narration* (London, 1643) has been reissued in a facsimile edition with critical notes and an introductory essay by Robert Paul (Boston, 1963).

[94] *Salvation In A Mystery* (London, 1644).

[95] Cf. L. Solt, *Saints in Arms* (Stanford, 1959).

them, to enable them to do Exploits."[96] Fairfax's victory at
Selby was celebrated on the twenty-third in similar fashion.
In printing his discourse, Joseph Caryl surveyed the practice and pronounced it good: "Let your pietie be as zealous
(in keeping the dayes of praise and thanksgiving) to record
blessings, as it hath bin (in keeping daies of Prayer and
Fasting) to procure them."[97] The scheduled fast followed
on the next day, and it, too, was observed with due
solemnity. In thanking John Greene and Edmund Staunton
for their participation, and while determining who would
be the preachers for the next regular fast, Commons en-
acted a 10/-fine for failure to attend the appointed church
on the days of humiliation.[98]

The stated pattern was next supplemented on July 18
when the Lords and Commons jointly assembled in an ex-
ultant thanksgiving for the victory over Prince Rupert at
Marston Moor, as well as for the subsequent surrender of
York. Scottish valor in the field was acknowledged through
Henderson's participation. Preaching upon Peter's deliverance, reported in Matthew 14, he reminded parliament that
God was author of their deliverance as well.[99] As a
"stranger," however, he could not resist remarking upon
three uncommon matters he had observed in the southern
kingdom which left him incredulous: that critics of Reformed Churches should be tolerated, sects and divisions allowed, and church reformation suspended.[100] Richard
Vines, who shared the pulpit with Henderson on that day,
but not the latter's reservations, rhapsodized over the victory as a manifestation of God.[101] Except for subsequent
appearances at regular humiliations of the Lords and a special sermon in 1645 by Gillespie, the Scottish Commissioners were extended no further opportunities to preach formally at the fasts and thanksgivings of the Long Parliament.

[96] *The Root of Apostacy* (London, 1644), 9, 10.
[97] *The Saints Thankfull Acclamation* . . . (London, 1644), "Epistle."
[98] *CJ*, III, 468.
[99] *A Sermon Preachd . . . 18 July 1644* (London, 1644).
[100] *Ibid.*, 21-22.
[101] *Magnalia Dei ab Aquilone; Set Forth* (London, 1644), 1off.

By the end of July 1644, however, the fortunes of the contending parties had been reversed, and Essex was in a difficult position in Cornwall. It seemed likely that Charles would be able to press his advantage. The houses at Westminster collectively responded with an extraordinary humiliation on August 13. Thomas Hill and Herbert Palmer did their best to "improve" the uncertain circumstances. Essex's fate still hung in doubt at the end of the month, and the sermons at the regular humiliation seem strangely silent and unedifying with respect to the military crisis. The surrender of the army after the commander's ignominious flight terminated the suspense, and that destiny "which befell the Army in the West" led to yet another joint humiliation of the houses on September 12. Thomas Coleman declared: "The sum of all is: Terrible answers harden the wicked, and make them irreconcilable to the waies of God. . . . But the same so prepare the Saints, . . . that they shall quickly perceive God in this way to be the preserver of men."[102] For his part, Matthew Newcomen resolved the experience according to the calculus of the Covenant.[103] Exhortation to soul-searching on the part of the people and magistrates marked the next regular fast on September 25.[104]

October 22 was devoted to an extraordinary humiliation. Strategy dictated the joining of the parliamentary armies in an attempt to counter the moves of Charles, who was intent on securing his position for the winter. Essex and Manchester, together with Waller, had actually combined forces on the twenty-first. Divine blessings upon this project of uniting the armies were sought through a battery of six sermons at Westminster. The Lords listened to Temple, Chambers, and Palmer, while Commons was exhorted by Calamy, Obadiah Sedgwick, and Vines. Only the latter three sermons were printed. In introducing his to the reader,

---

[102] *Gods unusuall Answer to a Solemne Fast* (London, 1644), 25.

[103] *A Sermon . . . Sept. 12. Anno 1644* (London, 1644), 32.

[104] N. Proffett, *Englands Impenitencie under Smiting* (London, 1645); L. Seaman, *Solomons Choice* (London, 1644).

Sedgwick made much of the positive contribution which he assumed the exercises had made to completion of the maneuver.[105] More striking, perhaps, was Calamy's doctrine that long-standing toleration of "Idolatry and superstition, is no good argument to maintain Idolatry and superstition."[106] Trevor-Roper sees in this sermon the beginning of the final episode in the fitful prosecution of Laud, a course of action abetted as well by the Commons preachers at the monthly fast on the thirtieth of the month.[107]

However closely related to this policy decision these sermons may have been, the more significant point for the purposes of this study is the considerable development in the parliamentary preaching institution that occurred at this time. The Lords now moved to adopt the formal monthly fast procedures which had been so fully articulated and utilized by the lower house.[108] Some consideration had already been given to this matter by the Lords on October 19.[109] On the twenty-fifth of the month it was voted "That the Peers do solemnize the Monthly Fast in the Abby Church at Westminster."[110] The Lords determined also to follow the practices of Commons both in requesting the preachers to participate in the program and in thanking them and inviting them to publish their addresses. In this fashion there originated another class of published exhortations to the Long Parliament. On one point, however, the Lords departed from the Commons institution: for the first fast, at least, it invited the Assembly to nominate the preachers. Edmund Staunton initiated the new series on October 30 with a sermon on *Phinehas's Zeal In Ex-*

---

[105] *An Arke against a Deluge* (London, 1644) , "Epistle."

[106] *Englands Antidote against the Plague of Civile Ware* (London, 1645) , 3.

[107] "Fast Sermons," 317-319.

[108] Up to this point, apparently, the Lords had observed the days of humiliation but had not construed them as integral to sitting in parliament. Thus reference to the practice was not included in its *Journals.* Only one printed sermon seems to have originated from the Lords's fasts prior to October 1644: Thomas Cheshire's *A Sermon Preached* . . . [June 29, 1642] (London, 1642) .

[109] *LJ*, VII, 29.   [110] *Ibid.*, 34.

ecution Of Judgment. Or, A Divine Remedy For Englands Misery.[111] Confessing inspiration from the "Citie Petition" for giving no quarter to captured Irish or papists, he defended the extraordinary means through which God thus poured out "his wrath upon his enemies," even in contravention of "the Magistrates due and regular execution of justice."[112] The subsequent destruction of Laud became, of course, a display of the parliament's "radical resolve."[113]

Both houses chose to take note of November 5 but also made their celebrations special thanksgivings for the recent (though incomplete) victory at Newbury and the delivery of Newcastle to the Scots. Anthony Burges, Charles Herle, William Spurstowe, and John Strickland did the honors, and all published their sermons. Exhortations at the end of the month, on the twenty-seventh, included pointed sermons to the Lords. Thomas Hill in defending "Right Separatists"—those who renounced "communion with any impurity"—may have been entering into the public record comments on the proceedings of the Assembly which had recently turned its attention to scriptural warrants for presbyters in the church.[114] Henry Wilkinson counseled that "persons of highest rank and quality" should "expend at the highest rate for God."[115] Commons heard variations on the theme that the godly, though experiencing troubles in this life, would finally know comfort and deliverance.[116]

Probably the most weighty issue focused within the Long Parliament during December 1644 was the mounting resolve to develop an adequate military posture. With Cromwell, Tate, and Vane taking the lead, a proposal for a self-denying ordinance was introduced.[117] As in the past, the puritan preachers were called upon to play their role in

---

[111] (London, 1645) .   [112] *Phinehas's Zeal* . . . , 9.
[113] Trevor-Roper, "Fast Sermons," 318-319.
[114] *The Right Separation Incouraged* (London, 1645) , 24; W. A. Shaw, *op.cit.*, I, 181.
[115] *The Gainefull Cost* (London, 1644) , (2) .
[116] G. Gipps, *A Sermon Preached* . . . (London, 1645) ; B. Pickering, *A Firebrand Pluckt out of the Burning* (London, 1645) .
[117] S. R. Gardiner, *The History of the Great Civil War*, II, 28ff.

supporting this bold maneuver. A private fast was thus hastily arranged for December 18, to be held in the chapel of Lincoln's Inn. The faithful Thomas Hill, Obadiah Sedgwick, and Stephen Marshall lent their energies to the work of the day. Although all were thanked, none were invited to publish their sermons—additional evidence that the intention underlying the service was to bring pressure to bear upon parliament. The ordinance in its original form was not passed, of course, although by April a modified version would enable a reorganization of the parliamentary forces to take place.[118] The routine fast sermons of December perhaps reflected the immediate (if not eventual) failure of Vane's scheme. While Thomas Thorowgood was extolling moderation as a virtue before Commons, Edmund Calamy bluntly indicted England—and implicitly the Lords—"because of her selfe-murdering divisions."[119] Francis Cheynell's forthright remarks to the upper house some weeks later, on March 26, 1645, attest to the persistence of clerical lobbying in support of the ordinance.[120]

The regular fasts continued on schedule during the next months, supplemented with a thanksgiving on March 12. Many of these sermons to Commons were published, and numerous addresses before the Lords were also distributed by the booksellers. In several respects the institution of parliamentary preaching reached a plateau during the late spring of 1645 which lasted through that fall and winter, coming to an end with the defeat of Charles and the surrender of Oxford in July 1646. During this period monthly humiliations were balanced by thanksgiving celebrations of victories. Cooperation between, and joint action of, the two

[118] *Ibid.*, 6off. and 141ff. Trevor-Roper provides a full and vivid description of this event. I have followed his reconstruction of it. See his "Fast Sermons," 319ff.

[119] T. Thorowgood, *Moderation Iustified* (London, 1645) ; E. Calamy, *An Indictment against England* (London, 1645) . In passing, the latter took grim satisfaction in the circumstance that, since the last Wednesday of December was the twenty-fifth of the month, the hated feast (Christmas) had been buried in a Christian fast!

[120] *The Man of Honour, Described* (London, 1645) .

houses in these religious fasts and feasts were frequent. Clerical participation appears to have been willing and shows no signs of that reluctance which came to mark it in subsequent years. The significant changes in the ranks of the preachers, which would soon take place, had not yet begun.[121] Finally, publication of the exhortations remained the normal practice. For these reasons it is important to note that the flourishing of preaching before parliament was accompanied nonetheless, among at least certain of the participants, by a basic ambivalence toward the institution. This development was most clearly articulated by Joseph Caryl in a sermon he delivered to Commons. Speaking to a regular fast on May 28, 1645, he "arraigned" unbelief, identifying it as the "Grand Cause of our National Non-establishment."

> This neglect to keep fasts, and negligent keeping of them, is so grosse and notorious, that it makes many hearts to bleed while they think of it. Hence some have thought it most safe, to move for the supersedeating of these duties, fearing that such setled [regular] fasts will but more unsettle the Kingdom, and rather provoke the Lord, then pacifie him towards us. Reasons may be given for laying down of these Monethly, and the keeping only of occasionall fasts: though in one sense our monethly fasts are occasionall, the great occasion why they began [the Irish crisis], continuing to this day.[122]

Caryl's frank indictment did not immediately lead to basic changes in the institution, although his analysis was essentially confirmed by the subsequent evolution of the preaching program. In any case, during the succeeding years the pulpit seems to have been less carefully "tuned," certainly less fully orchestrated.

Beginning with the May fast the Scottish Commissioners

---

121 See Trevor-Roper, "Fast Sermons," 323-324, where this phenomenon is noted. See *infra*, Ch. IV: "Parliamentary Sponsors and the Puritan Preachers."

122 *The Arraignment of Unbelief* (London, 1645), 24-25.

appeared before the Lords in the same order which they had taken before Commons one and a half years previously. By this time the "new-modeling" of the parliamentary forces had been carried out through a judicious combination of financial planning, military discipline, and religious ardor, and the preaching mirrored the consequent tensions. Thus, in the sermons they delivered at the May fasts, Caryl and Whitaker extolled Christ and belief in him as the proper foundation for the parliamentary cause.[123] Alexander Henderson, by contrast, explicitly criticized Independency and sought to clarify the peers' understanding of Christ's kingdom.[124] At a special thanksgiving on June 19 for the victory at Naseby and the regaining of Leicester, Marshall paid special tribute to the role of the "people."[125] Fairfax's rout of Goring prompted separate thanksgivings in the houses three days later on July 22. The one published sermon originating from them played upon the "extraordinary providence in favour of a wretched people."[126] Ecstatic praises for the New Model Army were sung by Thomas Case at the thanksgiving on August 22: "The Lord of Hosts can make better Souldiers in a few days, then the Prince of Orange can do in many yeers."[127] Robert Baillie, preaching on the thirtieth of July, in the context of this widespread parliamentary optimism (and reflecting disapproval of the hegemony established by the Independents), instructed the Lords in the errors and hardness of heart which constituted the "Great Sins and the Great Judgments of the Time."[128]

If the Scottish Commissioners were frustrated at the turn taken by the wheel of their fortune, which required them

[123] J. Caryl, *The Arraignment of Unbelief*; J. Whitaker, *The Christians Hope* (London, 1645).

[124] *A Sermon Preached . . . 28. of May 1645* (London, 1645), "Preface."

[125] *A Sacred Record* (London, 1645).

[126] J. Ward, *The Good-Will of him that Dwelt in the Bush* (London, 1645), 4.

[127] *A Sermon Preached . . .* (London, 1645), 21.

[128] *Errours and Induration* (London, 1645), title page.

to endure the political ascendancy of the Independents during these months, they must have been equally dismayed to discover among ostensible "Presbyterians" that continuing strain of Erastianism which played so prominent a role in the religious life of the English people. Thomas Coleman took up this matter in his controversial sermon to Commons during the same July fast day (the thirtieth) on which Baillie was addressing Lords. Basically he proposed settlement of the church (and therefore the commonwealth) through placing its government in the hands of Christian magistrates.[129] George Gillespie, taking his turn before the peers at the next monthly fast on August 27, worked out his measured doctrines on the "right Reformation of the Church."[130] To this sermon he appended a denunciation of Coleman's Erastianism.[131] The burden of both was the urgent necessity to place the church under the authority of Christ—whatever the civil consequences. Gillespie did preach again before Commons at an extraordinary fast on September 5 occasioned by the miseries of Scotland, but neither his sermon nor any of the others delivered on the same day was published. Aside from this minor exception, Trevor-Roper seems to be correct in asserting that never again (in the course of the fast sermons before the Long Parliament) "was a Scotsman invited to preach to the English Parliament."[132] One additional innovation in the Commons institution during this period was the explicit nomination of a divine to offer prayer as colleague to the two preachers.[133]

While the basic fast program continued, further voices echoed Caryl's concern about its appropriateness: "Take heed of turning these monethly humiliations into formalities, lest we provoke God more by our hypocriticall mock-fasts, then by any other our sins, for which we pretend to

---

129 *Hopes Deferred And Dashed* (London, 1645), esp. 24ff. Cf. Trevor-Roper, "Fast Sermons," 322-323.

130 *A Sermon Preached* . . . (London, 1645), 10.

131 "A Brotherly examination," *ibid.*, 31ff.

132 "Fast Sermons," 323.

133 *CJ*, IV, 284 (Sept. 24, 1645).

be humbled on such daies as these."[134] Nonetheless, the routine ground on relentlessly, although the pulpit certainly failed to speak with a single voice. One preacher reiterated theories of limited monarchy which seemed to be the necessary outcome of the civil struggles.[135] Independents, like Jeremiah Burroughs, at times entered forthright pleas for latitude or toleration as a way to settle religious issues within the kingdom.[136] John Dury put in an appearance before Commons, opening *Israels Call To March Out Of Babylon Unto Jerusalem.*[137] Another participant directed his remarks to the goal of Charles's restoration and the resolution of differences with him.[138]

Beginning in January 1645-6 the tempo of supplementary humiliations and thanksgivings again advanced. On the fourteenth the Lords, Commons, and the Assembly gathered in St. Martin-in-the-Fields, resolved to work for the settlement of the church in view of the King's repudiation of the proposal that formal organization of the English church be "presbyterian." Marshall was joined by Jeremiah Whitaker for this event. Thereafter victories at Dartmouth, Chester, and Torrington were each duly celebrated in separate thanksgivings for the two houses. On April 2, Fairfax's victory in Cornwall and the disbandment of Hopton's Army were celebrated in a joint thanksgiving which served to ease relationships between parliament and the City of London.[139] Joseph Caryl, who preached on frequent occasions throughout the decade, enlarged upon the divine mercies vouchsafed to the faithful.[140] But it was undoubtedly Hugh Peter who dominated the occasion in

---

[134] C. Burges, *The Necessity of Agreement with God* (London, 1645), 46.

[135] F. Taylor, *Gods Covenant The Churches Plea* (London, 1645), 18.

[136] *A Sermon Preached . . . 26. of Novemb. 1645* (London, 1646). Cf. R. P. Stearns, *The Strenuous Puritan: Hugh Peter, 1598-1660* (Urbana, Ill., 1954), 237-240.

[137] (London, 1646).

[138] J. Foxcroft, *The Good of a good Government* (London, 1645).

[139] S. R. Gardiner, *The History of the Great Civil War*, II, 456.

[140] *Englands Plus ultra* (London, 1646).

"opening" *Gods Doings, And Mans Duty*.[141] Arguing that "the faithful have God for their preserver, whilst the proud doer by the same hand receives wages proportionable to his work," the army chaplain, fresh from the field, recited a catalogue of numerous special providences which proved the point.[142] Peter's participation, which basically mirrored a profound shift in the parliamentary position and sentiment, anticipated a new phase in the fast program. As "vicar-general of the Independents," Peter was ubiquitous in his activity during the next several years.[143] Trevor-Roper likens his role at Westminster during the last years of the decade to that of Marshall at the beginning of the civil struggles. The latter, of course, was the agent of "King" Pym, whereas Peter served "King" Oliver.[144] Without denying the existence of grounds for the parallel, it is important to observe that Peter never dominated the formal humiliations as Marshall did: the scale on which Marshall took part in the work of the fasts was never matched by any man. Peter's sermon does suggest, however, that different preachers would soon appear formally before the houses in duties which were thus no longer explicitly restricted to a closed fraternity. At the very next fast, for example, Commons would be exhorted by James Nalton and John Owen—neither one a member of the Assembly. When the latter published his *Vision of Unchangeable free mercy*,[145] he boldly appended a treatise and an essay, both on the government of the church.

Charles was, during this period, contriving his flight to the Scots—done with the knowledge of their Commissioners in London.[146] By the beginning of May he had placed himself in their hands and thus, unwittingly, began his captivity. When the surrender of Oxford was marked by Commons at a thanksgiving on July 21, another "intruder" held forth in the pulpit during the afternoon. Walter Cradock

---

141 (London, 1646).   142 *Gods Doings* . . . , 4, 19ff.
143 See R. P. Stearns, *op.cit., passim.*
144 "Fast Sermons," 323-325.   145 (London, 1646).
146 S. R. Gardiner, *The History of the Great Civil War*, II, 469ff.

preached a sermon entitled *The Saints Fulnesse Of Joy in their fellowship with God.*[147] Probably the most flagrant breach of the convention which had restricted the pulpit to divines who were sitting in the Assembly occurred with William Dell's participation in the monthly fast of November 25, 1646. Railing against the carnal or external reformation of the church, Dell identified it with the Mosaic dispensation which, he alleged, simply covered inward corruption with outward conformity.[148] Only a purging of sin from the body would suffice, and only the righteousness of Christ was adequate for this purpose.[149] Such a furor was provoked by this performance that Commons explicitly refused to "thank" the preacher; nor did it "desire" him to publish the remarks. Dell did have the sermon printed, though, with a preface intended to clarify his position. This tactic only served to render it more obnoxious to Commons. Both preacher and printer were subpoenaed by the house to answer for their deed. Thus were radical voices heard in a forum theretofore exclusively reserved to "Presbyterians" and conservative "Independents."

A related development is to be found in the attitude taken by at least some preachers toward invitations from the parliament. The members of the Assembly who had preached frequently, elders of the brotherhood who had originally contributed to the growth of the institution and who had dominated it, ceased to participate as regularly as they once had. One example will illustrate the emerging pattern. On May 27, 1646, Edmund Calamy was asked to preach at the next scheduled fast.[150] Two days later he was excused on the grounds of ill health, and it was proposed that Stephen Marshall be asked to take his place.[151] On May 30, Marshall too was excused, because of a "Multitude of Businesses."[152] Finally William Spurstowe preached with Peter Smith on June 24, but typically

---

[147] (London, 1646).
[148] *Right Reformation* (London, 1646), 3f.
[149] *Ibid.*, 4ff.   [150] *CJ*, IV, 556.   [151] *Ibid.*, 558.
[152] *Ibid.*

neither sermon appears to have been printed.[153] It may be that Calamy was seriously ill, for he declined to preach to the Lords on July 29 of the same year[154] and, again, to Commons at its fast on August 26.[155] But the reluctance may also be observed in numerous other instances. In the early years of the institution few appear to have asked to be released from the invitation, and then only for specific cause. After 1645, however, the more sober heads within the brotherhood seem to have become disenchanted with the parliamentary fast sermons; at any rate, at least many seem not to have coveted the opportunities to preach. When they did preach during these years, they were also less likely to print their exhortations, especially those addressed to the Lords.

More important than the infrequent appearance of radicals like Peter and Dell was the regular participation in the institution by a younger generation of puritan preachers, now risen to prominence, who were in one way or another identified with the Independents. William Strong, minister to the Abbey, became a regular preacher before both houses in their fasts. Peter Sterry, no conventional "mystic," also frequently preached in the program. Perhaps John Owen came to be best known. He is generally considered to have been a prime mover in the emergence of the "Congregationalists" as a coherent body at the end of the Interregnum. The "dissenting brethren" of the Assembly took their turns as well: Thomas Goodwin, William Bridge, Philip Nye, and, until his death (1646), Jeremiah Burroughs. The external record of the preaching to parliament thus mirrors the religious changes taking place in the realm. The failure to establish a viable national Church of England through the Westminster Assembly was directly reflected in this institution of preaching before parliament. To be sure, the clerical Presbyterians were victims of their own designs, as well as the prey of religious forces which could not be ordered into the so-

---

[153] *Ibid.*, 585.   [154] *LJ*, VIII, 435.   [155] *CJ*, IV, 629, 635.

cial and political system they desired. The clerical Independents, on the other hand, marginal and overshadowed during the early years of the first civil war, emerged into prominence on the shoulders of Cromwell as a group which appeared to be earnest of the future.

These developments, finally, are manifested in the extraordinary humiliations and thanksgivings. During the years of obvious peril they had been a form of corporate ritual religious behavior in which the houses represented the kingdom through their protestations (although also joined by parts of it). The occasion for a formal fast held on March 10, 1646-7, reveals one of the fundamental social changes which contradicted the basis program—a humiliation for the growth of heresy. The tenuous religious consensus which had contributed to the conduct of the first civil war ceased to be effective, paving the way for the divisions and realignments of the second war and the Interregnum.

The net effect of this metamorphosis in the character of the preaching program is that the fast sermons are rendered less useful as a window through which to view the Long Parliament. One extreme example may be cited from that important period at the beginning of December 1646 when the courses of action open to the Scots and Charles were under consideration. It is not surprising that each house should have held an extraordinary humiliation on the ninth—but the fast was actually directed toward obtaining relief from excessive and unseasonal rain! The one published sermon of the four delivered, one by Francis Roberts, extolled the virtue of a broken spirit.[156] Even those sermons which appeared during the stretches when the fast exhortations were being published with comparative regularity seem not to represent either a useful or a consistent perspective on the struggles within the Long Parliament. Stephen Marshall confessed that confusion which seems to have been general: "Know then our present times. . . . are such times, as I thinke never were before us in the World . . . I meane, our times are so full of various admin-

---

[156] *A broken Spirit, God's Sacrifices* (London, 1647).

istrations, such a concurrence of all kinde of Providences and Administrations, as seldome were ever knowne in so few yeares."[157] Unprecedented experiences were construed (in the absence of human comprehension) by Matthew Newcomen, at the same December fast, as an argument for divine omniscience. "This knowledge which God hath of all things, is not a potentiall, partiall, imperfect knowledge, but an actuall, comprehensive, perfect knowledge. God with one infinite, individed act of his understanding, knows at once, all things that ever were, are, or shall be, yea infinite things that never were, nor ever shall be."[158] Further witness to the confusion is provided by sermons from the January fast. Arrowsmith portrayed "a lively Picture of the Militant Church," while Obadiah Sedgwick diagnosed "the Nature and Danger of Heresies."[159] Hodges and Vines returned to the latter subject on March 10 at a special humiliation.[160]

If the sermons which are available from the following years seem less useful for study of the Long Parliament, it is in part because the fast program had clearly ceased to be so instrumental in the affairs of Westminster. Coincidentally and correlatively, power was plainly moving away from parliament, the realm in this way coming under the control of the victorious army. The religious complexion of the troops, fully disclosed in the debates at Putney in the fall of 1647, provided small comfort to traditionalists in the ranks of the puritan clerics.[161] Much of the preaching to Commons during the preceding spring which reached print—no sermon to the Lords between February 24, 1646-7, and March 29, 1648, having done so—avoided this issue by working over general and conventional themes or by emphasizing the prerogatives of the "saints." One

[157] *The Right Understanding Of The Times* (London, 1647), 30.

[158] *The All-Seeing Unseen Eye of God* (London, 1647), 12.

[159] J. Arrowsmith, *A great Wonder in Heaven* (London, 1647); O. Sedgwick, *The Nature and Danger Of Heresies, Opened* (London, 1647).

[160] T. Hodges, *The Growth and Spreading Of Haeresie* (London, 1647); R. Vines, *The Authours, Nature, and Danger Of Haeresie* (London, 1647).

[161] See A.S.P. Woodhouse, *Puritanism and Liberty* (London, 1938), for the Army Debates.

preacher at the June fast, however, did express in a blunt fashion the point of view of an earlier generation of puritans. Nathaniel Ward, very recently returned from New England, was invited to occupy the pulpit on the thirtieth when Cawdrey, the original nominee, sought to be excused.[162] His remarks inadvertently reveal the deep gulf which had opened during the 1640's between the settlers of Massachusetts Bay Colony and their alleged confreres, the English Independents. Ward contemptuously portrayed England as "a State [which] hath brought it selfe to that passe that the Scepters of authority, and powers of Government are wasted and weakned." The specifics he included— for example, a reference to the army as "mounted upon . . . Saddles of John a Leyden's make"—made the sermon into a *cause célèbre* in all quarters, and neither the conventional thanks nor request to print his sermon was extended to him.[163] Within little more than a month the Army had come up to London and put an end to "Parliament as an effective body in politics."[164] Marshall pronounced his benediction on the move at a special thanksgiving, declaring that the avoidance of civil war was a gift of divine mercy.[165]

Formally speaking, the fast program continued uninterrupted during the fall and winter of 1647 and the spring of 1648, although only a very small number of exhortations was published, chiefly those by the favored Independents. Peter Sterry, for example, published two in the course of a six-month period—one of them the last sermon delivered to a regular Lords humiliation which would be printed. November 5, 1647 was also celebrated; William Bridge reiterated the common theme of warning implicit in divine

---

[162] *CJ*, v, 204.

[163] *A Sermon Preached* . . . (London, 1649), 5-6, 22.

[164] Trevor-Roper, "Fast Sermons," 329. Trevor-Roper is mistaken in thinking that Nathaniel Ward was the first preacher not to receive an invitation to print his sermon; cf. Dell's sermon, esp. the introductory "Letter," noted *supra*, 88.

[165] *A Sermon Preached . . . Aug. 12. 1647* (London, 1647), 7. Trevor-Roper places great emphasis upon Marshall's role in political maneuvering during these months. See his "Fast Sermons," 327-329.

clemency. His text was taken from Psalms (106:8), and the message was ominous: "When God doth save his people with a Notwithstanding [all their sin and unworthiness], he doth then leave such Marks, and Characters, of his Infinite Power upon their Deliverance to Salvation, that he may be Fully, Clearly, Plainly known to the Sons of men."[166] Only one extraordinary affair graced these spring months: a day of praise on May 17 for the victory in Wales after the reopening of hostilities. William Bridge and Stephen Marshall were the Commons preachers. On this occasion they exulted in "Christs coming" to, and God's presence with, their people in perilous times.[167]

The hostilities of the second civil war during July and August 1648 are reflected in the few published exhortations from the fasts. Thomas Manton attributed the renewed struggle to the decay of godliness. The friends of religion had made it odious, a stalking-horse for every self-seeking design.[168] John Bond, at a thanksgiving on July 19, proposed this interpretation of the second war: in the first struggle God's sieve had been coarse, and He had accomplished only the sifting out of the profane party; but in the second struggle the mesh of His sieve was fine, and with it He was separating the faithful from the formalists.[169] Marshall returned on the twenty-eighth to warn that "the sinne of hardning the heart against God, is a certain forerunner of utter destruction."[170] At a humiliation for blessing upon the Treaty of Newport, William Gouge offered his directions "For Obtaining good Successe in a weighty Enterprise."[171] He urged, as an incidental matter, that the "set fasts" be continued since the original cause for them remained unresolved in spite of their long use.[172]

---

[166] *England Saved* . . . (London, 1648), 16.

[167] W. Bridge, *Christs coming* . . . (London, 1648); S. Marshall, *Emmanuel* . . . (London, 1648).

[168] *Englands Spirituall Languishing* (London, 1648), 20ff.

[169] *Eshcol* . . . (London, 1648), 1.

[170] *The Sinne Of Hardnesse Of Heart* (London, 1648), 8.

[171] *The Right Way* (London, 1648), subtitle.

[172] *Ibid.*, 30.

Trevor-Roper brilliantly argues that "on one last occasion the system returned to life," that is to say, the pulpit became a direct instrument of propaganda for a new policy within the Long Parliament.[173] Ireton's *Remonstrance*, drafted in response to the continuing and indecisive negotiations with Charles, advocated bringing the King to trial. On November 20 the *Remonstrance* was submitted to Commons, which postponed consideration of it. The monthly fast, on the twenty-ninth, was in the hands of Obadiah Sedgwick and a London Independent, George Cokayn, who was a recent (and substitute) nominee for the duty. Only the latter's sermon was printed. Its subtitle suggests the argument he mounted: "God himself, supplying the room of withered Powers, judging and inheriting all Nations."[174] His doctrine, innocent insofar as it expressed personal piety, was ominous when taken in an activist and collectivist sense: "The neerer you are to God, the dearer you are to him."[175]

So inspired, the radicals pressed on. Charles was secured on the first of December, and the parliament was decisively purged by Colonel Pride on the sixth. A special fast on the eighth with all the hallmarks of a private and internal session, was staffed by Marshall, Caryl, and Peter.[176] The Rump was subjected to another fast on December 22, with Peter again taking a leading role. None of these sermons reached print. With the regular fast on the twenty-seventh of the month came further exhortation to persevere in the radical course of action: "Upright hearts will hold on in the wayes of God, and in the wayes of well-doing, notwithstanding all afflictions, troubles, and discouragements they meet withall."[177] Thomas Brooks, author of this encouragement, was accompanied in the pulpit by a London Presbyterian, who made bold to criticize the bloody course on

---

[173] "Fast Sermons," 329.

[174] *Flesh Expiring, And The Spirit Inspiring In The New Earth* (London, 1648).

[175] *Ibid.*, 9.

[176] *CJ*, VI, 95.

[177] *Gods Delight In The Progresse Of The Upright* (London, 1649), 2.

which the leaders had resolved. The nomination of Thomas Watson to preach had preceded the purge, and his argument was not calculated to please those members who remained. His discourse, entitled *Gods Anatomy Upon Mans Heart,*[178] laid bare the hypocrisy of the Rump. "The most secret Cabinet-designes of mans heart are all unlocked and clearly anatomized before the Lord."[179] Both the usual "thanks" and invitation to print were pointedly omitted.[180]

No official parliamentary fasts took place during the month of Charles's trial and condemnation, although radical preachers like Peter were exceedingly active.[181] Indeed, the execution of the King on January 30, a Wednesday, led to the postponement of the regular humiliation to the following day—the first time any such delay had occurred. At that point Marshall addressed the Lords, thus apparently condoning the act, but he did not commit his sermon to print. The Commons preachers, John Cardell and John Owen, on the other hand, both published their sermons. The first assured the members of the Rump that "God will certainly order all the great Affairs of the world in that way, which may chiefly tend unto the advancement of his own Glory, and the good of his own People."[182] Owen searched Jeremiah for his text and explored "darke and difficult dispensations of Providence." He concluded that "God will certainly give prevailing strength, and unconquerable defence unto Persons constantly discharging the duties of Righteousnesse, especially when undertaken in times of difficulty and opposition."[183]

With the purge of December, the institution of the Commonwealth in January, and the killing of Charles and the abolition of the House of Lords shortly thereafter, the character of the Long Parliament had so changed that its pulpit

[178] (London, 1649).
[179] *Gods Anatomy* . . . , 4.
[180] This episode is treated at some length and with dramatic effect by Trevor-Roper in his "Fast Sermons," 333-335.
[181] R. P. Stearns, *op.cit.,* 330-336.
[182] *Gods Wisdom Justified* . . . (London, 1649), 6.
[183] *A Sermon Preached* . . . (London, 1649), 22.

inevitably was drastically affected. A monthly fast in continuation of the set pattern was held on February 28, 1648-9. This proved to be the last of the regular monthly humiliations, for the next one was postponed several times until finally it was held on April 19 as a solemn humiliation for "settlement of the nations freedom." One of the speakers, John Warren, proposed that "God can deal with any people or Nation, as the potter dealeth with his clay."[184] Owen, who also preached, published his discourse, to which he had given the title *Ouranon Ourania. The Shaking and Translating of Heaven and Earth.*[185] A motion was introduced on the twenty-third of April to terminate the monthly fasts. Thus, as it turned out, their end came some six months before their ostensible occasion—the crisis in Ireland—was at least temporarily resolved.[186] Suppression of political preaching in general followed soon afterward, for the Rump did not need to be reminded of what Charles had painfully learned: "certainly if the pulpits teach not obedience . . . the King will have but small comfort of the militia."[187]

Such occasional humiliations and thanksgivings as were authorized during the next years seldom found their way into print. Owen and Sterry each did publish several, and Vavasor Powell produced the one additional sermon formally distributed to the public. But the exercises had ceased to be in any sense a sounding board through which parliamentary policy was transmitted to the realm. No less had they failed to make credible the puritans' political convictions. It is evident that the preaching institution was no longer expressing all of the puritan hopes as early as 1646, when the promise latent in the fasts failed to materialize. Continuing exhortation made sense while the desired future appeared to be a possible outgrowth of forces

---

[184] *The Potent Potter* (London, 1649), 6.

[185] (London, 1649).

[186] Trevor-Roper delights in this irony, "Fast Sermons," 340-342. See *An Act For setting apart A Day of Solemn Fasting and Humiliation; And Repealing the former Monethly-Fast* (London [1649]).

[187] Charles I to his wife, Nov. 30[21?], 1646, in *Charles I in 1646*, ed. J. Bruce (Camden Society, 1856), 79.

at work in the present. But on this point there was no consensus after 1646. Thus the fast institution languished, not only because it had outlived its usefulness within parliament and the realm but because its premise—that political men could submit themselves and their interests to divine purposes—was cruelly refuted for all but the most radical and obdurate of believers. Certainly by the time of Charles's death, and probably several years before, the constructive political phase of the movement which may be termed English Puritanism had been effectively ended. Members of the brotherhood had lost their collective vision, which had enabled them to have a comprehensive grasp of men and events. This was what had previously distinguished the movement and made it a compelling option in the common life. In this way the materials provided by the preaching before the Long Parliament suggest possibilities for study of civil war Puritanism. Thus the significance of the fast sermons extends well beyond the formal institution of humiliations and thanksgivings, however remarkable and even notable that exercise of piety may have been.

IV

Parliamentary Sponsors and the Puritan Preachers

MONTHLY fast preaching to the Long Parliament supplemented by extraordinary humiliations and thanksgivings represented a significant opportunity for puritan preachers to declare their views before the houses at Westminster between 1642 and 1649. The circumstance that over one-half of the sermons were published and are still available presents the possibility for extensive study of them. Thus Hugh R. Trevor-Roper has proposed that the pulpit in the Long Parliament was used to "declare the general party line, [and] also, on particular occasions, [to] prepare the way for dramatic episodes."[1] His article on "The Fast Sermons of the Long Parliament" adroitly substantiates this hypothesis, directing attention to the preachers' rhetoric in relationship to both policy determination and general discipline within parliament. In this fashion he opens the way to a broader appreciation of how Charles's rebellious parliament actually functioned.

It is important to ask, however, whether other perspectives on the fast system may not be necessary. Since it was, after all, basically a continuing routine within the Long Parliament, perhaps it could be studied most fruitfully as a periodic exercise irregularly supplemented as occasion warranted. Though subordinate to the houses, this was intended to be a national institution replicated throughout the realm. Publication of the sermons must be interpreted accordingly. The exercises at Westminster were at once reppresentative of England's piety before a biblical God and paradigmatic for the nation. In this perspective dramatic utilization of the fasts by Pym or Cromwell was an intru-

[1] "Fast Sermons," 296.

sion upon, or appropriation of, the basic system. Considering the phenomenon as a program, then, the present chapter will review the role of sponsors (indicating those members who appear to have played prominent parts in arranging the humiliations and thanksgivings) and, more important, will identify the preachers who participated.

THE SPONSORING MEMBERS

Several circumstances render difficult the attempt to identify those members of parliament who explicitly sponsored the fasts. As a consequence, the conclusions reached from such a review are not as useful as might be wished. These difficulties are inherent in the available materials. One major limitation derives from the type of entries made in the *Lords Journals*, in contrast with the kind that appear in the *Commons Journals*. The Lords formally adopted the fast program during the fall of 1644. As a rule the entries in its *Journals* do not identify the member of the upper house who conveyed invitations and thanks to the clerics, if any did. The entries in the *Commons Journals*, on the other hand, usually do indicate, along with the preacher nominated for the next monthly fast, the member(s) of the house instructed to extend the invitation. Wherever it is recorded that a nominee refused or declined, subsequent entries record orders for the same or different member(s) to ask another preacher for the fast. Following the humiliation it was customary for the preachers to be thanked in person and invited to publish their sermons. Again, a delegate from Commons was often specified as bearer of the formal message. It sometimes happened that the same member of the house would extend both invitation and thanks to a preacher at a particular fast. But it was not unusual for different members of Commons to discharge these duties. Normally the *Journals* records the assignment of responsibility for thanking a preacher at an extraordinary humiliation or thanksgiving, but it does not always note who initially invited him. Thus, whereas references to the sponsors in the lower house, especially for the monthly fasts, are reasonably consistent and therefore useful, the practice followed in keeping the records of the Lords makes any systematic study of sponsors in the upper house virtually impossible. Since, however, the monthly fasts were developed in the lower house, extraordinary occasions were most common there, and the sermons to Commons were those most frequently published, these limitations on data, while unfortunate, do not render pointless a review of the sponsors.

The entries in the *Commons Journals* do, nevertheless, exhibit certain features which make it advisable to exercise caution in drawing major conclusions from a survey of the sponsors even in the lower house. In the first place, there seems to be sufficient confusion in the records so that any particular entry may be suspect even though, taken as a whole, they are probably relatively reliable. In all references, for instance, the surname usually stands alone—unless there is a title. In the second place, a preacher was frequently asked and thanked by different individuals, so it may well be that multiple or joint sponsorship of nominees was a common practice. On certain occasions three or four members were involved in the conventional communications with a single cleric, suggesting that there *may* have been several aspects of the procedure. Thirdly, if the member who was held responsible for staffing a particular fast failed to secure the initial nominee, it seems that often the same member was expected to propose and invite a substitute if the house approved the selection. But on other occasions this procedure does not seem to have been followed. In the fourth place, individual members who were repeatedly sponsors in the program were not consistently charged with soliciting the participation of the prominent preachers who were most active in the system and with whom they may have had close personal ties. An exception was Sir William Masham, who either "asked" or "thanked" Stephen Marshall at least seven times. Finally, there are the obvious reasons why members of Commons were assigned

these tasks, namely, identical surnames,[2] known friend-
ships,[3] and ties to the same or neighboring locations.[4] In
light of these considerations, participation in arranging the fasts suggests complicity in the program and general support for its ends, whereas on the whole the correlation of preacher with sponsor does not necessarily appear
to reveal common political sympathies or shared convictions.[5]

A great many of the individual members of the House of
Commons took part in actually proposing, inviting, or
thanking the preachers. The *Journals* records that over one
hundred different representatives discharged the duties of
sponsor, and undoubtedly a significant additional number

[2] E.g., A. Goodwin thanked Thomas Goodwin when the latter
preached on April 27, 1642; Sir John Corbett asked and thanked
Edward Corbett for the fast of December 28, 1642; W. Spurstowe
thanked William Spurstowe for his sermon on July 21, 1643; Sir John
Temple thanked Thomas Temple for his sermon on August 31, 1647.

[3] Sir Thomas Barrington provides a good illustration. Since he was
an active member of the Eastern Association and had close ties to the
Earl of Warwick, it was natural that he should have been the one to
sponsor Stephen Marshall during September and December of 1641.

[4] Thus M. Corbett, member from Great Yarmouth, asked William
Bridge, who had been town preacher at Yarmouth, to commemorate the
anniversary of the Powder Plot on November 5, 1647, as well as to
preach at a fast in May 1648.

[5] The following example, provided by Trevor-Roper, indicates the
kind of correlations between sponsors and preachers which might be
attempted: Thomas Watson preached at the monthly fast on December 27, 1648, shortly after Pride's Purge; John Rolle, a London merchant, had been his sponsor and was probably excluded from the house
in the purge. "Fast Sermons," 334-335. Trevor-Roper delights in emphasizing the drama implicit in Watson's denunciation of hypocrisy
before the Rump from which his sponsor was missing. (The *Journals*
entry is *CJ*, VI, 91. The performance by Thomas Brooks, the other
preacher of the day who was thanked, was quite different. See *CJ*, VI,
107.) It is more important, though, to recognize that the fast system
was such an established routine in the Long Parliament that it was not
disturbed or the nominees changed *in spite of* the drastic alteration
of the house through the purge. Thus, while the specific content of the
sermon *may* reflect Rolle's sponsoring of Watson before the purge,
the incident also suggests that the house considered itself constrained
to continue to honor a nomination *if there was* any expectation that
an "unacceptable" sermon might be forthcoming.

did so without there being historical records of their deeds. Some accepted the assignment once, or perhaps several times at most. Others, however, found themselves serving as sponsors relatively often. Still, frequent participation was not widespread. The *Journals* records that only some two dozen members of Commons were instructed to ask or thank preachers (or both if the same occasion was involved) five times or more. These entries total over two hundred "charges" to members of the house. Of these two dozen men, one-third carried out the task ten times or more, conveying over one hundred invitations, thanks, or both. The high incidence of participation on the part of these eight members suggests that they identified themselves closely with the continuing institution.[6] Furthermore, having been members of the Long Parliament from its early months, if not original members, these men played the role off and on over a considerable span of time. By no means, however, did all of these eight men survive Pride's Purge to sit in the Rump.

Francis Rous (1579-1659) was the most conspicuously active member of Commons in arranging fast preaching before the Long Parliament. He had already sat in three previous parliaments. As early as 1628 he was known for his strong ecclesiastical opinions. After receiving a bachelor's degree from Oxford, he had done additional study in theology, and he continued to display an intense subjective piety throughout his career. It is perhaps more to the point to mention that he was a half-brother of John Pym, although the bulk of his activity on behalf of the fast system took place after the latter's death (December 1643).[7] Sir Robert Harley (1579-1656) was also consistently directed to invite and thank preachers. He had served in five prior parliaments, and, like Rous, he was very active in the

---

[6] Five of the eight, including the first four listed below (Rous, Harley, Masham, and Salwey), were lay members of the Westminster Assembly.

[7] M. F. Keeler, *The Long Parliament, 1640-1641: A Biographical Study of Its Members* (Philadelphia, 1954), 329; *DNB*.

committee work of the Long Parliament. He was eventually secluded from the parliament, but as late as July 1648 he conveyed its thanks to Stephen Marshall. Harley is worthy of note particularly because he had been instructed to invite preachers prior to inauguration of the fast system—Marshall for November 17, 1640, and Calamy for December 22, 1641. Thus his participation in the institution spanned virtually the entire program of monthly preaching to the Long Parliament.[8]

Two other very active members were Sir William Masham and Humphrey Salwey. Confusion surrounds their roles in sponsoring fast preaching because another Masham and a second Salwey joined the Long Parliament as recruiters. Sir William and Humphrey Salwey, however, seem to have been the individuals with those surnames who chiefly undertook to invite or thank preachers. Salwey (1575-1652) was a member of that generation to which Rous and Harley belonged, and he was, like them, a strong parliamentarian. He did sit in the Rump, although he refused nomination to be one of the King's judges.[9] Sir William was somewhat younger (b. 1592). Like Salwey, he also declined to take part in the King's trial yet retained his seat in the Rump, serving on the Council of State between 1649 and 1652.[10] Salwey's active participation in the fast program may have lapsed as early as the fall of 1646; Masham's continued until 1648.

Four more members are referred to ten or more times in connection with the institution. John Blakiston (1603-1649) was a prosperous Newcastle merchant and an outspoken puritan who was declared elected to the Long Parliament on the death of his opponent (and the winner of the election) Sir John Melton. Between the summers of 1643 and 1648 he asked or thanked at least ten preachers. Blakiston,

8 Keeler, 203; *DNB*; D. Brunton and D. H. Pennington, *Members of the Long Parliament* (London, 1954), 23.

9 Keeler, 332; *DNB*. Cf. article in *DNB* on Richard Salwey (1615-1685), a son.

10 Keeler, 268-269; Brunton and Pennington, 120-121, 123.

a member of the Rump, signed the warrant for Charles's death.[11] Sir Peter Wentworth (1592-1675), who was generally more conspicuous in the house than Blakiston, refused to act as commissioner at the King's trial but remained in the Rump nevertheless. His participation in arranging the preaching program extended from the spring months of 1643 to those of 1648.[12] William Wheeler, or Wheler (1601-1666), was apparently considered an authority on ecclesiastical questions in the Long Parliament, and he served as a lay member of the Westminster Assembly. Between September 1644 and July 1648, when secluded from the house, he was a frequently delegated by Commons to secure preachers.[13] Also quite active was William Ashurst, or Ashenhurst, about whom little appears to be known. A member from Newton, Lancashire, he took a role in the fast program from 1643 through 1647. He ceased to sit at Pride's Purge.[14]

Other members, though less active in numerical terms than these eight, clearly played important roles in sponsoring the exhortation of Commons. Sir Thomas Barrington (ca. 1589-1644), for instance, the representative for Newtown, Isle of Wight, a puritan leader and close business and political associate of John Pym and the Earl of Warwick,[15] early took a large share of responsibility for the preaching program in the Long Parliament, securing clerics for several of the sessions prior to the institution of the regular fasts. Sir Anthony Ireby (1605-1682), regular representative of Boston, was an active reformer with special interests in ecclesiastical matters.[16] On at least seven occasions he was instructed to ask or thank preachers. Richard Knightley (1617?-1661), who had explicitly associated himself with leaders of the opposition which formed ranks after the dissolution of the Short Parliament, was also a frequent spon-

11 Keeler, 109; Brunton and Pennington, 61f.
12 Keeler, 385; *DNB*.
13 Keeler, 386-387.
14 See article on Henry Ashurst, a brother, in *DNB*.
15 Keeler, 97-99; Brunton and Pennington, 123f.
16 Keeler, 230-231; Brunton and Pennington, 71.

sor within the fast program.[17] He later sought to work against bringing Charles to trial. Similarly, Anthony Nichols (1611-1659), a nephew of John Pym and Francis Rous, ceased to sit at Pride's Purge.[18] He too was responsible for inviting and thanking a number of clerics. Sir Edmund Prideaux (1601-1659), who continued to sit in the Rump, was directly involved in arranging fasts between 1644 and 1646. Oliver St. John (ca. 1598-1673), an early leader of the opposition to Charles and later a member of the Assembly of Divines, extended at least eight invitations or thanks; he was the one who solicited William Dell's sermon in November 1646.[19] Finally, Sir Christopher Yelverton (ca. 1602-1654) was active in sponsoring fasts between 1642 and 1647.[20]

Additional examples may be cited to provide further illustration of the widespread support for the institution among the members of parliament. One or both of the Allens—probably Francis rather than Matthew—who were recruiters asked or thanked some eight divines between 1646 and 1648. Francis was Treasurer of the Army and became a financier of the Commonwealth.[21] Sir Simonds D'Ewes several times extended invitations or thanks on behalf of the house. Sir Gilbert Gerard, colleague of Pym and St. John in overseas ventures, represented Commons in thanking Marshall in November 1640 and played the same role during the monthly program between 1642 and 1648 when he was secluded.[22] Denzil Holles was instructed by the house to serve as delegate to clerics on at least six occasions between 1642 and 1646, after which he was disabled through impeachment by the Army.[23] John Pym, whose hand Trevor-Roper discovers guiding and directing the fasts until his death in 1643, apparently invited only one preacher

17 Keeler, 243; *DNB*. Cf. article in *DNB* on Richard Knightley (d. 1639), a relative.
18 Keeler, 285; *DNB* (Nicoll or Nicolls).
19 Keeler, 330-331; Brunton and Pennington, 131; *DNB*.
20 Keeler, 403-404.
21 Brunton and Pennington, 59-60.   22 Keeler, 185-186.
23 Keeler, 220; Brunton and Pennington, 155-159.

himself—Cornelius Burges for November 17, 1640. Finally, the younger Vane, whom one might expect to have participated frequently, seems to have been charged only once with summoning a preacher—Joseph Caryl for the August fast in 1645.[24]

The conclusion seems evident that the program of humiliations and thanksgivings in the lower house of the Long Parliament came to have something of a life of its own, as institutions are wont to do when established on a regular basis. Even if, as Trevor-Roper argues, the preaching at times directly served the immediate purposes of Pym during the early years of the parliament and of Cromwell during a later period, its more basic function was to make possible continuing exhortation of the members of the houses by puritan clerics. Broad support for the program was expressed in the activity of the sponsors, important members as well as those of lesser stature, who were engaged in arranging for both regular fasts and extraordinary services. No royalists extended invitations during the few months in which they might have done so. Beyond this limitation, however, sponsorship seems to have been widespread. Many original members of the parliament who invited or thanked preachers survived the metamorphosis into the Rump, some having been instrumental in Charles's death. Recruiters also proved to be active in the institution. But it would be wrong to conclude that the fast program was consistently a sounding-board for a radical caucus within Commons. Many members who had been vigorous in its support were excluded at Pride's Purge, and some were clearly out of favor during the Commonwealth and worked for the return of the Stuart line.[25]

[24] Of these additional Commoners, Barrington, Gerard, Prideaux, Pym, St. John, and Vane were lay members of the Westminster Assembly.

[25] In discussing members of the Long Parliament, such religio-political labels as "Independent" and "Presbyterian" should be used only with reference to a specific context (rather than as a general party designation) and then with great care. Therefore, these terms have been avoided in this section since their use would have confused the

Parliamentary Sponsors and Puritan Preachers

In general, then, the system seems to have had considerable support within the lower house, at least prior to a waning of interest after the middle of the decade. It is clear that the leaders of the parliament basically gave it strong support. Pym promoted it indirectly, partly through the direct participation of his associates. By no means, however, was it entirely their creature, responsive to their wishes. To be sure, the party bias of a sponsor was sometimes plainly reflected in the preachers he invited or thanked. So it was with Francis Allen. Certainly his active role in the Commonwealth during the next decade can be correlated with his prior sponsorship of such Independent preachers as William Bridge, Joseph Caryl, and William Strong. But the pattern is not general. More active supporters—Sir Robert Harley and William Wheeler, for example—demonstrated or betrayed no such immediate partiality in the fulfillment of these duties. They served as delegates to a variety of clerics, Scottish Commissioners, English Erastians, Presbyterians, and Independents. Whatever special purposes the preaching may have served in the designs of some, the institution as a whole proved to be a broadly supported, although a distinctly puritan, presence before the parliament in rebellion against the King. For this reason it is important to review the corps of preachers whose participation was sought and, in most cases it seems, willingly given.

---

general point that the fast program, though it undoubtedly served special interests, seems not to have been exclusively dominated (or captured) by any of them. The initial discussion of this problem was charted by J. H. Hexter in "The Problem of the Presbyterian Independents," *American Historical Review*, XLIV/1 (Oct. 1938) —reprinted in *Reappraisals in History* (London, 1961). Cf. the following recent articles and further references cited there: David Underdown, "The Independents Reconsidered," *The Journal of British Studies*, III/2 (May 1964); Lotte Glow, "Political Affiliations in the House of Commons after Pym's Death," *Bulletin of the Institute of Historical Research*, XXXVIII/97 (May 1965); Valerie Pearl, "Oliver St. John and the 'middle group' in the Long Parliament," *English Historical Review*, LXXXI/320 (July 1966); George Yule, "Independents and Revolutionaries," *The Journal of British Studies*, VII/2 (May 1968).

The Chief Preachers

The formal preaching opportunities within the Long Parliament through January 31, 1648-9, fell to about one hundred and twenty-five different clerics. More than one hundred and ten of these men published sermons which they had preached in this "pulpit."[26] Some broad generalizations can be made about the preachers in this latter group since nearly all of them can be identified through their publications. The vast majority were members of the Westminster Assembly. Thus, even though the restriction of the pulpit to members of the Assembly was relaxed in the later years of the institution, the fast program as a whole was dominated by Westminster divines. This point may be simply illustrated. Certain individuals were especially prominent in the program. Approximately one-half of the printed sermons, for example, were penned by twenty-seven men, who were each responsible for three or more. These preachers were all members of the Assembly, and most were active in the proceedings of that body. A few others who preached several times, such as John Owen, though technically not members of the Assembly, were nevertheless closely associated with parliament. Practically all those who published more than one sermon delivered before the Long Parliament were members of the Assembly.

A second generalization underscores the significance of the monthly Commons fasts as the basic element in the system. Almost every one of the preachers who had a sermon printed appeared before the lower house in its series of regular humiliations, and a high proportion of those who

[26] The qualifications are introduced to allow for the uncertain status of some occasions (e.g., the special humiliations of December 8 and 22, 1648), the confusions in the *Journals* of both houses when no publication was forthcoming, and, finally, the difficulties involved in identifying preachers from the entries in the *Journals* or, in a very few instances, in attributing authorship.

Those who failed to publish any sermons they delivered to the Long Parliament are a diverse group. Three appear to have preached twice without publishing, the rest once only. They are identified, insofar as possible, in a footnote on 130.

did speak there published at least one of the exhortations they delivered. Construing the same point another way, we may say that preachers at the Lords monthly fasts (after October 1644) or at extraordinary occasions before Commons or Lords generally had already been—or soon would be—participants in the monthly fast series in the lower house. This is further evidence, in addition to its historical precedence and its numerical dominance, that the regular Commons program of fasts was the basic forum in which preaching to parliament took place.

Without controverting these generalizations, it is imperative to recognize, nevertheless, that the roles played by those preachers who took part in the humiliations and thanksgivings varied greatly. A few individuals were deeply involved in the program, and a number contributed substantially to the fast system. On the other hand, many filled conventional rules only, and still others were simply marginal participants. Thus it will be necessary, as well as useful, to study the preachers in terms of different groupings. This procedure will indicate the diverse patterns of their association with, and participation in, this formal preaching institution.

Four individuals seem to have constituted something of a class by themselves. They contributed so extensively to the preaching program that they deserve individual attention. The preeminent one among them, Stephen Marshall, was without peer as preacher to the Long Parliament. It will be recalled that he preached at the initial fast in November 1640, again at a special thanksgiving in September 1641, and then in December of that year at a fast preceding the institution of the monthly system. Thereafter he appeared at five regular Commons fasts between February 1641-2 and 1648, as well as at three of the regular Lords fasts, the last on the day following Charles's death. Besides these labors, his preaching was enlisted for some ten extraordinary occasions, as well as for the funeral of John Pym. Marshall evidently had no inhibitions about publishing his exhortations: sixteen of the above were printed. He delivered two more sermons, neither of which were published, to the Rump during November 1649 and March 1652-3.

Born about 1594, Marshall entered Emmanuel College, Cambridge, as a "sizar." By 1625 he was settled in the parish at Finchingfield, Essex. At Westminster during the 1640's, his presence was effectively employed behind the scenes in the Long Parliament. In the public view he served as chaplain to Essex and as a member of the delegation to Scotland which negotiated the Solemn League and Covenant. Of course, he took a hand in the work of the Westminister Assembly. Trevor-Roper has emphasized the manifold services he rendered to the leaders of the Long Parliament; clearly he was a clerical politician of the first order.[27] In 1651 he received an appointment as town preacher to Ipswich. Marshall died in 1655 and was buried in Westminster Abbey. As a mark of royalist hatred for him, his remains were disinterred at the Restoration.[28] William Haller has vividly portrayed the dominant role Marshall played during the decade of the 1640's.[29] This role was probably possible because Marshall—whether from an instinctual preference for mediation or out of simple opportunism—was at once moderate in his Presbyterianism and open toward Independency. Thus he appears to have served as a broker within the ranks of the brotherhood and in this capacity proved his great usefulness to parliament.

Three other preachers—Joseph Caryl, Obadiah Sedgwick, and Richard Vines—did not quite rival Marshall, but their contributions to the parliamentary preaching were so numerous that they must rank near him in this first group.

Joseph Caryl (or Carrill) was born early in the century (sometime between 1602 and 1604) and received his BA

27 "Fast Sermons," *passim.*
28 *Alumni Cantabrigienses,* compiled by John and J. A. Venn (Cambridge, Eng., 1922-1927) ; *DNB.*
29 *Liberty and Reformation in the Puritan Revolution, passim.*

from Exeter College, Oxford, in 1624-5. From 1632 to 1647 he was preacher at Lincoln's Inn and from 1649 to 1660 at Westminster Abbey. Caryl was one of the most prominent clerical Independents.[30] He delivered his initial sermon to parliament at the third monthly fast (April 27, 1642). He preached next at a Covenant-taking ceremony in October 1643. Thereafter he participated in many of the monthly fasts of the lower house and became a favorite choice as preacher for extraordinary humiliations and thanksgivings, too. He graced the Lords regular fasts once or twice. Of some fourteen sermons he gave between 1640 and 1649, one-half were published. Caryl also preached frequently to the Rump, participating in some six special humiliations of that body.

Obadiah Sedgwick, apparently not related to William of the same name, was born about 1600. Awarded his BA by Magdalen Hall, Oxford, in 1620, he first became preacher at St. Mildred's, Bread Street, London, then vicar of Coggeshall, Essex, in 1639, next rector of St. Andrew, Holborn, in 1645-1646, and finally minister at St. Paul, Covent Garden, in 1646. He died before the Restoration, in 1657 or 1658.[31] Sedgwick preached at the May fast to Commons in 1642, early in the series. Although he appeared once more in that sequence and several times in the Lords regular fasts, he made his basic contribution to the program on extraordinary occasions, delivering sermons to nine or ten of them between 1643 and the early fall of 1648. Of these fourteen or fifteen sermons, he published only five, none of which were preached later than 1646-7.

Richard Vines, the fourth member of this group of clerics, was born about 1599. He earned his BA from Magdalene College, Cambridge, in 1622-3 and served as rector at Weddington, Warwickshire, from 1628 to 1644. He was at St. Clement Dane in London for a short time

---

[30] *Alumni Oxonienses*, compiled by Joseph Foster (Oxford, 1891); *DNB*. Cf. G. Yule, *The Independents in the English Civil War* (Cambridge, Eng., 1958), 141.

[31] *Alumni Oxonienses*; *DNB*.

(1643-1645) and then held office as Master of the Temple between 1644 and 1647. In 1650 he moved to St. Laurence, Jewry in London and remained there as minister until his death in 1655-6.[32] Vines first contributed to the program of exhorting the Long Parliament in the fall of 1642. He preached a second and a third time to monthly fasts for Commons and once to one of the Lords regular humiliations. Like Sedgwick, however, he did the bulk of his additional preaching at extraordinary occasions, seven in all. Vines also preached at the funeral for Essex in 1646. As late as June 1648 he was still active in the fast program. But, again like Sedgwick, he did not participate in humiliations of the Rump.

Obviously these four men were mainstays of the system throughout the decade of the 1640's. Together they delivered over sixty sermons in the pulpit provided by the Long Parliament. In addition, Marshall and especially Caryl continued to associate with the derivative institution which graced the Rump. In other respects they proved representative of the preachers as a whole. All were born within five or six years of the turn of the century, and all received their BA's close to 1620. Two studied at Oxford, including the youngest and most radical, and two at Cambridge. Finally, all embarked on their clerical careers in the closing years of James's reign and came to professional maturity under the Laudian repression of puritans during the decade of the 1630's. This experience drove them into close association with the mounting opposition to Charles and his government. Marshall's ties to Essex and the leaders of the Eastern Association and Caryl's role in the Inns of Court illustrate these connections. Thus these particular preachers, who did so much to sustain the fast system, were in many respects typical of the ranks of the brotherhood from which the pulpit in parliament was staffed during the decade of civil struggles.

A group of thirteen additional puritan clerics regularly contributed to the fast program. All preached on no fewer

[32] *Alumni Cantabrigienses*; *DNB*.

than four, and some on as many as eight, occasions. Most began early in the decade and remained participants in the program at least through 1646-7. Several continued almost up to the time of the King's trial and execution. None of this group preached to the Rump.

Charles Herle, Anthony Burges, and Jeremy Whitaker are especially prominent within this group. Herle, born in 1598, received his BA from Exeter College, Oxford, in 1615.[33] Later he became prolocutor to the Assembly and a chaplain to the House of Commons. While Herle published only a few sermons from early in the program, he preached at a monthly Commons fast as late as October 1647. Thereafter he apparently took no active role in the system. Burges, who represented Warwickshire in the Westminster Assembly, was vicar of St. Laurence, Jewry, during 1644-1645.[34] He too preached as many as eight sermons in different classes yet published but a few of them. Burges did sign *A Testimony to the Truth of Jesus Christ*,[35] which is usually taken to be indicative of Presbyterian ties, although within the Assembly he seems to have been sympathetic to the Independents. In any case, it was probably Anthony, rather than Cornelius, who preached twice after publication of the *Testimony* in May and September of 1648. Burges held his BA from Cambridge (St. John's College, 1627).[36] Jeremy Whitaker preached seven times between late 1642 and March 1648, publishing only the three earliest of these sermons. Born in 1599, he graduated with a BA from Sidney Sussex College, Cambridge, in 1619-20. At the beginning of the Assembly he was rector of St. Mary Magdalene, Bermondsey, Middlesex.[37]

Thomas Case and Simeon Ash were only slightly less active in the fast system. The former printed all six of the exhortations he delivered between 1642 and May 1647. He was born in 1598 and received his BA from Christ Church

[33] *Alumni Oxonienses.*
[34] *Calamy Revised*, ed. A. G. Matthews (Oxford, 1934).
[35] (London, 1647).
[36] *Alumni Cantabrigienses; DNB.*   [37] *Ibid.*

College, Oxford, in 1620. Case was lecturer at St. Martin-in-the-Fields from 1641 on. He also served as a parliamentary chaplain and as rector of St. Mary Magdalen, Milk Street.[38] Ash, educated at Emmanuel College, Cambridge, preached five or six sermons, publishing four of them. His participation extended from March 1642 through February 1647-8. He is considered to have been one of the leading Presbyterian ministers in London.[39]

Eight others in this group preached at least four or five times in the parliamentary pulpit, participating as late as 1647 and 1648. They were Samuel Bolton, Gasper Hickes, Thomas Hodges, John Ley (or Leigh), Lazarus Seaman, William Spurstowe, Thomas Valentine, and Henry Wilkinson.[40] All published one or more of their sermons, and all but three took part in extraordinary occasions, as well as the regular Lords and Commons fasts. They all belonged to the Westminster Assembly, and most were distinguished within the brotherhood. Henry Wilkinson, for example, was Lady Margaret Professor of Divinity at Oxford from 1652 until the Restoration. Samuel Bolton was Master of Christ's College, Cambridge, between 1646 and 1654 and was Vice-Chancellor during 1651 and 1652. John Ley was made President of Sion College in 1645. William Spurstowe had been one of the authors who jointly wrote as "Smectymnuus."[41]

Within this group John Ley and Thomas Valentine were older than the others, having been born in 1585 and 1586 respectively. The others were born at the turn of the century or later. Thus Bolton, Burges, Hickes, Hodges, Seaman, Spurstowe, and Wilkinson all received their BA degrees during the middle or late 1620's. Eight

[38] *Alumni Oxonienses*; *Calamy Revised*; *DNB*.

[39] *Alumni Cantabrigienses*; *DNB*.

[40] Information on all of these men is taken from the *Alumni Cantabrigienses*, *Alumni Oxonienses*, and *Calamy Revised*.

[41] The others were, of course, Stephen Marshall (*supra*), Edmund Calamy, Matthew Newcomen, and Thomas Young (*infra*). See W. Haller, *The Rise of Puritanism* (New York, 1938), 329; *Liberty and Reformation in the Puritan Revolution* (New York, 1955), *passim*.

were from Cambridge and the rest from Oxford. Emmanuel College, Cambridge, with three—Ash, Seaman, and Spurstowe—was the only college to have more than two representatives in this group. None of these men continued to be associated with humiliations during the Rump, and in general most of these preachers were considered Presbyterians.

A somewhat smaller number of preachers collectively resembles the last group in most respects, except that their participation in the fast system was terminated rather earlier, in no case later than 1646. These men were Cornelius Burges, Edmund Calamy, Thomas Coleman, Thomas Hill, Herbert Palmer, Matthew Newcomen, and Andrew Pearne. Each preached four or more times; all participated in the regular Commons humiliations, and most in both the Lords fasts and the extraordinary occasions. Early withdrawal from the program is explained in two instances by death. Thomas Coleman (b. 1598) received his BA from Magdalen Hall, Oxford. A renowned Hebraist, and generally thought to be Erastian, he was a member of the Assembly and preached at one of the Covenant-conventions in 1643. Coleman became rector of St. Peter's, Cornhill, just prior to his death in 1646.[42] Herbert Palmer was also born near the turn of the century (1601). Granted a BA by St. John's College, Cambridge, he was made a lecturer at Westminster Abbey in 1643 and shortly thereafter was appointed President of Queens' College, Cambridge, a post he held until his death in 1647.[43]

For the withdrawal of the others there seems to be no such ready explanation. Cornelius Burges was an early favorite, preaching with Marshall at the initial fast, at the first commemoration of the Powder Plot (November 5, 1641), and at the second monthly fast as well. He was also active as chaplain to Essex's regiment during 1642. But after his sermons during 1645 at Lords and Commons fasts

[42] *Alumni Oxonienses.*
[43] *Alumni Cantabrigienses; DNB.*

he appears not to have graced the institution again.[44] Burges, incidentally, was very much opposed to the execution of Charles I at the end of the decade. Edmund Calamy, born in 1600, graduated with a BA from Pembroke College, Cambridge, in 1620. He preached with Marshall at the special fast for the Irish crisis in December 1641, as well as at the first monthly fast. Calamy was counted a staunch Presbyterian. Like Burges, he seems to have made his final contribution to the program sometime during 1645. Thomas Hill also appeared among the preachers at early fasts (July 1642). He exhorted the Lords and preached at several extraordinary occasions as well. Recipient of a BA from Emmanuel College, Cambridge, in 1622-3, he was an original member of the Assembly. Hill became Master of Trinity College in 1645 and at the same time served as Vice-Chancellor until 1647. He died in 1653.[45] Matthew Newcomen was a younger man; he received his BA from St. John's College, Cambridge, in 1629-30. Newcomen, in sympathy with the Presbyterian cause, signed the *Testimony* in 1648.[46] Finally, Andrew Pearne, born in 1594, was graduated from Peterhouse, Cambridge, in 1617-8. He accepted a position as rector of Wilby, Northamptonshire, in 1627 and thereafter represented that county in the Assembly. He was sequestered to St. Dunstan-in-the-West during 1643-1645.[47] Like the others in the group, Pearne participated frequently in the early years of the program but then discontinued his activities and did not preach before parliament again.

In many respects these clerics resemble those of the immediately preceding and somewhat more active group, except for the generally earlier dates at which those of the

[44] Late *Journals* references to "Mr. Burges" I generally identify as intending Anthony. Apparently Cornelius was invited to preach to Commons in 1646 and 1647, but was excused. Cf., *CJ*, v, index. Cornelius Burges received his BA from Wadham College, Oxford, in 1615. *Alumni Oxonienses*; *DNB*.

[45] *Alumni Cantabrigienses*; *DNB*.

[46] *Ibid.*; *Calamy Revised*.

[47] *Alumni Cantabrigienses*; *DNB*.

latter ended their involvement with the system. In terms of their ages, their educations at Oxford and Cambridge, and their membership in the Assembly, there are no manifest differences. The high proportion of Presbyterians among both the thirteen regular preachers discussed above and these seven is noteworthy. The metamorphosis of the fast program after 1646, to which allusion was made in Chapter III, may be correlated with the observation that these twenty pillars, who had staunchly supported the institution during its early years, apparently no longer continued to uphold it shortly before, or soon after, the end of the first war. For this reason it is important to turn our attention to another group of preachers whose major contributions to the fast system were made during its later years.

Nine additional preachers were as active in the fast institution as those in the previous groups: John Bond, William Bridge, Daniel Cawdrey, William Carter, Thomas Goodwin, Philip Nye, Peter Sterry, William Strong, and John Ward. Each preached at least three times—and most of them more—prior to the execution of Charles, both at Commons and Lords monthly fasts and, in the case of most of them, at extraordinary occasions as well. All were members of the Assembly. What distinguishes these men, collectively, is that, although some did preach during the early years of the institution, their chief efforts came during the years following 1645. If the preceding group of seven preachers participated in the fast system exclusively during its early years, this group of nine was primarily associated with the program during its later years. Furthermore, seven of the nine preached to the Rump—William Strong on as many as five occasions, John Bond on four.

William Bridge, Thomas Goodwin, and Philip Nye were all "dissenting brethren" of the Assembly, closely identified with the Independent party both religiously and—insofar as it is possible to gauge it—politically. Each, moreover, had been an expatriate in the Low Countries during the late 1630's. Bridge, who earned a BA from Emmanuel

College in 1622-3, was a representative of Essex Puritanism and during the decade was town preacher at Yarmouth, Norfolk.[48] Thomas Goodwin, born in 1600, graduated from Christ's College, Cambridge, in 1617.[49] In 1649 he became a minister in attendance, lodging at Whitehall. Philip Nye received a BA from Magdalen Hall, Oxford, in 1619.[50] He represented Huntingdonshire in the Assembly and with his father-in-law, Stephen Marshall, assisted in the negotiations at Leith from which issued the original draft of the Solemn League and Covenant between England and Scotland. Neither Nye nor Bridge preached as frequently in the program as Thomas Goodwin, although Bridge published more of his sermons to parliament than either of the other two.

With the exception of Peter Sterry, the remaining five preached often during the fast program. John Ward of Ipswich and Brampton, it appears, delivered eight exhortations.[51] He was a replacement appointee to the Assembly and seems to have been the John Ward who received his BA from Cambridge in 1612-3. If so, he was from 1617 vicar of St. Michael at Plea, Norwich. Between 1645 and 1665 he was rector of St. Clement's, Ipswich.[52] William Strong also preached some eight times. Awarded a BA from St. Catharine's College, Cambridge, in 1630-1, he joined the Assembly in 1645, was a preacher at the Abbey, and became minister of St. Dunstan-in-the-West in 1647 or 1648. He died in 1654 and was buried in the Abbey; his body suffered the fate of Marshall's in being exhumed at the Restoration.[53] John Bond received his BA from St. Catharine's College in 1631-2 and was thus a close contemporary of Strong's. He was named to take Ussher's place in

---

[48] *Ibid.*   [49] *Ibid.*

[50] *Alumni Oxonienses*; *Calamy Revised*; *DNB*.

[51] There is some possibility of confusion here with Nathaniel Ward, who preached on June 30, 1647. The latter had recently returned from New England, however, and he so angered the members that it is most unlikely that he received any subsequent invitations to preach to the Long Parliament.

[52] *Alumni Cantabrigienses.*   [53] *Ibid.*; *DNB*.

the Assembly and became minister, then Master, of the Savoy and of Trinity Hall, as well as professor of law at Gresham College.[54] William Carter, who probably earned a BA in 1616 at Trinity College, Oxford, was rector at St. John Zachary, London, between 1625 and 1630.[55] During the 1640's he was termed "Minister of God's Word," a title frequently used by Independents at this time, and he seems to have been located in London. Peter Sterry, holder of a BA from Emmanuel College (1633-4), represented London in the Assembly. He became a favorite of Oliver Cromwell, serving as his chaplain. Surprisingly he was not as active in the fast system as one might expect him to have been. He preached on three occasions and in addition, appeared once before the Rump.[56] Daniel Cawdrey completes this group. He was, it seems, older than most of these active preachers, having probably been born about 1588. Cawdrey received his BA from Sidney Sussex College, Cambridge, in 1610. He replaced John Harris, D.D., of Winchester in the Assembly and during this period probably served as vicar at St. Martin-in-the-Fields.[57] Cawdrey published only the first of his sermons, which he delivered to Commons in 1643-4. Thereafter he preached once more to Commons in their monthly program, in 1646, and thrice at extraordinary affairs during 1645 and 1646. Cawdrey seems, however, to have exhorted the Lords at monthly fasts some half-dozen times, four of them during 1648 (N.S.). This concentrated activity in the upper house may be interpreted in light of his having signed the *Testimony*, commonly taken to be positive evidence of Presbyterian convictions. It might be surmised that his frequent appearances, exclusively before the Lords, during the last year or so of the institu-

[54] *Alumni Cantabrigienses*; *DNB*. Bond preached chiefly at extraordinary affairs.

[55] *Alumni Oxonienses*.

[56] *Alumni Cantabrigienses*; *Calamy Revised*; *DNB*.

[57] *Alumni Cantabrigienses*; *Minutes of . . . the Westminster Assembly*, ed. A. F. Mitchell and J. Struthers (Edinburgh, 1874); list of members, lxxxii-lxxxiv.

tion indicate lack of sympathy with Commons and the course of action it was following.

What is significant about the preachers in this group is not their ages—although perhaps they may have been slightly younger on the whole than the preceding ones. Nor does the pattern of their university connections stand out: it resembles those of the other groups. Rather, the important point is that, with the exception of Daniel Cawdrey (for which an explanation has been suggested) they all seem to have been "Independent puritans." This, in conjunction with the observation of their frequent participation in the later fasts, implies that, to some extent at least, the system became increasingly dominated by that party from 1646 onward. It was exclusively controlled by them, of course, when continued in truncated form as an instrument of the Rump. That there was a correlation between the political ascendancy of the Independent party and the increasing frequency of involvement in the fast system on the part of the clerical Independents is in no sense surprising. With respect to patterns of participation in the fast program, however, the contrast between this group of preachers and the preceding ones (except for the first) is striking and important to note.

The four groups of preachers already discussed include thirty-three men. Together these men carried the major burden of the humiliations and thanksgivings as far as preaching to the Long Parliament was concerned. Between the beginning of the sitting and the execution of Charles, they collectively delivered over two hundred and fifty sermons within the program. Of this number approximately one hundred and forty were published, so that some sixty percent of their exhortations are available for study. In general these preachers seem to have readied for publication their early sermons and been less concerned to print later ones. The remaining preachers, especially those who published sermons, fall into several additional categories.

LESS FREQUENT PARTICIPANTS

A large number of individuals who preached in the fast program may be described as relatively conventional participants, that is, as members of the Assembly who exhorted both Commons and Lords monthly fasts, and possibly an extraordinary occasion. Many of these sermons were published. The men who constitute this group are differentiated from their colleagues discussed above in that generally they seem not to have been asked to preach at additional fasts or thanksgivings—or else turned the offer down if they were invited to do so. Thus their participation in the system seems to have been correlated with the fact that they belonged to the Assembly. (Of course, Commons had early moved to restrict this pulpit to members it appointed.) We can identify a further category which consists of members of the Assembly who, for whatever reason, seem to have been marginal participants in the program, serving it only once or possibly twice. Still another class is composed of marginal participants who were not members of the Westminster Assembly.

Of those who played conventional roles in the fast system, none are more typical than the Scottish Commissioners, who together preached a dozen sermons in the program, ten of which were published. Alexander Henderson was the first to participate, contributing to the Covenant-subscribing ceremony on August 25, 1643. On that occasion Philip Nye served as representative English divine. Four months passed before the Commissioners began to preach at the Commons regular monthly fasts. Henderson exhorted the December humiliation, and his three colleagues—Samuel Rutherford, Robert Baillie, and George Gillespie—appeared in that order at the succeeding monthly fasts. At each event a member of the Assembly proper (from the English brotherhood) delivered the companion sermon. Henderson also preached—obviously in acknowledgment of the role played by Scottish troops—at the extraordinary thanksgiving for the victories at Marston Moor and York, held on July 18, 1644, sharing the pulpit with Richard Vines. In the following May the four Commissioners began taking their turns at the Lords regular fasts, which had been inaugurated in the preceding October (1644). They followed the same order, and an English member of the Assembly preached the other sermon on each occasion. The repetition of the formal order of seniority, as well as the careful pairing of the Scotsmen with English divines, suggests that their participation was viewed as a requirement of protocol rather than as unqualified and routine preaching within the fast system of the Long Parliament. Both Henderson and Gillespie gave sermons at special Lords and Commons humiliations for the "miseries of Scotland" on September 5, 1645, appearances requiring no further explanation. Thereafter the Commissioners did not have access to the pulpit.

Nineteen additional English preachers may be categorized as conventional participants. Collectively they delivered over fifty sermons, of which thirty-seven were published. These men were by no stretch of the imagination a homogeneous group, having in common only their membership in the Assembly and participation in the fast system on several occasions. Two of these clerics suffered untimely deaths which abbreviated what would probably have been more extensive careers within the institution. The first, Jeremiah Burroughs (or Jeremy Burrows), was counted a "dissenting brother" in the Assembly along with the other leading Independents. After receiving a BA from Emmanuel College, Cambridge, in 1620-1, he served as a rector in Norfolk until deprived of his post by Bishop Wren in 1636. At Rotterdam for several years, he returned to be preacher at Stepney and Cripplegate between 1641 and his death in 1646.[58] Had he lived, Burroughs might well have played a very active role in the program during the years which immediately followed, as did Goodwin, Nye, and

---

[58] *Alumni Cantabrigienses*; *DNB*.

Bridge. The second, John Whincop, died in 1647. He was awarded a BA by Trinity College, Cambridge, in 1621-2 and held a position at St. Martin-in-the-Fields, London, from 1642-3.[59]

Other members of this group of conventional participants were significantly older than the average age of the preachers to parliament. Such a one was the indomitable William Gouge, a patriarch of the brotherhood, who preached to Lords as late as September 12, 1648, at a special humiliation for the successful outcome of the negotiations then being undertaken with Charles. A long-time preacher at St. Anne, Blackfriars, in London, he had been born about 1574 and had received his BA from King's College, Cambridge, in 1598-9.[60] Thus he clearly represented an older generation than most of the clerical leaders within Puritanism during the civil war period. Robert Harris (b. 1581), who had preached to an earlier parliament as the practice was developing, resembles Gouge in this respect. Graduated with a BA from Magdalen Hall, Oxford, in 1600, he was rector of Hanwell, Oxfordshire, from 1607 until the beginning of the civil war. Thereafter he was minister of St. Botolph, Bishopsgate, before becoming President of Trinity College, an office he held between 1648 and his death in 1658.[61] Francis Taylor also was a decade older than most of the others. Born in 1590, he received his BA from Christ's College, Cambridge, in 1609. He was preacher at Canterbury Cathedral before his death in 1656.[62] Peter (or Brockett) Smith, who received a BA from Pembroke College, Cambridge, in 1605-6 and an MA from Oxford in 1610, was apparently about the same age.[63]

Of the rest, nine seem to have been born within a year or so of the turn of the century, thus being roughly of the same

[59] *Alumni Cantabrigienses.*
[60] *Alumni Oxonienses; DNB.*
[61] *Ibid.*
[62] *Alumni Cantabrigienses.*
[63] *Alumni Oxonienses.*

age as the preceding groups of preachers.[64] As alumni they were almost equally divided between Oxford and Cambridge, and no single college was represented by more than two in this group. A few points are worth mentioning about them individually. Sidrach Simpson was generally considered a "dissenting brother," and John Strickland signed the *Testimony.* Thomas Wilson preached to "sundry of the House of Commons" during the spring of 1641. John Arrowsmith had a distinguished career at Cambridge. Staunton represented Surrey in the Assembly, and Maynard represented Sussex. Humphrey Chambers was allegedly directly involved in the civil strife, maintaining "a horse and man at his own charge in actual service against the king."[65]

Four members of this group of conventional participants in the fast system remain to be considered. Francis Cheynell and Francis Woodcock were both younger than any of the nine men above. Cheynell, born in 1608, was a graduate of Balliol College, Oxford, and a chaplain to Essex during 1644. He became Lady Margaret Professor of Divinity at Oxford in 1648 and held that chair until 1652.[66] Woodcock was even younger. Born in 1614, he was also an alumnus of Oxford, having received his BA from Brasenose College in 1632-3. Made a lecturer at St. Laurence, Jewry, in 1641, he was added to the Assembly. Woodcock became rector of St. Mildred, Poultry, and then,

[64] This number includes:

> John Arrowsmith, b. 1602, BA St. John's College, Cambridge, 1619-20.
> Humphrey Chambers, b. ca. 1602, BA University College, Oxford, 1618.
> William Goode, b. 1600, BA Pembroke College, Cambridge.
> John Maynard, b. 1600, BA Queen's College, Oxford, 1620.
> Sidrach Simpson, BA Queens' College, Cambridge, 1621-2.
> Edmund Staunton, b. ca. 1598, BA Corpus Christi College, Oxford, 1619-20.
> John Strickland, b. 1601, BA Queen's College, Oxford, 1622.
> Thomas Temple, BA Dublin, 1620.
> Thomas Wilson, b. 1601, BA Christ's College, Cambridge, 1621-2.

[65] *Alumni Oxonienses.*
[66] *Ibid.; DNB.*

in 1646, of St. Olave, Southwark.[67] Stanley Gower has not been precisely identified. His published sermon, however, terms him "Preacher of Gods Word at Martins Ludgate, London."[68] He was nominated to Trinity, Dorchester, in December 1648.[69] John Greene, who took the similar title "Minister of Gods Word," was identified with Pencombe, Herefordshire.[70] Greene was probably an Independent.

These conventional participants share many characteristics with the foregoing groups of men. All were members of the Assembly. They generally belonged to the generation which had been born at the turn of the century, and nearly all received their university training at various Oxford and Cambridge colleges. It may be essentially accidental that their preaching in the fast program was less frequent, or there may be rather mundane explanations. Perhaps, for example, their rhetorical powers were less vaunted. Possibly, too, some may not have had the connections and associations with sponsors which certain of the more active preachers obviously did. In any case, these divines did participate more frequently than another larger group of preachers from the Assembly most of whom participated only once, a few twice, within the parliamentary fast system.

Twenty-eight members of the Assembly each played a very marginal role in the program. For them, as for the previous group, there were probably a number of different factors that determined—and thus would help to explain —the frequency of their participation. Together they preached some thirty-four times within the system, chiefly between 1642 and 1645, and each published exactly one sermon. Age, and perhaps death, probably limited the ac-

67 *Alumni Oxonienses.*

68 *Things Now-a-doing* (London, 1644), title-page.

69 W. A. Shaw, *A History of the English Church . . . 1640-1660* (London, 1900), II, 363. Apparently a son, Humfrey Gower, matriculated at St. John's College, Cambridge, in 1655. *Alumni Cantabrigienses.*

70 *Nehemiah's Teares and Prayers . . .* (London, 1644), title-page; *The Churches Duty, for received Mercies* (London, 1647), title-page.

tivities of some. John White, the puritan patriarch of
Dorchester, preached only once, for example, and that
was to the Lords. Born in 1575, he earned his BA from New
College, Oxford, in 1597. He served as assessor of the Westminster Assembly and died in 1648.[71] Oliver Bowles was
White's contemporary. His only sermon was delivered at
the extraordinary fast when the Assembly was convened
on July 7, 1643. Recipient of a BA from Queens' College,
Cambridge, in 1596-7, he represented Sutton, Bedfordshire, where he had been rector since 1607. He died in
1646.[72] Thomas Carter was a younger man, who had
been awarded his BA by St. John's College, Cambridge, in
1604-5. He also died in 1646.[73] He was replaced in the Assembly by Robert Johnson (Johnston), who was an alumnus
of Trinity College, Cambridge (1622-3), and rector of
Rise, Yorkshire.[74] The lateness of Johnson's single sermon, given only in 1647, is thus easily explained. Edward
Reynolds, at least formally a member of the Assembly,
preached at the Commons fast of July 1642 and thereafter had no further association with the institution. Graduated from Merton College, Oxford, in 1618, he was
preacher at Lincoln's Inn from 1628 until 1631 and vicar
of St. Laurence, Jewry, London, from 1645 through 1662.
Dean of Christ Church College, and Vice-Chancellor of
Oxford during 1648-1650, he became chaplain to the King
in 1660 and served as Bishop of Norwich from 1661 until
1676.[75] Reynolds was one of the few preachers to the Long
Parliament who embraced the Restoration settlement of
the church in this unequivocal manner.

Additional members of this category could be identified in the text and references to them multiplied at

[71] *Alumni Oxonienses; Minutes of . . . the Westminster Assembly*,
lxxxii.
[72] *Alumni Cantabrigienses; Minutes of . . . the Westminster Assembly.*
[73] *Alumni Cantabrigienses.*
[74] *Ibid.*   [75] *Alumni Oxonienses.*

some length.[76] But it is more important for our purposes simply to direct attention to the way in which Westminster divines were mobilized for the support of the fast system, especially through 1646. Secondarily, the concentration of puritan preachers from the generation born during the last years of Elizabeth's rule and early in James's should be noted. Thus the predominant number of these participants, like their colleagues considered in the other groups, attended university during the second and third decades of the century. With reference to the persons comprising this group of preachers—more than those in the groups previously reviewed—the connections with Cambridge are par-

[76] The following are included in this group with the above (* = replacement or substitute member of the Assembly; see *Minutes of . . . the Westminster Assembly,* lxxxiv):

*Richard Byfield, b. 1598, BA Queen's College, Oxford, 1619.
John Conant, b. 1608, BA Exeter College, Oxford, 1631.
*Edward Corbett, b. 1602, BA Merton College, Oxford, 1622.
John Foxcroft, b. 1594-5, BA Emmanuel College, Cambridge, 1614-5.
Samuel Gibson, BA Emmanuel College, Cambridge, 1599-1600 or 1627-8.
George Gippes, BA St. John's College, Cambridge, 1610-1.
William Greenhill, b. 1598, BA Caius College, Cambridge, 1618-9.
Henry Hall, BA Trinity College, Cambridge, 1624-5.
*Humphrey Hardwick, b. 1602, matriculated at Jesus College, Oxford, 1621.
Richard Heyrick, b. 1600, BA St. John's College, Oxford, 1619.
John Langley, probably BA Clare College, Cambridge, 1612-3.
William Mewe, probably BA Emmanuel College, Cambridge, 1622.
Benjamin Pickering, probably BA Sidney Sussex College, Cambridge, 1615-6.
William Price, perhaps BA Emmanuel College, Cambridge, 1625-6.
Nicholas Proffettfi BA Emmanuel College, Cambridge, 1618-9.
William Reyner (Rayner), BA Corpus Christi College, Cambridge, 1614.
Arthur Salwey, b. 1606, BA Brasenose College, Oxford, 1623-4.
Henry Scudder, MA Christ's College, Cambridge, 1606.
Christopher Tesdale, b. 1591, BA New College, Oxford, 1614.
Thomas Thurgood (Thoroughgood), BA Queens' College, Cambridge, 1613-4.
Anthony Tuckney, b. 1599, BA Emmanuel College, Cambridge, 1616-7.
George Walker, BA St. John's College, Cambridge, 1608-9.
Thomas Young, b. 1587, MA St. Andrews, 1606.

ticularly interesting. Probably fifteen received BA's there whereas seven attended Oxford, and one took his degree at St. Andrews. Moreover, as many as six of these preachers were apparently trained at Emmanuel College, Cambridge that notorious "nursery" of Puritanism.

The other group of marginal participants is somewhat less extensive.[77] These twenty-one preachers seem not to have been official members of the Assembly. Only three of them—Thomas Horton, William Jenkyn, and Thomas Manton—were responsible for two exhortations to the Long Parliament within the decade covered by this study. Three others—Matthew Barker, Thomas Brooks, and Nicholas Lockyer—each of whom participated in the system only once prior to the death of Charles, apparently did preach to the Rump one or more times during the next decade. It might be surmised from the preceding discussion that the preachers who were *not* members of the Assembly prob-

[77] The following preachers constitute this group:

Samuel Annesley, b. 1620, BA Queen's College, Oxford, 1639.

Matthew Barker, BA Trinity College, Cambridge, 1637-8.

Walter Bridges (see W. A. Shaw, *op.cit.*, II, 305; *CJ*, II, 933).

Thomas Brooks, matriculated at Emmanuel College, Cambridge, 1625.

John Cardell, b. 1609, BA Brasenose College, Oxford, 1628-9.

George Cokayn (Cockayne), b. 1619-20, BA Sidney Sussex College, Cambridge, 1639-40.

John Ellis, BA St. Catharine's College, Cambridge, 1634.

Daniel Evance (Evans), b. 1613, BA Sidney Sussex College, Cambridge, 1633-4.

Nathaniel Hardy, b. 1619, BA Magdalen Hall, Oxford, 1635.

Thomas Horton, BA Emmanuel College, Cambridge, 1626-7.

George Hughes, b. 1604, BA Corpus Christi College, Oxford, 1622-3.

William Hussey (see W. A. Shaw, *op.cit.*, II, 354; *LJ* X, 193, 236).

William Jenkyn, BA St. John's College, Cambridge, 1632.

Richard Kentish, BA Hart Hall, Oxford, 1630-1.

Nicholas Lockyer, b. 1611, BA New Inn Hall, Oxford, 1633; MA Emmanuel College, Cambridge, 1636.

Thomas Manton, b. 1620, BA Hart Hall, Oxford, 1639.

James Nalton, BA Trinity College, Cambridge, 1619-20.

Francis Roberts, b. 1609, BA Trinity College, Oxford, 1628-9.

William Sedgwick, b. 1610, BA Pembroke College, Oxford, 1628.

Samuel Torshel, b. 1604, BA Christ's College, Cambridge, 1624-5.

Thomas Watson, BA Emmanuel College, Cambridge, 1638-9.

ably participated in the institution—and more often in the lower than in the upper house—mostly during the later years of the decade. This was manifestly the case. Three of this group did preach during the first year of the system: namely, Walter Bridges, John Ellis, and William Sedgwick. But none of the remaining eighteen delivered any sermons earlier than 1645-6, and they all preached most frequently during 1647 and 1648. Every member of this group seems to have been born within the seventeenth century, and a good proportion received their BA's during the 1630's—two in the last year of the decade. John Ellis, who exhorted Commons early in the program, probably became a royalist soon after his appearance. Many of the others were clearly Independents—for example, Barker, Brooks, Cardell, Kentish, Lockyer, and William Sedgwick—although a few seem definitely to have been Presbyterians, namely, Samuel Annesley (grandfather of John and Charles Wesley), George Hughes, Francis Roberts, and Thomas Watson. The Independents subsequently lent their talents to "King" Oliver and received appropriate appointments: Brooks was made chaplain to the parliamentary fleet, Lockyer preacher at Windsor Castle, and Cokayn chaplain to Fleetwood. "Doomsday" Sedgwick, of course, had been a prototypical fire-breathing chaplain to the parliamentary forces during the first war.

The differences in profile between this group and those who were also marginal participants but who held membership in the Assembly could be studied at great length. The decisive difference would appear to be, in any case, that these men generally belonged to a younger generation than those in the previous category and were not so much a part of the brotherhood which had come to maturity under James and which nourished Puritanism under his son. Nevertheless, all were Cambridge and Oxford graduates apparently, although—and here the circumstance of their ages may be crucial—they did not return to university careers as frequently as members of the other groups.

The classifications already set forth do not include the

few preachers in the program, identified from references in the *Journals*, who failed (for whatever reasons) to publish sermons they delivered under the auspices of the houses.[78] Logically all of them would belong to one or the other of the groups of marginal participants just reviewed. No additional notice will be taken of these men. Conceivably several others may have contributed to the program, but record of their participation has not been located.

SIGNIFICANT INDIVIDUALS

A few preachers not discussed hitherto require special notice because of their personal importance, notoriety, or the exceptional circumstances under which they participated in the fast system. None of the eight was a major preacher in the program, and collectively they were responsible for only eleven published and two more unpublished sermons to the Long Parliament. They have little in common aside from their unique roles in the humiliations and thanksgivings or their particular prominence in related activities.

Two of the eight were members of the Assembly. John Lightfoot was renowned as a Hebraist and seems to have

[78] The men identified below appear to have preached in the fast program but did not publish their sermons; additional individuals probably preached (* = members of the Assembly):

*Calibut Downing, BA Oriel College, Oxford, 1626. d. 1644.
"Esthorp," probably Reuben Esthorpe (see W. A. Shaw, *op.cit.*, II, 330, 368).
*Thomas Ford, BA Magdalen Hall, Oxford, 1624-5.
Fowler, perhaps Matthew or Richard (see W. A. Shaw, *op.cit.*, II, 546, 531).
* (?) Gibbons, perhaps "Dr." or John (see W. A. Shaw, *op.cit.*, II, 339, 336, 403).
A. Harford, perhaps Anthony (see W. A. Shaw, *op.cit.*, II, 529).
Jaggard, perhaps Richard, BA Magdalen Hall, Oxford, 1623.
*Christopher Love, BA New Inn Hall, Oxford, 1639.
*"Rathband" (see *Minutes of . . . the Westminster Assembly*, lxxxiv replaced G. Morley in the Assembly).
Ralph Robinson (?), BA St. Catharine's College, Cambridge, 1638-9.
Joseph Symonds, BA Emmanuel College, Cambridge, 1623-4.
*William Twisse, BA New College, Oxford, 1600, d. 1646.
"Whitcott," probably Benjamin Whichcote, 1609-83, Cambridge Platonist.

delighted in his posture of detachment from the parties of the puritan brotherhood. Born in 1602, he acquired his BA at Christ's College, Cambridge, in 1620-1. Between 1630 and 1642 he was rector at Ashby, Staffordshire, which he left to come to St. Bartholomew-by-the-Exchange in London. He returned to Cambridge in 1650 as Master of St. Catharine's College, remaining there until his death in 1675.[79] Lightfoot preached to monthly Commons fasts in 1643, 1645, and 1646-7. Also technically a member of the Assembly, John Dury (or Durie), the Scottish proponent of international Protestant union, was added to it on the death of Calibut Downing, although he seems not to have been very active in its business. Trevor-Roper gives a great deal of attention to Dury as a "philosopher" of Pym's party.[80] The one exhortation he delivered in this program was to a regular Commons fast in 1645. One further nonpolitical figure was Ralph Cudworth, chiefly known as a Cambridge Platonist (with Benjamin Whichcote). His one sermon in this series was delivered to Commons in 1647. Cudworth's participation in this fundamentally puritan institution is a reminder that his early development took place under the guidance of his stepfather, the puritan patriarch John Stoughton.[81]

Two other preachers are remarkable because they managed to provoke Commons into denying its thanks and withholding its invitation to print the offending sermons.[82] William Dell, recipient of a BA from Emmanuel College, Cambridge, in 1627-8, served as rector at Yeldon, Bedfordshire, between 1641 and 1662. He also contributed his talents to the Army and, as a result, was invited to be

79 *Alumni Cantabrigienses*; *DNB*.
80 See the *Minutes of . . . the Westminster Assembly*; H. R. Trevor-Roper, "Three Foreigners: The Philosophers of the Puritan Revolution," in *The Crisis of the Seventeenth Century* (New York, 1968), 237-293.
81 See J. C. Whitebrook, "Dr. John Stoughton the Elder," in *Transactions of the Congregational Historical Society*, VI (1913-1915), 89-107, 177-187.
82 A similar provocation, involving Thomas Watson, happened at the December 1648 fast. See Trevor-Roper, "Fast Sermons," 334-335.

Commons fast preacher for November 1646. His radical comments and ill-chosen words so scandalized and infuriated some members of the house that it refused to take conventional notice of his appearance. Not to be silenced in this way, Dell published his sermon without authorization, and he and his printer were required to answer for their presumption. A similar incident occurred on another occasion. This time, however, the preacher took an unduly conservative line. Nathaniel Ward was of an older generation and had seen a good deal of the world. Born in 1578 and graduated from Emmanuel College in 1599-1600, he had traveled on the continent and studied law. Suspended by Laud in 1633, he journeyed to New England and contributed to the formulation of its penal code.[83] He returned to England in 1646 and was invited to preach at the June 1647 fast. His caustic and critical remarks were not appreciated by the members. Denied the conventional acknowledgment, he too had his sermon published.

Hugh Peter and Walter Cradock provide further examples of Army preachers installed in the parliamentary pulpit to signalize victories. Peter exhorted a joint celebration of both houses for Fairfax's success in Cornwall, held on April 12, 1646. On this occasion he brought an eyewitness account of the victory. Cradock preached at the thanksgiving on July 21, 1646, which acclaimed the surrender of Oxford. As a chaplain, like Peter, he brought his own report of the victory. Cradock soon afterward accepted appointment as a "Minister of the Gospel to South Wales," a commission extended by the parliament.[84] Peter's career, of course, was to keep him at Westminster. Granted a BA by Trinity College, Cambridge, in 1617-8, he had been an expatriate in Rotterdam during the early 1630's. Journeying to New England, he served a parish at Salem and then returned to England proper in 1641. Tech-

[83] On both Dell and Ward, see *Alumni Cantabrigienses*. Nathaniel Ward is best known for *The Simple Cobler Of Aggawam* (London, 1647).

[84] See G. F. Nuttall, *The Welsh Saints, 1640-1660* (Oxford, 1957), 10 (also *passim*); W. A. Shaw, *op.cit.*, II, 323, 329, 540.

nically he was chaplain to the Army between 1644 and 1649, but he was perhaps even more active as an agent for Warwick, Fairfax, and Cromwell. He preached several additional times on important occasions before 1649.[85] Very active in Westminster in the weeks preceding Charles's death, he became a preacher at Whitehall in 1650. Thereafter he formally preached to the Rump at least once. Peter was, of course, held to be a regicide at the Restoration.[86]

John Owen is a final and a very important figure in the parliamentary pulpit. With a BA earned from Queen's College, Oxford, in 1632, he was installed in Essex at Fordham and Coggeshall. Coming to Westminster during the 1640's, he preached to Commons fasts twice, in 1646 and 1648-9. Thereafter he exhorted the Rump on at least eight special occasions. A favorite of Cromwell, he accompanied the Irish expedition and then became Dean of Christ Church College, Oxford, serving as Vice-Chancellor during the 1650's. In critical respects he led in the transformation of the Independency of the Interregnum into the "Congregational" nonconformity of the Restoration.[87]

CONCLUSION

The foregoing survey demonstrates the substantial character of the parliamentary fast program. Clearly it had widespread and influential backing among members of Commons. Furthermore, it was obviously a settled routine which consistently claimed parliamentary time, energy, and attention through 1648. As for the preachers, the burden of the program seems to have been carried by the generation whose members' births straddled the turn of the century. Puritan divines born during the last years of Elizabeth's reign and in the first few of James's dominated the

---

85 See Trevor-Roper, "Fast Sermons," 323-325.

86 *Alumni Cantabrigienses.* A modern critical biography is R. P. Stearns's, *The Strenuous Puritan: Hugh Peter, 1598-1660* (Urbana, Ill., 1954).

87 *Alumni Oxonienses; Calamy Revised.* A recent study of Owen is Dewey D. Wallace's "The Life and Thought of John Owen to 1660" (Ph.D. diss., Princeton University, 1965).

institution and were evidently its prime movers. This was the generation available for lectureships under the Feoffees scheme and fascinated by the New World ventures. It was also the generation which experienced most directly the rigorous hand of Laud; some responded by preparing for a European exile, which, of course, certain ones chose for a period. Contemporaries and friends, as well as a very few participants in the preaching institution, actually went so far as to retire across the Atlantic, some returning during the 1640's. A slightly younger generation made its lesser contribution to the system toward the end of the decade. The structure of the Westminster Assembly made it inevitable that the preachers would provide for, although only in nominal terms, geographical representation of the English counties. The important role taken by divines from Essex, however, and also the many and close associations with London before as well as during the period, should not be overlooked. It is, moreover, impressive that alumni of many of the Oxford and Cambridge colleges preached in the parliamentary pulpit. Thus there is need for caution in emphasizing superficial correlations between particular parties and individual colleges, at least without a far larger sample than lies beneath this study. Even so, the significance of Emmanuel College, Cambridge, as a "nursery" for this generation of puritans will have been obvious to the reader.

The material reviewed in this chapter underscores the importance of the monthly fast days celebrated by Commons. The preeminence of the regular humiliations is clear in terms of both the numerical tabulation of the preachers and the prevailing order of their appearances before parliament. The Commons routine was the heart of systematic humiliation in the Long Parliament. Though not necessarily surprising, it does indicate that in analysis of the content of the published sermons emphasis is appropriately placed upon exhortations from that class. It may be noteworthy that Independents appear to have preached before Commons more often than they did before Lords.

This striking involvement on their part, which started after the first war and developed during 1648 in the months immediately preceding Charles's death, should not obscure, however, a significant rate of participation in the program by Independents throughout the entire decade. Above all stands out the dominant role played by the Westminster divines. This was a puritan pulpit almost without exception, dedicated to instructing the representatives of England so that the national life might be conformed to the goals and the style of Puritanism. Most of these preachers were explicitly committed to reconstruction of the Church of England, and on the whole the preachers who did not participate in the Assembly may have been more radical in their views than its members were. The range of opinions among the clerics correctly reflects the constitution of Puritanism. In this sense, sectarian opinions did not belong to the movement however much they may have been derived from it, directly as well as indirectly. It therefore seems correct to denominate this a *puritan* institution, if that designation is at all permissible. In sum, within the preaching to parliament we might expect to find exemplification of puritan conceptions about the relationship between the claims of religion and political authority. The fast institution embodied, and was the occasion for the articulation of, the brotherhood's presuppositions and program. This point might seem trivial were it not for the difficulty of making discriminate judgments about the relationship of Puritanism to politics during that revolutionary era. By virtue of this extensive preaching institution we possess a remarkable repository of puritan addresses to the Long Parliament which have collective significance over and above whatever interest each may have in terms of its context or content.

In her survey of the early sermons, including those which preceded the monthly program, Mrs. Kirby remarks upon the tone of authority with which the preachers addressed the parliament. She thinks they were relatively insignificant

men whose presumption was great indeed. This chapter
(and the study generally) at least make it plausible to
argue that they were not as insignificant as she supposed.[88]
Their formal preaching took place against a background
of frequent and close relationships with the influential
members of the Long Parliament. The present point does
not pertain to their social position, of course, but rather
underscores the kind of authority in terms of which they
undertook to discharge their responsibilities. Commonly
designating themselves "Ministers of God's Word" or "Ministers of the Gospel," they apparently understood themselves to be preaching to political authorities on the basis
of a divine mandate which was not mediated by episcopal
appointment or a patron's favor. Failure to understand this
conception the puritan divines had of their role renders
their sermons essentially unintelligible. Considering themselves preachers of God's Word, they opened their texts and
instructed the Long Parliament through the rhetoric of
the "plain style." The next chapter will analyze the use
they made of this conventional sermon form, as well as
the scriptural warrants they assembled as authoritative
texts.

[88] E. W. Kirby, "Sermons before the Commons, 1640-42" *American
Historical Review*, XLIV/3 (April 1939), 524-531. To be fair to Mrs.
Kirby, it is important to recognize that she studied only the first
months of the formal fast program.

V

The Plain Style and
Puritan Texts

THERE are about two hundred and forty printed sermons which were originally preached to members of the Long Parliament at humiliations and thanksgivings before the death of Charles. On the basis of the discrimination between various classes of sermons set forth in the initial chapter, some will be excluded from further consideration. The sermons at the opening of the parliament, while properly representing the genesis of the preaching institution, do not for the most part embody its developed characteristics. For this reason no attempt will be made to assimilate them to the major classes. The informal sermons to sundry of the House of Commons during 1641, fascinating though they were both individually and as a group, should not be considered fully comparable to those which originated in the formal program.[1] The "Powder Plot" sermons stand apart from the mature institution, too, even though in most respects they were linked directly to exhortations which belong to the major classes. These will receive attention when appropriate. The Covenant-subscription sermons, manifestly a discrete group, will enter into the subsequent analysis insofar as they are pertinent, but the funeral sermons will generally not be accorded any further consideration. With the scope of the subject so defined, some two hundred and eighteen published sermons remain as representative of formal fast and thanksgiving preaching to the Lords and Commons through January 31, 1648-9. One hundred and twenty-nine of them were delivered to Commons in this series of regular monthly fasts which began

1 See the discussion in Appendix Three, "Sermons Preached to Sundry of the House of Commons, 1641," 275ff.

on February 23, 1641-2. Another thirty-six were delivered to the Lords beginning in October 1644. This class ceased to be represented in print after the publication of a sermon preached at the March fast in 1648. The remaining fifty-three exhortations were delivered to extraordinary or occasional fasts or thanksgivings. Some of these occasions were primarily (or even exclusively) arranged for either Commons or the Lords; others were joint affairs and at times also involved the Westminster Assembly and other constituted authorities. Grouped together, these more than two hundred sermons are the proper object for any analysis of the formal preaching before the Long Parliament, insofar as the sermons are available for study.

Literary studies written in recent decades have made us familiar with the different styles of preaching which characterized early Stuart England. The significance of these styles for interpretation of sermon literature from the period is evident. The most important volumes are those by J. W. Blench, W. Fraser Mitchell, and Perry G. E. Miller. Blench's *Preaching in England in the late Fifteenth and Sixteenth Centuries*[2] examines English sermons under the headings of Scriptural Interpretation, Form, Style, Use of Classical Allusions, and Themes. Discussion of the Elizabethan preachers isolates the distinctive elements which underlay the markedly divergent anglican and puritan preaching of the early Stuart era. In *English Pulpit Oratory*[3] Mitchell instructively reviews the "witty preaching" and elaborate verbal designs of those divines who cultivated the Stuart court. Perry Miller placed students of puritan preaching greatly in his debt through his analysis of that characteristic form of exhortation.[4] The contrast between the "witty" court preaching and the methodical "plain style" of the puritans is very sharp. An intelligent reading of the sermons preached before the Long Parliament presupposes recognition of that style which was so assiduously developed by the Assembly di-

---

[2] (New York, 1964).   [3] (London, 1932).
[4] *The New England Mind*, I (Cambridge, Mass., 1954), 331-362.

vines. The present chapter will discuss the distinguishing features of the "plain style" and also emphasize how that rhetorical procedure became a rather remarkable instrument in the preaching to the members of the Long Parliament.

THE PLAIN STYLE

Virtually all of the sermons delivered at parliamentary humiliations and thanksgivings display the general "method" of preaching commonly employed by most of the puritan clerics in Stuart England. This method may be traced in general outline to their patriarch, William Perkins.[5] Perkins had prepared a Latin treatise later translated as *The Arte of Prophecying, or, A Treatise concerning the sacred and only true manner and methode of Preaching.*[6] It discloses the strong influence which Petrus Ramus exerted upon the puritan method of preaching, if not upon the definition of subject matter.[7] Perkins had emphasized the release of the true "doctrine" from the biblical texts and toward this end had made use of techniques which became characteristic of those who followed him.

A further and more substantial debt the puritans owed Ramus (and Talon) was their rejection, following his lead, of the traditional separation of rhetoric and logic as independent domains each ordered by methods and procedures appropriate to it alone.[8] That traditional separation was mirrored in the anglican preaching within the Church of England. There the distinction between clergy and laity was

[5] On Perkins, see the *DNB* and H. C. Porter, *Reformation and Reaction in Tudor Cambridge* (Cambridge, Eng., 1958).

[6] The original was published in 1592; it was translated by T. Tuke in 1606. See W. S. Howell, *Logic and Rhetoric in England, 1500-1700* (Princeton, 1956), 206; also Miller, *op.cit.*, Chs. XI and XII.

[7] See Howell, 207. More precisely, the influence was transmitted through Omer Talon, Ramus's disciple, who had applied the latter's ideas to the discipline of rhetoric (Howell, 148-149). Yet see H. C. Porter's comment warning against exaggeration of Ramus's influence on the Cambridge puritans, *op.cit.*, 225, n. 8.

[8] Howell, 147-148.

perpetuated in such a way that the rigorous logic of doctrinal reflection (suitable to the theological mysteries) was reserved to the former while the latter were fed, consequently, on an essentially derivative rhetorical fare. The puritans, by contrast, assumed and insisted upon the intellectual priesthood of all believers. Thus merchants, lawyers, and gentry—whether sitting as members of parliament or not—were expected to share the staple diet of logic and not the sweet desserts of rhetoric alone. The vigor of Puritanism as a social movement was embodied in just this stance, its challenge to a theory of communication associated with a traditional and aristocratic society.[9] The assault was conceived to be in the service of both truth and utility. For this reason the assumptions undergirding Ramist logic (and the rhetoric conjoined with it) rendered it appealing to the puritans. In this sense, the kind of logic and rhetoric adopted was an integral element of Puritanism as a social movement and not simply an academic issue or a formal matter of style. The puritans' theory of communication was an expression of the struggle in which they were engaged, no less than were their concerns for social position, power, and influence—as well as for a mode of religious life congruent with, and expressive of, these goals.

In order to liberate true doctrine from a text and to structure purified teaching around it, most puritans resorted to the conventional homiletic devices perfected by their party. Their conception of the sermon was not, however, simply a transcription of Ramist theories. As with Perkins himself, a marked eclecticism characterized their relationships to the technical schools and disputes.[10] What developed as a result was a typical structure for the puritan sermon, or variations upon a typical structure. This was the "plain style" in which nearly all of the parliamentary sermons were preached—although it might be rendered explicit to varying degrees in any one of them. The

---

[9] *Ibid.*, 9-10.   [10] *Ibid.*, 207.

possibilities for variation within the structure were its great strength. Failure to use the method at all was very rare.

The initial text was "divided" so as to yield a suitable number of "doctrines." This act was regarded as an "opening" of the text for the purpose of extracting principles or general rules from biblical materials. The third element in the sermon was usually termed "reasons." This part of the sermon provided an explication of the "doctrine" and, in the extreme case, became a rationalization for it. It held a key position within the structure of the sermon, for it was at this point that the puritan preacher reached out beyond the one authoritative book to supplement it with the wisdom of classical antiquity and the experience of his contemporaries. The "reasons" proved the "doctrine (s) " not to be arbitrary. The final section of the sermon was generally termed "use" or "application." Its purpose was to manifest the contemporary relevance of the "doctrine," the cogency and truth of which had already been demonstrated. The "reasons" and "applications" (or "uses") might be as numerous as the sermon and its context required or rendered appropriate. In some sermons this triadic pattern would be repeated for each "doctrine" distilled from the text; in others the "doctrine (s) ," "reasons," and "uses" would be clustered separately. But, whatever the exact arrangement, the implicit, if not explicit, structure of almost every exhortation to the Long Parliament exhibited this method of preaching. The "plain style" was the universal mode of puritan sermons—at least in this pulpit.

Preaching in the "plain style," developed by the puritan party to carry their struggle into the realm of communication, was recommended in the *Directory* by the Westminster divines who were chiefly responsible for the preaching to parliament. According to them, it had been "found by experience to be very much blessed of God, and very helpfull for the peoples understandings and memories."[11] In giving this form to their sermons, the puritans explicitly recognized the utility of human arts and let-

11 *A Directory for The Publique Worship of God* (London, 1644) , 34.

ters.[12] In addition to "illumination of Gods Spirit, and other gifts of edification," the *Directory* noted that the preacher should possess "skill in the Original Languages, and in such Arts and Sciences as are handmaids unto Divinity, . . . knowledge in the whole Body of Theology, but most of all in the holy Scriptures. . . ."[13] The subject of the sermon was to be a suitable text, properly (if briefly) analyzed and divided. Doctrines were to be "raised" from the text with great care and expressed in "plaine termes," confirmed by parallel and pertinent citations from scripture. "The Arguments or Reasons are to bee solid; and, as much as may bee, convincing."[14] The preacher was not to "rest in generall Doctrine, . . . but to bring it home to special Use, by application to his hearers," namely, by the "Use of Instruction or information in the knowledge of some truth, which is a consequence from his Doctrine," the "Confutation of false Doctrines," the "Exhorting to Duties," "Dehortion, Reprehension, and publique Admonition," "applying Comfort," and "Notes of Tryall . . . whereby the Hearers may be able to examine themselves. . . ."[15]

There were certain assumptions underlying this conventional homiletics which should be brought to light. The most obvious is that in principle the preachers were tutoring their listeners in Reformed doctrine. Although the preacher might effectively attract or fascinate with interesting images and ready wit, these devices were at best a sweetening of an inherently bitter pill. Such exercises were tactics in the preaching, not examples of that fundamental literary strategy which had been adopted among the "witty" divines of the anglican party.[16] The preacher enlightened his audience with an eternal wisdom for the sake of its edification. Although this assumption might be clothed in gracious words, it stood forth boldly in the structure of the exhortation. Equally significant is the implicit claim to universal validity which was made on be-

---

[12] Cf. the discussion of the "plain style" in Miller, *op.cit.*, 331-362.
[13] *A Directory* . . . , 28.   [14] *Ibid.*, 30.
[15] *Ibid.*, 31-33.   [16] Cf. Miller, *op.cit.*, 331-335.

half of this inspired teaching through the "reasons." The scriptures were held to be authoritative but also self-authenticating according to the wisdom of the world rooted in the informed experience of rational men. Like their spiritual father Calvin, and unlike many post-Enlightenment Protestants, the puritans experienced no gulf between natural and revealed truth. More akin to Augustine than to Aquinas, they were closer to both than to later fundamentalists or liberals. The "doctrines" preceded the "reasons," but the latter made the former principles comprehensible and eminently rational.

Possibly the most fundamental of their assumptions was that scripture, with its particularity and provincial character, was to be comprehended in terms of precedents. Thus, in the final analysis, the "doctrines" explicated God's universal and normative precedents with respect to human history. The close relationship between this kind of reading of the Bible and a typological interpretation of scripture is evident. Some puritans actually developed a rigorous typology, the significance of which was summarized in the following terms by the Massachusetts Bay puritans:

> Whatsoever Ordinance of the old Testament is not repealed in the New Testament, as peculiar to the Jewish Paedagogie, but was of morall and perpetuall equitie, the same bindes us in these dayes, and is to be accounted the revealed will of God in all ages, though it be not particularly and expressly mentioned in the writings of the New Testament. . . . the Scriptures of the New Testament doe speake little in these cases; onely the Scriptures of the Old Testament doe give direction, and light about them.[17]

More common, however, was a less highly elaborated assumption that the history of Israel was precedential:

17 *An Apologie Of The Churches In New England For Church-Covenant* (London, 1643), 8.

Look on what we finde acted, or written of Gods goodnesse to his people, not as bare histories of things
done, but as Prognosticks and assurances of the like
again; as upon *Book-cases* adjudged, that may be vouched
unto God as Presidents in this time of trouble and danger. It is the great fault of too many, when they read
in Scripture of wonderfull protections and deliverances,
they behold them onely to admire the acts done, but not
to rowle themselves, by vertue thereof, upon God, for the
like.[18]

In many ways this particular use of scripture as normative precedent seems to have been the most basic theme
of puritan preaching to parliament, a position which locates Puritanism within the distinctive Reformed tradition of international Calvinism. John White articulated
this assumption in a sermon to the Lords:

Whatsoever things were written aforehand, were written for our learning, saith the Apostle, *Rom* 15.4. The
Lawes for our Direction: The Prophecies for Observation of their Accomplishment in answerable Events: The
Promises for our Comfort and consolation: The Examples of Evill for Caution, of Good for Imitation: And
lastly the Events, ordered by the Wisdome, and Providence of God, for Precedents and Patternes, representing our State and Condition, either What it is at Present, and Why so, or what wee are to Expect it may be
hereafter.[19]

Thus puritans did not read their scriptures as a collection
or collation of proof-texts, although many later Protestants
have tended to do just that. Each book and verse had its
particular significance within the status of the whole
corpus. That whole was the revealed Word of God. The
Word (Logos) was the fundamental structure of the world.
The diversity embodied within the Bible served to demon-

[18] C. Burges, *Another Sermon* (London, 1641), 57.
[19] *The Troubles Of Jerusalems Restauration* (London, 1646), 1.

strate its relationship to the multifarious events of history, while the fundamental unity of scripture at the same time brought order to that chaos. Edward Corbett directly echoed Calvin in making this point at the regular Commons fast in December 1642:

> Had we no other light but that of Nature, and no other writings but the book of the world, we might read a God and see his Providence: But to find a Saviour, to know a Gospell, to understand the mysteries of Salvation, is above the Art of humane learning, the spirit of God must be our Tutor therein, and the Holy Scriptures only can teach and give us such a lesson.[20]

The puritans did not have recourse, naturally, to the fourfold exegesis which had been characteristic of theology during the centuries preceding the Reformation. Allegorical interpretation of scripture presupposed a world conceived in idealistic and, usually, nonhistorical terms. Accordingly, their historical or precedential construction had a twofold connotation. In a manifest sense the precedent lay in the parallelism between the biblical text which gave substance to the "doctrine" and the situation to which it might be applied. In a latent sense the scriptural precedents had been baptized in Christ and transformed by His coming, so that the puritan might understand his age to be simply a living out of divine intentions. This premise gave vitality to the puritan exhortations, for the contemporary application of Old Testament precedents represented in this view, quite literally, new life in Christ. In the extreme case suggested above, these assumptions might lead to a typological reading of scripture in which the Old Testament shadows would be made flesh and blood in the New Testament. Construed in a doctrinaire fashion, this meant that the future course of history could be found "writ small" (and symbolically) in the apocalyptic literature. The more general and less rigorous use of scrip-

[20] *Gods Providence* (London, 1642), 1.

ture, however, was in the more moderate precedential sense. The puritans, it should be emphasized, did not consider these to be provincial assumptions; on the contrary, they believed them to be universal in scope. This proved to be the mold in which their thought was cast, and it provided the basic language in which they addressed the Long Parliament.

This fundamental structure is implicit in nearly all of the sermons to parliament which were published. Reading them, one cannot help being struck by the altogether remarkable flexibility which it afforded the preachers. Variations upon the pattern suggest its adaptability to text, occasion, preacher, and audience. The deficiencies which marred it, especially its failure to foster elegance of style and graceful expression, are evident. At the same time, this structure made the "plain style" of preaching an appropriate means of address to the parliament. It was a kind of exhortation that was perfectly suited to the political context of this preaching program, because it invited—that is, logically required—those who heard it to become involved in the matter of biblical norms and their direct application to a reforming nation. In a basic sense it was almost a pure form of political address. The puritan sermon, especially in its use before the Long Parliament, is to be judged as an engine of influence rather than as a literary creation subject to the canons of taste or style. Precisely in this manner the preaching before Commons and the Lords can be considered to have been a revolutionary rhetoric, since it systematically referred to an authority in terms of which the puritans sought to reconstitute Stuart society.

PURITAN TEXTS

The numerous references already made to specific sermons throughout previous chapters should have indicated that preachers selected texts according to their appropriateness for the particular occasion and the moral they wished to convey. At the same time a considerable burden was placed upon the cleric to "open" his text acknowledging its proper setting and to reinforce his doctrines with supporting citations from scripture. It should be obvious, then, that the texts were not simply proof-texts essentially removed from a suitable context and "opened" without reference to that locus. Rather, the puritan method of "plain style" preaching necessarily gave weight to the scriptural setting in both immediate and extended senses.

In this light it should be instructive to note the distribution of texts used in the parliamentary sermons, that is, their location in the scriptural corpus. What kind of doctrines did the preachers seek to extract from the Bible? What kinds of precedents were thought to be relevant and useful? One might expect, for example, that the exodus from Egypt would have provided imagery for the puritans who had recently experienced "captivity" at the hand of Laud, or possibly the recourse to rule by "judges" in ancient Israel would have seemed to justify rebellion against an established and alien authority. A Deuteronomic interpretation of history, too, would seem to have been apposite to the puritan experience.[21] Or the preachers could have styled themselves "prophets" delivering the "Word of the Lord" to the rulers of the day. Response might likewise be expected to the apocalyptic literature, which seemed to offer "knowledge" of the anticipated course of history, perhaps culminating in a millennial epoch. It would be interesting to discover, moreover, whether the New Testament could provide texts in any meaningful number which would be appropriate for the manifestly political context of preaching to the Long Parliament. In brief, a review of the distribution of scriptural texts is a prerequisite for any study of the sermons' form and contents.

A survey of the biblical books from which the parliamentary preachers drew their texts discloses both a wide assortment of sources and patterns of choice within them. Dis-

21 James Spalding recently proposed this as the appropriate biblical category for understanding the sermons. "Sermons before Parliament (1640-1649) as a Public Puritan Diary," *Church History* XXXVI/1 (March 1967), 24-35.

crimination between those texts used for sermons at regular Commons fasts (the majority of the sermons studied) and those of the additional major classes shows that the puritan preachers were generally consistent in their selection of scriptural texts as the bases for their sermons to the Long Parliament. The use of texts similar in substance or approximately identical is also noteworthy. The material for these considerations is the two hundred and seventeen sermons published by the preachers in the three major classes.[22]

Tabulation confirms the general impression that texts were culled from a wide variety of the books of scripture. The Old Testament especially was mined thoroughly: one hundred and sixty-two of the sermons were based upon it. The texts were taken from thirty-two of the thirty-nine books that puritans admitted to the Old Testament canon. Those not used at all were basically marginal ones —Ruth, Ecclesiastes, the Song of Solomon, Joel, Obadiah, Jonah, and Nahum. Adoption of texts from the remaining books of the Old Testament is even more impressive in that all but six of them supplied the Biblical grounding for at least two (and usually more) sermons[23] and all but five furnished scriptural basis for sermons to the regular fasts before Commons.[24]

Selection of texts from the New Testament books was broadly parallel but sufficiently distinctive to warrant separate notice. Fifty-five of the two hundred and seventeen sermons were based upon them. Of the twenty-seven books in the New Testament, however, only thirteen provided texts. All four Gospels and the Acts were sources

[22] This excludes J. Ussher, *Vox Hibernae* (*sic*) (London, 1642), a sermon which was pirated and published against his wishes and which he claimed was inaccurate and a misrepresentation of his exhortation.

[23] The six books of the Old Testament which each provided a text for only one sermon were: Leviticus, II Kings, Job, Lamentations, Habakkuk, and Malachi.

[24] The five Old Testament books each providing texts for published sermons to the Lords periodic fasts and to extraordinary occasions but not to the regular Commons fasts were: Joshua, II Kings, Lamentations, Amos, and Malachi.

for sermons, but of the Pauline corpus, only I and II Corinthians and Philippians were used, excluding altogether such conventional sources as the Letters to the Romans, Galatians, and (the disputed) Ephesians. Additional texts came from the Epistle to the Hebrews, the Letter of James, I John, II Peter, and Revelation. The sermons preached at the monthly fasts before Commons involved texts from all of the above sources except II Peter.

The readiness of the preachers to select texts from the broad range of the Old Testament in preference to the New Testament is evident. Thus the distribution of texts among the biblical books is interesting confirmation that the puritans, while reading their Old Testament in light of the New Covenant, yet were drawn back toward the earlier and richer materials in elaborating their conceptions of political and social life. It also provides specific evidence that the puritans construed ancient Israel's library as a source of "authoritative words." With the abundance of its teachings the Old Testament legitimated their many and various convictions.

Although the texts for parliamentary sermons were drawn from a wide range of biblical books, certain clusters emerged indicating patterns of choice. By far the greatest concentration of texts is from the book of Psalms, the classical expression of Israel's piety and her "hymn book."[25] In general, however, the thirty-nine texts from Psalms do not fall into any obvious groupings within that book itself. The explanation for the predominance of these texts is probably to be located rather in the genre, namely, address to God or acknowledgment of His power in the context of articulating individual as well as collective piety. For it does seem reasonable to assume that the mode of literature represented by Psalms was the basic factor responsible for the remarkable frequency (almost one

---

[25] The total is thirty-nine: twenty-one in sermons for the regular Commons fasts, six in the Lords monthly series, and twelve at the extraordinary occasions. Certain instances of the use of identical or contiguous texts from Psalms will be discussed below.

out of every five printed sermons) with which preachers turned to this book for their texts. The program, after all, was one of national humiliation and thanksgiving.

The next largest concentration of texts is from the book of Isaiah. Twenty-five sermons, approximately twelve percent of the total, were based on texts from this source. The proportion of these sermons from three major classes is roughly the same as the distribution of those preached upon Psalms: sixteen of the sermons in the regular Commons sequence, three in the Lords fast institution, and six at extraordinary occasions. Another parallel to the distribution of texts from Psalms is the breadth of selection, ranging over the entire Isaian corpus—a matter of some interest in view of the critical consensus that this biblical book was of manifold origin.[26]

Of the other prophetic works, only Jeremiah and Zechariah provided more than four texts apiece for published parliamentary sermons. Ten separate texts were derived from each of these books. Nine of the texts from Jeremiah, four from the fourth chapter alone, were selected for sermons preached to monthly Commons fasts. All of the ten texts from Zechariah, taken from seven different chapters, were chosen for sermons to regular Commons humiliations. The selection of these twenty texts for sermons to parliament is probably valid testimony to the role played in the puritan imagination by the exile from, return to, and rebuilding of Jerusalem, a theme especially congenial to the purposes underlying the Commons fasts.

The next most frequently used source was I Samuel, which afforded a total of six texts distributed among the three major classes of sermons. Many of the other Old Testament books provided two, three, or four texts each.

A similar pattern may be found in the selections from the New Testament. Revelation provided the largest number of texts, fourteen in all. It should be noticed that ten of

[26] In bald form the thesis is that material in Isaiah derives from two or three distinct sources and periods, which can be distinguished in the text. These are designated I, II, and III Isaiah.

these were used in sermons preached to monthly Commons fasts, and only four in sermons at irregular occasions. This distribution shows that texts were deliberately selected from Revelation for scheduled humiliations and not simply for use at extraordinary affairs. In other words, the eschatological framework of Revelation possessed general meaning for the puritans beyond whatever specific expectations they derived from it. Nine sermons were based on texts from Matthew; of these, five were delivered at monthly Commons humiliations. The gospel of Mark was the source for only one sermon text. Apparently there were no particular sections of these gospels that held any unusual fascination for the divines of the brotherhood. With the exception of the special relationships between certain sermons noted below, the several texts were essentially unrelated to each other aside from their positions in the scriptural corpus.

Special relationships between different sermons are worth noting, however, especially those of convergence, conjunction, and identity of texts. Occasionally, it seems, a progression in texts was arranged by two individuals scheduled to preach on the same day or, more rarely, by the same individual appearing at a series of separate fasts. Twice only—at least as far as published materials are concerned—was a parliamentary sermon preached on a text basically identical to one already used. Henry Hall spoke at a regular Commons fast in May 1644 on Matthew 11:12: "And from the days of John the Baptist until now the kingdom of heaven suffereth violence and the violent take it by force." He titled his sermon *Heaven Ravished*. Its chief point was that possibly the veritable rule of Christ was then upon them.[27] Stephen Marshall chose the same text for the monthly Commons fast of January 1647-8.[28] The other pair were based on Proverbs 23:23: "Buy the truth, and sell it not." Thomas Hill took this as his text for a sermon in July 1642.[29] John Maynard used it in

---

27 (London, 1644).   28 *A Sermon Preached* . . . (London, 1647).
29 *The Trade of Truth Advanced* (London, 1642).

February 1644-5.[30] In both instances it is difficult to attach any significance to this choice of the same texts, except insofar as it was an indirect confirmation, in the one case, that the symbol of the "kingdom" (or divine rule) was prominent in puritan analysis of the age and, in the other, that a well-known proverb draws attention to itself.

A great many sermons were preached on related or contiguous texts. In every instance, though, the separation in time between the sermons and the actual differences between the texts suggest that the connection was essentially accidental. The explanation appears to be simply that certain biblical contexts expressed themes which were especially congenial to the needs of the preachers in their office before parliament. Specific examples of close convergence or conjunction are given in detail below.[31] In

---

[30] *A Sermon Preached* . . . (London, 1645) .

[31] Daniel Evance's *The Noble Order* (London, 1646) , preached to the Lords in January 1645-6, was based on I Samuel 2:30d; William Strong's *The Way to the Highest Honour* (London, 1647) , delivered to the same body in February 1646-7, used for its text I Samuel 2:30c.

Thomas Young's *Hopes Incouragement* . . . (London, 1644) , addressed to a regular Commons fast in February 1643-4, developed a theme from Psalm 31:24; Hugh Peter's *Gods Doings, and Mans Duty* (London, 1646) , presented at an extraordinary fast in April 1646, took Psalm 31:23 as its starting point.

Thomas Coleman's *God's Unusuall Answer* . . . (London, 1644) , composed for an extraordinary fast in September 1644, was founded on Psalm 65:5a; William Carter's *Light in Darknesse: discovered* (London, 1648) , given before Commons at its November fast in 1647 took Psalm 65:5 as its text.

John Langley's *Gemitus Columbae: The Mournfull Note of the Dove* (London, 1644) , contributed to a Commons fast in December 1644, derived inspiration from Psalm 74:19-20; Francis Taylor's *Gods Covenant The Churches Plea* (London, 1645) , presented before the same house in October 1645, elaborated on a topic broached in Psalm 74:20.

William Sedgwick's *Zions Deliverance* . . . (London, 1642) , delivered to Commons in June 1642, took its subject from Isaiah 62:7; Matthew Newcomen's *Jerusalems Watch-men* . . . (London, 1643) , preached to both houses and the Assembly on July 7, 1643, had Isaiah 62:6b-7 for its text.

Jeremy Whitaker's *Ejrenopojos, Christ the Settlement of Unsettled Times* (London, 1642) , which Commons heard in January 1642-3,

none is there displayed any intention to rebut or correct a previous interpretation of the text in question. The occurrence of convergence or conjunction, then, appears to have been basically fortuitous.

Linkage by progression was more intentional. The body of published material discloses two instances in which preachers—apparently on purpose—used adjacent biblical passages as texts for related sermons. The practice of exegetical and expository preaching or lecturing common among the earlier Stuart puritans lies behind this arrangement. The practice seems to have been continued or even expanded within the brotherhood during this period, and these instances probably reflect it. Stephen Marshall provided the clearest example of this progression with a series of sermons which he delivered in 1645. On March 26 he preached to the Lords on Psalm 102:16-17.[32] At the next monthly fast he exhorted Commons, this time taking Psalm 102:17 as his text;[33] this sermon appears to have been essentially a continuation of the previous one. On June 19, finally, he spoke at an extraordinary thanksgiving of both houses on a theme derived from Psalm

built upon Haggai 2:7; William Reyner's *Babylons Ruining-Earthquake* (London, 1644), the sermon for a Commons fast in August 1644, made use of Haggai 2:6-7.

Robert Baillie's *Satan the Leader in Chief* (London, 1643), addressed to Commons in February 1643-4, interpreted Zechariah 3:1-2; Benjamin Pickering's *A Firebrand Pluckt out of the Burning* (London, 1645), given in November 1644 before the same body, borrowed its title and theme from Zechariah 3:2b.

Edmund Calamy's *Englands Antidote . . .* (London, 1645), which highlighted an extraordinary fast in October 1644, showed the contemporary relevance of Acts 17:30b; Lazarus Seaman's *The Head of the Church . . .* (London, 1647), delivered to the Lords in January 1646-7, adopted Acts 17:30b-31 as a text.

Joseph Caryl's *The Saints Thankfull Acclamation . . .* (London, 1644), preached before Commons in April 1644, sought guidance in Revelation 11:16-17; George Hughes's *Vae-Euge-tuba. Or, The Wo-joy-Trumpet* (London, 1647), the Commons sermon in May 1647, referred to Revelation 11:15.

32 *Gods Master-piece* (London, 1645).
33 *The Strong Helper* (London, 1645).

102:18.[34] The other preacher who sought to tie one sermon to another in this way was Cornelius Burges. In his use of progression, however, temporal contiguity was not a factor. For the second monthly fast, in March 1642, he had chosen to preach on Jeremiah 4:14. Three years later, in April 1645, he presented a sequel on Jeremiah 4:14b.[35]

Connections of a similar kind are illustrated by three sets of sermons in which different preachers apparently agreed to select closely related texts for their labors on the same days. Anthony Tuckney and Thomas Coleman collaborated in one such enterprise in their preaching before Commons in August 1643. Tuckney spoke in the morning on Jeremiah 8:22 in a sermon entitled *The Balme of Gilead.*[36] Coleman based his afternoon address, *The Christians Course and Complaint,*[37] on Jeremiah 8:20. Joseph Caryl and Richard Vines picked James 4:8 as a common text for the Commons fast on January 28, 1645-6. Caryl preached on *Heaven and Earth Embracing*[38] in the morning, and Vines on *The Purifying of Unclean Hearts and Hands*[39] at the afternoon sitting. Perhaps the most notable collaboration developed out of a topical fast, an extraordinary humiliation for the growth of heresy held on March 10, 1646-7. Richard Vines opened with *The Authours, Nature, and Danger of Haeresie,*[40] based on II Peter 2:1. Thomas Hodges in his turn took up the very next verse (II Peter 2:2) in *The Growth and Spreading of Haeresie.*[41]

In light of the instances cited above, it is curious that preachers did not cooperate in these various ways more often. That they did not may be additional evidence for the interpretation of Puritanism which has been advocated in this study, namely, that the identity of a puritan preacher was not derived so much from his reliance on special texts (or doctrines) as from a shared and self-conscious acceptance of scripture as normative in the na-

---

[34] *A Sacred Record* (London [1645]) .
[35] *Two Sermons* (London, 1645) .
[36] (London, 1643) . [37] (London, 1643) . [38] (London, 1646) .
[39] (London, 1646) . [40] (London, 1647) . [41] (London, 1647) .

tional crisis then being experienced. Thus the explication of diverse texts was rendered coherent through the common method of preaching according to the "plain style." This interpretation is supported further by attention to one additional matter. Those preachers who did publish a number of different sermons which they had preached to the Long Parliament betrayed through their selection of texts no special biases. Rather, they demonstrated a catholic approach to the scriptural canon. In his choices, for example, Stephen Marshall ranged from I Chronicles, Joshua, and Judges through the prophets and Psalms to Matthew and Revelation. Obadiah Sedgwick preached on texts from as diverse a group of books as Esther, Jeremiah, Hebrews, and Revelation. Richard Vines drew his sermons from Numbers, II Samuel, Deuteronomy, Isaiah, James, and II Peter. Thomas Case confined his choices to the Old Testament but within that compass covered the ground from Exodus through Hosea to Psalms. Joseph Caryl based his preaching on Isaiah, Psalms, Luke, James, and Revelation. In sum, the "authoritative book" was the source for numerous texts which were rendered coherent through the "doctrines" which were "opened" from them.

The Reasons and Uses for Doctrines

Thomas Watson preached to Commons in December at the next to the last fast formally included in this study. His sermon, *Gods Anatomy Upon Mans Heart*,[42] which boldly criticized the hypocrisy of Pride's Purge, made effective use of the "plain style." In moving from his text, Hebrews 4:12 (13b KJ), to his doctrine, he illumined the conventional procedures which undergirded the preaching institution before parliament: "In the Law, first the Lamps were lighted before the Incense was burned; To this I may allude, First the Judgement is to be enlightened by Doctrine, before the Affections are set on fire. We must first be shining, and then burning Lamps."[43] While not denigrat-

---

[42] (London, 1649).   [43] *Ibid.*, 2.

ing the importance of the affections, he insisted that the first and most basic concern of the preachers to the parliament was to address the "judgment."[44] The internal structure of the puritan sermon, therefore, turned upon the "doctrine." Logically it was the center of the sermon, however much energy might be expended subsequently to bring it to the hearts of those who heard it through the "uses" or "applications." The doctrine was the articulation of a general principle on the basis of a specific biblical text which gave it warrant. The status of the scripture permitted the doctrine, though drawn from a particular passage, to be identified as a universally valid precept, proved through "reasons" to be consistent with the sober experience of all ages. The doctrine, a medium which rendered general the particular and prescriptive scriptural text, was thus simply puritan teaching in its purest state. It expressed rationally, and usually in propositional form, the truth that puritans believed resided in scripture. It was buttressed by reasons and applied through uses to the condition of the auditors. Thus the doctrine served as a pivot on which the whole sermon was carefully balanced.

Watson's sermon exemplifies most features of the primordial pattern. From his opened text he framed one doctrine: "The most secret Cabinet-designes of mans heart are all unlocked and clearly anatomized before the Lord."[45] After citing additional texts to substantiate his doctrine and to amplify it fully,[46] he devoted several pages of the printed text to the reasons.[47] Finally he came to the uses,[48] in which he criticized, among other things, freedom of conscience and religious libertinism.[49] Typical applications of doctrines included confutation, humiliation, information, examination, consolation, admonition, and exhortation.[50] Not every doctrine was made to fulfill all these or all possible uses, although, recognizing the

---

[44] Cf. Miller, *op.cit.*, 344. [45] *Gods Anatomy* . . . , 4.
[46] *Ibid.*, 4-6. [47] *Ibid.*, 7-10. [48] *Ibid.*, 10-25. [49] *Ibid.*, 17.
[50] This particular list is taken from Simeon Ash's *God's Incomparable Goodnesse unto Israel* (London, 1647), 13-34.

ingenuity of the preachers, one has good reason to suspect that each one might have been so construed!

A sermon at the second monthly fast (March 30, 1642) illustrates equally well the way in which the conventional structure was balanced upon the basic doctrine or, in this case, doctrines. Simeon Ash preached on Psalm 9:9 (KJ): "The Lord also will be a refuge for the oppressed, a refuge in times of trouble."[51] His two doctrines, through clarification, confirmation, and application of the text, carried the burden of his exhortation: "That oppression and trouble may be in this world the portion of Gods children";[52] "The Lord will be a refuge in times of trouble."[53]

A sermon entitled *England's Preservation*,[54] which Obadiah Sedgwick delivered at the May fast in 1642, highlights other common variations in the method of "plain style" preaching. Sedgwick took his text from Jeremiah 4:3 (KJ): "For thus saith the Lord to the men of Judah and Jerusalem, Break up your fallow ground, and sow not among thorns." The verse had two members following the parallelism of Hebrew poetry. Thus each of the counsels— to "serious humiliation" and to "dextrous reformation"— yielded a doctrine.[55] The first doctrine stated that "the breaking up of sinfull hearts, is a singular meanes to prevent the breaking downe of a sinfull Nation."[56] Sedgwick applied a common variation of the general method in analyzing immediately and in great detail both the substance of the doctrine and the means through which its precept could be realized. Then followed the conventional reasons and applications before his discussion of the second doctrine.[57] This provided a positive injunction: "That all penetentiall and reforming worke must be so managed and acted that it may not prove a vaine and fruitlesse worke, but may come to be a successfull and profitable work."[58] At this point Sedgwick energetically enumer-

---

[51] *The Best Refuge for the Most Oppressed* (London, 1642).
[52] *Ibid.*, 4.   [53] *Ibid.*, 18.   [54] (London, 1642).
[55] *England's Preservation*, 4ff.
[56] *Ibid.*, 7.   [57] *Ibid.*, 30.   [58] *Ibid.*, 33.

ated the "pretending penitential agents" whose sowing was superficial and therefore of no worth. He omitted formal reasons. The application of this doctrine was a direct exhortation to the divines and the members of Commons in the name of ecclesiastical reformation.[59]

The basic structure as outlined above was dominated by the doctrines, but the possibility of variations upon the pattern must be stressed. Although many preachers rested content with one or two (numerous examples of which could be produced), the impulse to multiply doctrines on the basis of a fruitful text and an appropriate occasion seldom seems to have been denied. A good example of the proliferation of doctrines is provided in Edmund Calamy's sermon at the first of the regular monthly humiliations (February 23, 1641-2). It illustrates the conventional manner in which a series of closely interrelated doctrines could be derived from a single text. *Gods Free Mercy to England*,[60] a distinctively evangelical exhortation,[61] was based upon Ezekiel 36:32 (KJ): "Not for your sakes doe I [do] this, saith the Lord God, be it known unto you: be ashamed and confounded for your owne waies, O house of Israel." From this verse, which is set in the context of Ezekiel's prophetic words of restitution, Calamy framed a progression of four doctrines:

[1] That God doth sometimes shew mercy to a Nation when it least deserves it, and least expects it.[62]

[2] That the deliverances that come to a Nation, come from Jehovah Adonai. Nationall mercies come from the God of Nations.[63]

---

59 *Ibid.*, 40ff.

60 (London, 1642).

61 Calamy's expression of his evangelical intention is striking: "Now my purpose is to lay the sins of England against God in one scale, and the mercies of God to England in the other scale, and to call upon you this day to be humbled, and ashamed, and broken in heart before the Lord, that ever you should sinne against such a God." *Gods Free Mercy to England*, 2.

62 *Ibid.*, 3.   63 *Ibid.*, 8.

[3] That Nationall Mercies come from free grace, not from free will; Not from mans goodnes, but from Gods goodnes.[64]

[4] That the contemplation of Gods free mercy to Nations and persons ought to be a mighty incentive, and a most effectuall argument to make them ashamed, and ashamed, ashamed for sin for the times past, and ashamed to sinne for the time to come.[65]

The application of this exhortation is easily imagined since it expressed, indeed completed, the inner logic of the doctrines. Thus the doctrines of this sermon, as in nearly all of the other parliamentary sermons, served as structure for the whole.

A sermon preached by Edmund Staunton exhibits one typical manner in which devices were used to "open" and "frame up" texts into the doctrines. *Phinehas's Zeal In Execution Of Judgment. Or, A Divine Remedy For Englands Misery*[66] was delivered to the Lords on October 30, 1644. The text was Psalm 106:30 (KJ): "Then stood up Phinehas, and executed judgment: and so the plague was stayed." Staunton identified four particulars as a way of framing the doctrines: circumstance of time (*quando*), agent (*quis*), what he did (*quid*), and fruits or issues (*quid inde*).[67] These distinctions enabled him to offer his "observations" (=doctrines), which were sustained with "arguments" (=reasons) and then applied. His doctrines, corresponding to the particulars, were:

[1] The Magistrates due and regular execution of justice, bindeth not up Gods hands from powring out of his wrath upon his enemies, in wayes something strange and extraordinary.[68]

[2] When God hath work to do, he can finde out workmen, a Phinehas.[69]

[64] *Ibid.*, 17.   [65] *Ibid.*, 22.   [66] (London, 1645).
[67] *Phinehas's Zeal* . . . , 8-9.
[68] *Ibid.*, 9.   [69] *Ibid.*

[3 & 4] Execution of judgment, is Gods way to pacifie Gods wrath and to stay his judgements.[70]

Without exception in preaching according to the "plain style," the heart of the exhortation was located in the doctrines.

Attention to other variations of the method will underscore its extraordinary flexibility, especially in the service of preaching to the Long Parliament. Simeon Ash addressed a regular humiliation of Commons in 1647 on the subject *God's Incomparable Goodnesse unto Israel. Unfolded and Applyed.*[71] For this occasion he had selected Psalm 73:1 (KJ) as his text: "Truly God is good to Israel, even to such as are of a clean heart." He offered one main doctrine: "That the mighty God, Father, Sonne and holy Ghost, is really, constantly, singularly good in his administrations to his Church and people."[72] From this assertion he passed to a full application according to conventional "uses."[73] More significant, at least for analysis of the central role played by doctrines within the "plain style" method of preaching, was Ash's preliminary discrimination of five subordinate or intermediate doctrines, also termed "observations" by some. This procedure made possible a logical means of transition from the text to the central doctrine—a transition which, however, might not always be self-evident! Rhetorically, of course, this tactic facilitated development of a crescendo mounting toward the final doctrine:

[1] That the sufferings of Gods servants, tend to the Churches advantage.

[2] The prosperity of the wicked is sometimes a matter of offence unto suffering Saints.

[3] That notwithstanding the sorest assaults of Sathan, the world, and corruption, the servants of the most High shall get the victory.

[70] *Ibid.*, 10.   [71] (London, 1647).
[72] *God's Incomparable Goodnesse . . .*, 7.   [73] *Ibid.*, 13ff.

[4] The more deliverances, and the better successes, a gracious heart receives, the more it admireth and advanceth God.

[5] That a personall experience is improved to an universall advantage.[74]

A closely related technique is displayed in a sermon preached by Peter (or Brockett) Smith at the May fast in 1644.[75] His text was Psalm 107:6 (KJ): "Then they cried unto the Lord in their trouble and he delivered them out of their distresses." Smith developed three "observations" regarding the text. He pointed out first that "all the saints on earth are subject unto changes, and varietie of condition, and no man knoweth, what shall be on the morrow."[76] Next he remarked that God provided diverse ways for men to "cry" unto Him.[77] And, finally, he noted that God had not condemned all repetition in prayers and praises: "There are repetitions which are not accounted vain."[78] In these preliminary "observations" Smith offered low-level generalizations which allowed a gradual transition to his full doctrines for which, implicitly, universal validity was claimed:

[1] That the Condition of the Church, or its most usuall lot, is to lie under sorrows and afflictions.[79]

[2] Earnest prayer, or crying to the Lord, is an effectuall meanes to get helpe, and full deliverance in troubles and distresses.[80]

[3] Deliverances from distresses is from the Lord.[81]

The "observations," like the subordinate doctrines employed by Ash, essentially formed a bridge between the text and the doctrinal proposition(s) around which the

---

[74] *Ibid.*, 2-4.
[75] *A Sermon Preached* . . . (London, 1644) .
[76] *Ibid.*, 2, citing James 4:14.
[77] *Ibid.*, 5-6.
[78] *Ibid.*, 7.   [79] *Ibid.*, 8.   [80] *Ibid.*, 21.   [81] *Ibid.*, 37.

sermon was constructed.[82] A close parallel is available in *Solomons Choice*,[83] a sermon preached by Lazarus Seaman in September of the same year.

The converse may be observed in another interesting sermon by Lazarus Seaman. *The Head of the Church, the Judge of the World*[84] was presented before the Lords at a monthly humiliation in January 1646-7. The text was taken from Acts 17, the alleged address to the citizens of Athens by Paul, whom the preacher styled "Professor of Divinity in the University of Athens." From the text Seaman directly derived his single doctrine that "God hath appointed a day wherein he will judge the world, &c."[85] The remainder of the sermon consisted, in effect, of a deduction of propositions logically entailed by the main doctrine. They comprised six affirmations: (1) There would be a day of judgment. (2) It was already set. (3) The Judge had been appointed. (4) It would be Jesus Christ. (5) The world was to be judged by him. (6) The judgment would take place according to the will of God in his righteousness. Though rhetorically less elegant than the conventional order, the explicit text made Seaman's construction quite appropriate. The cardinal point to bear in mind, of course, is the flexibility of the "plain style" method of preaching which made such variations possible in the first place.

Further metamorphosis of the essential procedure may be noted in certain of the sermons. A few of them, for instance, pay stricter attention to the text itself and consequently deemphasize both doctrines, opened from the text, and reasons. One example is an exhortation delivered by William Gouge to the monthly fast in June 1642. The patriarch titled his sermon *The Saints Support*,[86] but his subject—at least as he developed it—would have been more accurately described as "the Patterne of a good Patriot."[87]

---

82 Cf. O. Sedgwick, *An Arke against a Deluge* (London, 1644). In that sermon he terms his doctrines "propositions."
83 (London, 1644).   84 (London, 1647).
85 *The Head of the Church* . . . , 7.   86 (London, 1642).
87 *The Saints Support*, "Dedicatory Epistle."

His text was Nehemiah 5:19 (KJ): "Think upon me, my God, for good according to all I have done for this people." Gouge devoted a large proportion of his sermon to a close exposition, clarification, and interpretation of the text, for he conceived Nehemiah to be a "pertinent patterne for Justification of what ye have done, and direction for what remains yet to be done."[88] Thus Gouge enumerated in detail some twenty qualities or characteristics which Nehemiah exemplified.[89] The transition to a formal observation—"God is the support of Saints"—came late in the sermon.[90] Thereafter it was applied in a largely conventional manner. John Lightfoot's *Elias Redivivus*,[91] originally delivered to the March Commons fast of 1643, manifests in certain respects the same concern with a very detailed exposition of the text prior to development of a doctrine or doctrines.

A comparable deemphasis of the basic method may be found in the sermon which John Owen preached at the Commons humiliation on the day following Charles's death.[92] His text was Jeremiah 15:19d-20 (KJ): "Let them return unto thee, but return not unto them. And I will make thee unto this people a fenced brasen wall; and they shall fight against thee, but they shall not prevail against thee, for I am with thee to save thee and to deliver thee, saith the Lord." Owen carefully placed these words in the context of the entire chapter. He then developed a series of ten observations, that is, propositions allegedly implied in the text. Although one of them was eventually singled out as more general, that status essentially reflected its appropriateness to the occasion rather than any logical priority within the series: "Plausible complyances of men in Authority, with those, against whom they are employed, are Treacherous contrivances against the God of Heaven, by whom they are employed."[93]

[88] *Ibid.*, 14.   [89] *Ibid.*, 14ff.   [90] *Ibid.*, 29-30.
[91] (London, 1643).
[92] *A Sermon Preached . . . January 31.* [1648-9] (London, 1649).
[93] *Ibid.*, 15.

A close parallel to this sermon is *A Divine Ballance to weigh Religious Fasts in*,[94] contributed by Humphrey Chambers to the Commons periodic fast of September 27, 1643. The text from Zechariah (7:5-7) was carefully opened in the conventional manner. Chambers then "framed up" a series of ten doctrines, which might indeed be used as "scales" to gauge the significance of the program in which he was participating. He made no serious attempt, however, to actually apply his criteria to the system in a precise way.

These sermons, which exhibit deemphasis of the "plain style" method, suggest the temptation which might overcome puritan preachers on occasion even though they had been schooled in universities and trained in the techniques, namely, to attempt the direct application of scripture to their present situation without making discriminating use of the whole method here under discussion. If "doctrines" and "reasons" were dropped, direct "application" or "use" of the text became inevitable given the assumptions of the "plain style." That this transformation proved irresistible to some puritan divines preaching under other circumstances—exhorting Roundheads before battle, for example—is not surprising. That it should have characterized the shrill sermons of the sectarians and tub-preachers is to be expected, too. But that certain members of the elite brotherhood, even some delegates to the Westminster Assembly, could occasionally succumb to the temptation while preaching to parliament is remarkable indeed. One partial example of this phenomenon—and there are very few available—is provided by Samuel Bolton in his *Hamartolos Hamartia: Or The Sinfulnes of Sin*,[95] preached to Commons on March 25, 1646. His text was Matthew 1:21b (KJ): "He shall save his people from their sins." "Branching out" the text, Bolton in effect applied it for his audience without the intermediate structure of doctrines and reasons. The most striking example of the virtually direct application of scripture to occasion, however, we owe to Samuel Rutherford. The dean of the Scottish

[94] (London, 1643).   [95] (London, 1646).

Commissioners, whose colleagues assiduously utilized the formal method, apparently wholly ignored it in his parliamentary sermon on January 31, 1643-4.[96] In this disjointed and passionate exhortation Rutherford made a number of points in a very blunt manner, which he thoughtfully summarized for the reader in his preface. It seems impossible to discover, however, any formal recourse to the "plain style" procedure. His anger at the English for not having already perfected their religious reformation is evident. Their failure to suppress heresy especially troubled him—Crisp had recently published the notorious *Christ Exalted*.[97] Rutherford's exhortation was essentially a direct application to his own present of the text which he had selected. It was Darius's decree, from Daniel 6:26 (KJ): "For he is the living God, and steadfast forever, and his kingdom that which shall not be destroyed, and his dominion shall be even unto the end." Apparently, if the occasion were appropriate, such a majestic text could literally consume the method.

Thus the members of the puritan brotherhood subscribed to a procedure in their preaching which set them apart from their contemporaries in the Church of England. Through it they sought to approach the judgment or the understanding of their audience—in this instance, the members of the Long Parliament—by use of "doctrines" or "propositions." Texts from the one authoritative book were translated into propositions. They were thought to render the texts sufficiently comprehensible to be both universal and credible. The resulting exhortation was taken to be compelling. For this reason the sermons preached before parliament help to illumine the way in which Puritanism rendered intelligible the time of civil war and revolution for those who accepted its terms of reference. To that end a systematic study is required of those doctrines which were framed during the whole program of humiliations and thanksgivings. That is the subject of the next chapter.

[96] *A Sermon Preached* . . . (London, 1644).
[97] *Ibid.*, 32.

VI

Puritan Piety for a Covenanted Nation

THE SERMONS preached before the Long Parliament, when viewed collectively, explicated puritan teaching about the national crisis of the 1640's. The doctrines of the sermons "framed up" or articulated the preachers' conceptions of the relationship between religious faith and political behavior in the public realm. The parliamentary preaching in this way exhibits the structure of piety advocated before representative England sitting at Westminster during the decade of the 1640's. The manifest function of the program, then, was the definition of corporate, collective, or national piety, and the explicit goal was an England conformed to the will of God, even united to Christ. Such concerns had not been wholly absent from Puritanism prior to the civil war, although circumstances generally served to deemphasize this theme, at least in the literature which survives.[1] By contrast the profound discipline of personal piety expected of the saint has been visible and has received appropriate attention in recent studies of Puritanism. Perhaps uniquely in the sermons preached to the Long Parliament we have available a means of examining systematically how the members of the brotherhood collectively understood the relationship between their religious convictions and the development of national life in the context of the civil wars.

Frequently the exhortations made direct references to the times, which they were intended to illumine and in-

[1] The special interests giving rise to secondary studies of Puritanism and puritan subjects—e.g., the origins of liberal political assumptions, denominational beginnings, theories of economic development, literary figures, etc.—have also helped to veil puritan concern for corporate piety.

fluence. Especially on the occasion of extraordinary fasts and thanksgivings, the preacher might "improve" particular events—much as Hugh Peter did on April 2, 1646, when he preached at a thanksgiving for Fairfax's success in Cornwall to which he had been a witness.[2] On balance, however, the preachers resisted this temptation more than might be expected. They appear to have been constrained by the formal pulpit, and they consequently approached their subjects "methodically." As full as their "applications" and "uses" might be, the latter essentially continued to be subordinate to the explicit texts and "doctrines." In view of the political and social turbulence of the period, and the remarkable energies invested by the puritans in the preaching before parliament, this restraint may be surprising. Without doubt, of course, the members of the Long Parliament were prepared to reprimand any preacher who ventured to address them on subjects thought not to be within his competence.[3] At the same time, the most regular, and presumably the most favored, preachers showed appropriate deference to the prerogatives of parliament, apparently without considering this an unwarranted limitation on the pulpit. Stephen Marshall, to cite an example, managed within the terms of the institution to give sermons that were morally relevant and edifying while never failing to make it clear that his authority was of a different species than that of his auditors. The preachers did not presume, generally, to speak with immediate political authority. Their teaching was basically derived from theological assumptions. They offered saving knowledge, rather than political advice and counsel, at the humiliations and thanksgivings. In this manner the divines of the brotherhood sought to shape a pious nation. From this perspective the sermons collectively constitute a remark-

[2] *Gods Doings, And Mans Duty* (London, 1646).

[3] An official rebuke was addressed to William Dell for his sermon on November 25, 1646. Others, like Nathaniel Ward and Thomas Watson, were not asked to print their sermons. Murmurings of disapproval arose on the other occasions as well—see N. Hardy, *The Arraignment* . . . (London, 1647), "Epistle."

able source of primary materials for study of Stuart puritan conceptions of the relationship between religious authority and political life. The doctrines of the parliamentary sermons provide the fundamental means of access to that teaching. Disagreements, indeed disputes, did develop among the participants, eventually destroying Puritanism as a movement. To be rendered intelligible, however, this disintegration of the brotherhood must be understood in light of the basic and common structure of puritan teaching.

COVENANTED SALVATION

The first premise on which the preachers rested their views of corporate piety was that God governs the destinies of individuals and nations alike. Presupposed in most of the sermons, this teaching was explicitly affirmed on certain occasions. Richard Vines, for example, used David to exemplify the complete dependence of the creature upon the creator: "David resolves all events into God, whether pro or con, for good or evill."[4] In a more philosophical vein Edmund Corbett declared that "Gods will hath an effectuall Influence upon all the Creatures."[5] According to this conventional position, "the rule whereby all things are dispensed here below . . . is the determinate will and counsell of God."[6] The universal dependence upon God of all creation did not exclude Christ from the puritan vision. By one construction he was—as God and man— the agent through whom God supervised all the works of men.[7] In other constructions the will of God was said to triumph through the hand of Christ as vice-regent.[8] In any case, Jesus Christ was explicitly identified with divine agency in and over history.

This interpretation of divine providence or agency took the nation to be an object of divine intention. Indeed,

---

[4] *The Posture of Davids Spirit* (London, 1644), 4.
[5] *Gods Providence* (London, 1642), 2.
[6] J. Owen, *A Vision of Unchangeable Free Mercy* (London, 1646), 7.
[7] J. Caryl, *The Workes of Ephesus* (London, 1642), 3ff.
[8] See Nicholas Lockyer, *A Sermon Preached . . .* (London, 1646), and J. Maynard, *A Shadow of the Victory of Christ* (London, 1646).

Calamy argued at the initial regular fast "that the deliverances that come to a Nation, come from Jehovah Adonai. Nationall mercies come from the God of Nations."[9] Thomas Case even proposed that a nation or a kingdom could stand "in a conjugal relation unto God."[10] His text, it need hardly be added, was taken from Hosea. A nation might be scourged for its sins, but it was expected, however slowly, to respond to divine initiative.[11]

Although the conception of the "nation" was central to the doctrines of the preachers, other notions of collective entities were even more prominent within the puritan construction of salvation. The "church" and "God's people," frequently defined in explicitly federal language, were the fundamental collective terms. Ancient Israel, of course, provided the model for puritan thinking on the subject. The emphasis placed upon the "people" of God is striking. Obadiah Sedgwick argued that "the salvation of Gods people belongs to God,"[12] and Thomas Coleman that God's people were always in pursuit of their desired condition.[13] Marshall affirmed, during the course of a thanksgiving sermon to both houses (June 1645), that "in all ages God will have a people for his praise" and that "the whole work of Gods redeemed people, is to provide that God may alwayes, and every where have the glory of it."[14] Late in the series of parliamentary sermons, Simeon Ash expressed the opinion that "God . . . is really, constantly, singularly good in his administrations to his . . . people."[15] The parallel to Israel was stressed by Richard Vines at an extraordinary occasion in March 1644-5. In *The Happinesse of Israel*[16] he contended that the ancient nation was above comparison with any other people in that par-

9 *Gods Free Mercy to England* (London, 1642), 8.
10 *Spirituall Whoredome* . . . (London, 1647), 4.
11 C. Burges, *Two Sermons* (London, 1645), 7-20.
12 *A Thanksgiving Sermon* (London, 1644), 4.
13 *The Christians Course* (London, 1643), 4ff.
14 *A Sacred Record* (London [1645]), 11-12.
15 *Gods Incomparable Goodness* . . . (London, 1647), 7.
16 (London, 1645).

ticular—as well as most others.[17] The implicit assumption
underlying use of this symbol was that worship was owed
to God by the people for His acts of power and goodness.[18] Typically the argument ran that the redeemed and
blessed people had an obligation to build up the church.[19]
(Logic could also run the other way: one might hold that
God would prosper those kingdoms which dealt well
with His people.) [20] Thus "church" and "people" were related as form and substance, or as explicit and implicit aspects of divine administration. It is manifest that during
the decade of the civil wars the puritan preachers fundamentally sought a national church as the expression of a
faithful people, at once object of and reason for divine
blessing.

Federal concepts played a major role in the definitions
of both "people" and "church." In this respect the significance of the Solemn League and Covenant must not be
passed over lightly. Besides being of tactical importance
in bringing the Scots into the struggle, it was also the
most effective means—that is, useful language—for articulating the interrelated religious, political, and social goals
of the Long Parliament, goals wholeheartedly embraced
by the preachers: "The glory of God, and the advancement
of the Kingdome of our Lord and Saviour Jesus Christ, the
Honour and happinesse of the Kings Majestie, and His
posterity; and the true publique Liberty, Safety and Peace
of the Kingdomes, wherein every ones private condition
is included."[21] If Henderson, the Scotsman, believed that
the Covenant was to be a vehicle for divine providence
in its workings, Nye, the English puritan who preached on
the occasion of its subscription, declared it to be, in effect,

[17] *The Happinesse of Israel*, 2.
[18] See J. Caryl, *The Saints Thankfull Acclamation* . . . (London,
1644) , 8.
[19] See S. Marshall, *A Sacred Record* (London [1645]) .
[20] See T. Goodwin, *The Great Interest of Saints & Kingdomes* (London, 1646) , *passim*, esp. 7.
[21] *The Covenant: with a Narrative of the Proceedings* (London,
1643) , 1f.

the realization of the hope of all ages.[22] In defending the Covenant, Thomas Coleman acknowledged that the "New Testament affords but rare instances" of covenanting, although the Old Testament provided ample precedents for the step.[23] The fullest analysis of the presuppositions underlying the Solemn League and Covenant was provided by Joseph Caryl in *The Nature, Solemnity, Grounds, Property, and Benefits, of a Sacred Covenant*.[24] He defined a covenant as a "solemne compact or agreement betweene two chosen parties or more, whereby with mutuall, free, and full consent they binde themselves upon select conditions, tending to the glory of God and their common good."[25]

For Caryl and his colleagues the Solemn League and Covenant had certain instrumental uses. It would make possible, for example, the drawing of distinctions between different sorts of men and in this way facilitate separation of the precious from the malignant and the vile. It would help "congregate" the "homogeneall" in uniting the kingdom and would bring together "sincere" Christians in diverse lands with God. Above all, the Covenant promised to create a holy and a happy people.[26] In this sense it rendered sociologically specific the common theological conceptions, and to this extent the Covenant was implicit throughout the entire program of humiliations and thanksgivings. It was the means both of defining England's special intimacy with God and of identifying her particular sufferings under His administration.[27] In these ways federal conceptions were fundamental to the pattern of corporate piety advocated by the puritans.

In this connection it is important to note that the preach-

---

[22] *Ibid.*, 15, 34.

[23] *The Hearts Ingagement* (London, 1643), 20.

[24] (London, 1643), preached on October 6, 1643.

[25] *The Nature . . .* , 7.

[26] *Ibid.*, 18-29.

[27] See, e.g., F. Taylor, *Gods Covenant The Churches Plea* (London, 1645); J. Nalton, *Delay of Reformation . . .* (London, 1646); F. Taylor, *The Danger of Vowes Neglected* (London, 1646).

ers developed concepts of particular leadership roles. Basically all men were assumed to be servants or stewards of God: "All men, even those in the highest Place, and greatest Honour, are but Stewards unto God."[28] At the same time, however, the puritans readily acknowledged differentiation within the servant people according to their contributions in fulfilling the necessary offices of civil and religious government. With regard to the latter, Henry Scudder stated explicitly what the preaching institution took for granted, namely, that God spoke to his people through his prophets and ministers.[29] The more vital question concerned civil authority; here the answer was less self-evident in the context of the parliamentary preaching. On this point the preachers argued for the divine origin of governors and magistrates as rulers or stewards held accountable to God.[30] The Lord could and would raise up leaders ("Judges"), even unexpected ones, when reform was made necessary by laws contrary to those of Christ.[31] The people and the commonwealth were committed to the care of such governors.[32] It was the duty of divinely ordained magistrates to sponsor appropriate reform of the church.[33] Thus religious and righteous magistrates and rulers constituted a blessing to God's people.[34] In this mode, and on the basis of this logic, the preachers specifically pointed to the need for reforming magistrates in light of the particular situation of a covenanted people. Governors in authority, possessed of a divine office, yet were to be tutored by the preachers who spoke with the voice of religious authority. Superimposed upon the English civil wars, this theory lent itself to radical interpretation by the

[28] W. Strong, *The Trust and the Account of a Steward* (London, 1647), 4.

[29] *Gods Warning to England* (London, 1644), 6.

[30] See W. Strong, *The Trust and the Account of a Steward.*

[31] See W. Hussey, *The Magistrates Charge, For the Peoples Safetie* (London, 1647).

[32] L. Seaman, *Solomons Choice* (London, 1644), 17f.

[33] A. Burges, *The Reformation of the Church* (London, 1645), 3.

[34] G. Hickes, *The Glory and Beauty of Gods Portion* (London, 1644), 33.

regicides. Within the program of preaching to parliament, however, the theory was typically applied in a more conservative fashion.

A related and very significant phenomenon was the preachers' reconstruction of English history and legend in accordance with these doctrines. It became a cardinal assumption that the English were a nascent people of God who fundamentally lacked only the full presence of God's church in their midst. One preacher, for instance, proposed that "the stability of all our blessings must come by the true religion. Gods presence is the best security, who is most powerfully present where there is most power and purity of religion. Would you have a flourishing Kingdome, advance the Kingdome of Christ in it. Let the State maintaine Religion, and Religion will blesse the State."[35] Many parallels to Thomas Hill's plea could be found among the exhortations in this series. It was thus possible, indeed necessary, to construe the events of the previous centuries as tending toward that reformation of church administration and life which the Westminster Assembly was completing.[36]

A basic framework was at hand, of course, in John Foxe's *Book of Martyrs* where England's election had been charted.[37] His interpretation had been continued by the reforming party with reference to succeeding events. One function of the preaching institution itself was to project a compelling image of the contemporary parliamentary cause against the background of the theory that God had "elected" England even as a new Israel. Simeon Ash, for example, apparently without any sense of the blasphemy which might be involved, assimilated his own present to Israel's past in a recitation of providential events:

[35] T. Hill, *The Trade of Truth Advanced* (London, 1642), "Epistle."
[36] Some of the common legends are reflected in the preaching. See H. Hall, *Heaven Ravished* (London, 1644), 20.
[37] W. Haller's *The Elect Nation* (New York, 1963) is an excellent recent discussion of the book and its significance.

[We should recall] Gods former famous acts for his servants safety. . . . Israel's experience . . . is on record in
holy Writ for our encouragement. We may add from
Gods dispensations in this Kingdome. Who in the year
Eighty-Eight sunke and scattered the Spanish Navy
called invincible? Who broke the necke of the Popish
powder-plot, and brought to light those under ground
workings of the traiterous, bloudy Papists? And who
lately composed the dangerous differences betwixt England and Scotland, which threatened the desolation of
both Kingdomes?[38]

The "application" which Ash made was no less straight-
forward: "Remember that your Saviour is the Lord of
Hosts. . . . What though Papists, Atheists and Divels were
in combination to destroy us, yet the Generalissimo who
manageth all forces and maketh all motions, is the Lord of
Hosts our maker, and Comforter."[39]

The argument ran that the past augured well for the
future, realization of which rested upon faithful performance of obligations by those invested with authority
in the present. This construction of English history was an
effective and concrete means of representing those crucial
concepts underlying the doctrines espoused by the preachers; providence, people, covenant, church, leadership
as stewardship. At the same time, it was a nationalistic
language to which English members of the Long Parliament
could be expected to respond.

THE SINS AND THE SIGNS OF THE TIMES

The preachers' interpretation of England's history
as holy history, that is, according to a course of covenanted salvation, contrasted starkly with the ambiguous
status of the parliamentary cause. Whereas the victories in
the field which led to conclusion of the first civil war, for
example, could be framed within their theological calculus

[38] *The Best Refuge for the most Oppressed* (London, 1642), 51-52.
[39] *Ibid.*, 51.

(thereby serving to confirm it), defeats and divisions were also experienced which, it might be thought, would have called that framework into question. Thus there was an evident need to come to terms with the times.

William Sedgwick articulated one common approach to the uncertainties, advocating that the troubles be embraced, when he asserted in June 1642 that "the Church in the beginnings of her deliverance is subject to shakings."[40] A variation on the theme was the argument that all nations had their times of shaking but that some were meant for reform while others were meant for ruin.[41] The same point was echoed by William Reyner two years later: "Great concussions, shakings and alterations of States and Nations, great warres and sometimes desolations both of civil and ecclesiasticall State doe in the course of Gods administration often times goe before great and notable restaurations and Reformations of the Church."[42] This view could be framed as well in the striking terms of Revelation, or as the dramatic struggle of twins in the womb.[43]

The experience could equally lead to resignation in the face of the troubles, often accompanied by a hope for the future though there might not be apparent ground for it in the present. Thus Walter Bridges deplored civil war and surmised that victory might well turn out to be sorrowful.[44] Similarly, George Gipps averred that "it is the Portion of Gods Church and Children to finde in and through this life very present . . . great and aboundant troubles."[45] An index of the cynicism which might be occasioned by the times was Francis Cheynell's declaration that men of position "do too often behave themselves more like Beasts then Men."[46] These responses did not, how-

[40] *Zions Deliverance* . . . (London, 1642), 6.
[41] See J. Whitaker, *Ejrenopojos, Christ the Settlement* . . . (London, 1642), 31ff.
[42] *Babylons Ruining-Earthquake* (London, 1644), 5.
[43] See J. Arrowsmith, *A Great Wonder in Heaven* (London, 1647), 38.
[44] *Joabs Counsell* . . . (London, 1643).
[45] *A Sermon Preached* . . . (London, 1645), 5.
[46] *The Man of Honour, Described* (London, 1645), 14.

ever, represent the basic and systematic teaching on the times that the puritan preachers promulgated in their sermons to the Long Parliament.

Just as a set of "doctrines" established the terms in which the past was comprehended, so the experiences of the present were stereotyped and catalogued in order to explain its disjunction from the anticipated course of salvation. The preachers' fundamental skepticism of externals and appearances fed their obsession to identify causes ("reasons") for the present uncertainty and distress. It is useful to distinguish between three different, though overlapping, kinds of explanation they employed. One group of reasons alleged for the disappointing fortunes of the cause involved suspicion of self, that is, acknowledgment that shortcomings and failings characterized the parliamentary insurgents as agents both individually and collectively. A second constellation of explanations for present disconfirmation of their expectations clustered around the figure of the "enemy." Finally, and most basically, distress was attributed to the judgments of God. These doctrines of collective piety were not mutually exclusive, but they supplemented as well as complemented each other—a characteristic kind of relationship in theological reflection. All were means of rationalizing the contradiction the preachers perceived between a legendary past full of promise and a painful and ambiguous present.

One obvious explanation for the troubles of the time lay in failures of the people to uphold the obligations of the covenant bond. In a sermon at a Commons humiliation as early as April 1643, William Greenhill explicitly analyzed God's forebearance toward a sinful people, arguing that judgments were exactly proportioned to offences.[47] Generally speaking, however, the theme of inadequacy on the part of the people and nation became prominent only later in the series, especially during 1645. The reason for emergence of this emphasis may have been directly related to the frustrations then being experienced by the West-

[47] *The Axe at the Root* (London, 1643), 9ff.

minster Assembly. It was making little headway in its efforts to reach agreement on reformation of the church and growing restive under parliament's circumscription of its authority. In any case, preaching to the Lords in December 1644, Edmund Calamy maintained that "Divisions, whether they be Ecclesiasticall, or Politicall, in Kingdomes, Cities, and Families, are infallible causes of ruine. . . ."[48] A year later Richard Vines, in a sermon entitled *The Purifying of Uncleane Hearts and Hands*,[49] charged in his initial doctrine that "A corrupt and wicked life argues a man to be a stranger to God, and God him."[50] Doubleminded men must be purified to enable them to approach God.[51] In the same vein Stephen Marshall, preaching late in the series, offered the ominous warning that "the sinne of hardning the heart against God, is a certain forerunner of utter destruction."[52] Some comfort was provided by Robert Baillie, who contended that "children of God" experience their sins more deeply than any affliction laid upon them.[53] But this argument was double-edged, and others repeatedly asserted the knowledge God has of all sin to be "clear and distinct"—indeed a source of terror to sinners.[54]

Sin, corruption, and wickedness might void the covenant expectations. Equally, false teaching might alienate people, nation, and church from the promises of salvation. The first sermon to place primary emphasis on heresy and schism was delivered at the monthly fast in January 1644-5. George Walker assaulted "every Band, Company, and faction of wicked men, whether evill Counsellors, unjust Judges, and corrupt Officers in a Church or State, or wicked instruments, and men of violence conspiring and

[48] *An Indictment against England* (London, 1645), 4.
[49] (London, 1646).
[50] *The Purifying . . .* , 9.
[51] *Ibid.*, 22-24.
[52] *The Sinne of Hardnesse of Heart* (London, 1648), 8.
[53] *Errours and Induration* (London, 1645), 14.
[54] M. Newcomen, *The All-seeing Unseen Eye* (London, 1647); P. Sterry, *The Spirit Convincing of Sinne* (London, 1645); W. Strong, *Humera Apokalupseus. The Day of Revelation* (London, 1645); T. Horton, *Sinne's Discovery and Revenge* (London, 1646).

working with them to doe hurt and mischiefe to Gods people, and to persecute his Church. . . ."[55] Walker was confident that such schemes would be frustrated by God. At the regular Commons fast in January 1646-7, Obadiah Sedgwick "opened" *The Nature and Danger of Heresies.*[56] Defined as "an erroneous or false opinion, repugnant unto and subverting of the doctrine of faith revealed in the Word, as necessary unto salvation," heresy was alleged to constitute the serpent's flood foretold in Revelation 12:15-16. Sedgwick was convinced, nevertheless, that the Lord would raise "fresh succours for the Church."[57] A special fast or humiliation for the growth of heresy was finally scheduled by Commons for the following March 10. On that day Thomas Hodges delineated the characteristics of heresy and described also the fascination the errors held for the faithful.[58] Richard Vines's contribution was to argue that false teachers might be expected in gospel churches "as there were false Prophets in the Church of olde."[59] He further explicitly attributed schism to heretical opinions.

The effectiveness of enemies was equally an explanation of the discomfiture of God's people and the frustration of England's reformation. This theme was, quite naturally, especially pronounced in the anniversary sermons which celebrated the failure of the "Powder Plot."[60] Thomas Case gave sustained attention to the subject in October 1642. He offered as a doctrine the view that "the Church of God ever had, and will have enemies and haters," who must therefore be God's enemies.[61] He went on to assert that, although for a season "God . . . seems sometimes to lie still, and sleep," He would awake and rise.[62]

[55] *A Sermon Preached* . . . (London, 1645), 7.

[56] (London, 1647).

[57] *The Nature and Danger of Heresies*, 8.

[58] *The Growth and Spreading of Haeresie* (London, 1647), 14ff.

[59] *The Authours, Nature, and Danger of Haeresie* (London, 1647), 6.

[60] See M. Newcomen, *The Craft and Cruelty* . . . (London, 1643), 2ff.

[61] *Gods Rising, His Enemies Scattering* (London, 1644), 2-6.

[62] *Ibid.*, 13, 17.

At the fast in the following July, John Conant argued that tribulation at the hands of enemies precedes deliverance —if rightly "improved."[63] William Bridge counseled the same patience in November 1643, alleging that God suffered enemies to rise against His church as He prepared reformation.[64] On the same occasion William Mewe insisted that the depredations of enemies were inflicted upon the faithful by God and urged that their meaning be recognized.[65] This point was also made by John Strickland at the next regular humiliation, when he reassured the members of parliament that God himself would "take in hand his peoples enemies, when they have done as much as he intended against his Church."[66] Nicholas Proffet carried the argument a step further, attributing an enemy's smiting of a covenant people directly to the Lord.[67]

Although enemies might be finally understood as instrumentalities of God and their victories construed as authored by Him, it remains true nonetheless that puritan doctrine on the subject exhibited a certain fascination with them beyond what this interpretation called for. Edmund Staunton betrayed such an interest in *Rupes Israelis, The Rock of Israel,*[68] which he delivered at the regular Commons humiliation in April 1644. The rock (=superstition) of the Egyptians (=the kingdom of Satan), he averred, bore no comparison to the rock (=God) of Israel (=the church).[69] Similarly, Stephen Marshall observed "a Concord, Harmony, and Unity of Spirits, and endeavours in the enemies of the Church."[70] He emphasized reassuringly, however, that God would send these enemies to their ruin and destruction.[71] The destruction of cunning enemies

[63] *The Woe and Weale of Gods People* (London, 1643), *passim.*
[64] *A Sermon Preached* . . . (London, 1643), *passim.*
[65] *The Robbing and Spoiling of Jacob and Israel* (London, 1643), 18, 32.
[66] *Gods Work of Mercy* . . . (London, 1644), 33.
[67] *Englands Impenitencie under Smiting* (London, 1645), 6.
[68] (London, 1644).
[69] *Rupes Israelis* . . . , *passim.*
[70] *Emmanuel* . . . (London, 1648), 8.
[71] *Ibid.,* 15ff.

might indeed become a source of awe, in this way redounding to God's glory.[72] Finally, the divines argued that "the experience of former mercies and successes" in triumphing over enemies was ground for present hope, if not for total reassurance.[73] Thus Francis Woodcock proposed that Joseph in Egypt was the appropriate scriptural figure to employ in comprehending England's situation.[74]

Implicit in the above teaching about the times was its interpretation in terms of divine judgment. Acknowledgment of sin, corruption, heresy, and the reality of enemies was essentially possible—and also made necessary—because God's intentions were believed to underlie them. Divine providence assumed for these preachers a manifold complexion, and to it they ascribed a variety of particular events. Accordingly, they expended great energies in trying to "read" properly, or to place a correct construction upon, the troubles they experienced. In this way the teaching about the present became sufficiently flexible and ingenious to anticipate almost any contingency; that is to say, present judgments could not disconfirm the basic covenant faith.[75] Doctrines were framed, then, reaffirming for the saints (whether in parliament or not) that, whatever the appearances, their own ultimate vindication and their enemies' final doom were certain. Three issues require further attention: particular and general judgments, the double effect of judgments, and judgment as experienced by the saints themselves.

The theme of God's particular judgment in the present

---

[72] See H. Wilkinson, *Miranda, Stupenda. Or, The Wonderfull and Astonishing Mercies* (London, 1646).

[73] J. Caryl, *Englands Plus ultra* (London, 1646), 16.

[74] *Joseph Paralled by the present Parliament* (London, 1646).

[75] Perry Miller's dictum regarding the "Jeremiad" as it developed in New England later in the century may be appropriate with reference to the sermons preached before the Long Parliament between 1640 and 1648: "The federal covenant does not shield a federated people from the wrath of God: it makes that wrath intelligible." *The New England Mind: From Colony To Province* (Cambridge, Mass., 1953), 24. Rendered in the present context, the point would read: the preachers did not promise the Long Parliament exemption from divine judgments, but they did claim to explain them.

ran throughout the series of sermons before the Long Parliament. It was, for instance, fitted to specific occasions. Stephen Marshall professed to see Christ pouring out the "vials of wrath" (from Revelation) in the discovery of a plot against parliament and London during the spring of 1643. Such judgments, great and wonderful to behold, were clearly attributable to the Lord.[76] On the same day Obadiah Sedgwick preached on Haman's plot as laid out in the book of Esther. He submitted that God could make the contrivances of "Church-destroying adversaries" hurtful to themselves.[77] Broader judgments, in the form of war, for example, were thought to be similarly the work of God in avenging himself on those who quarreled with the covenant.[78] The Lord, moreover, enlisted "workmen" or agents to execute His justice.[79] Judgment could also take the less dramatic form of "deep sleep," a very sore affliction.[80] The preachers were supremely confident that the great Judge was ingenious in His administration of justice: "God will finde a time and a way to bring evill upon those that rise up against the righteous, and are the authors and fomentors of an unjust war, and that without respect of persons."[81]

The parliamentary sermons demonstrate as well the preachers' conviction that divine judgment might simultaneously work good for His people and church while bringing ill upon their enemies—a theory of double effect or function. Thomas Case framed this doctrine most concisely in a thanksgiving sermon in August 1645 which celebrated victories at Bath, Bridgewater, and elsewhere: "In the mighty concussions and subversions of the Empires and Monarchies of the World, God carries on the designes of his Churches deliverance and enlargement."[82]

[76] *The Song of Moses* (London, 1643), *passim*, esp. 10.
[77] *Haman's Vanity* (London, 1643), 18.
[78] J. Arrowsmith, *The Covenant-Avenging Sword* (London, 1643), *passim*, esp. 4-5.
[79] See E. Staunton, *Phinehas's Zeal* . . . (London, 1645), 9.
[80] See W. Jenkyn, *A Sleeping sicknes* . . . (London, 1647), 10.
[81] S. Gibson, *The Ruine of the Authors* . . . (London, 1645), 15.
[82] *A Sermon Preached* . . . (London, 1645), 8.

Others expressed confidence in the economy of God's general judgment in equally striking terms. Stanley Gower, for example, advanced the obverse proposition that "the same times, and troubles in them, which make godly wise men better, make wicked men worse."[83] Again, Thomas Coleman argued that "terrible consequences" were consonant with the righteousness of God, in fact might be the way "whereby God to a Land becomes a saving God."[84] However terrible the judgment might be, if its ground was in divine righteousness, the saint could rest assured that God was "a God of their salvation still."[85] Indeed, one preacher taught that the delivery of the church occurs "not usually till it come to great extremity."[86]

The troubles immediately besetting the saints or their cause posed a more difficult issue for them. These were resolved into consequences of divine justice in several ways. William Bridge explored one possibility, that "God hath his dayes of anger, there is wrath and anger with God."[87] He went on to declare that, although God was usually "willing to hide his own people in evill times," it was his way sometimes to "leave them at great uncertainties," with no more than a *"may be* of their salvation."[88] Simeon Ash early in the fast series addressed himself to the same problem. He suggested that "oppression and trouble may be in this world the portion of Gods children."[89] To be sure, God was finally a "refuge" for Ash.[90] John Whincop rang changes on this theme by acknowledging the "sore judgment" sustained in the deprivation of the ordinances, as well as in the experience of exile among "scoffers and mockers," but he observed that judgments were "commonly . . . proportioned to mans sinne."[91] Eventu-

83 *Things Now-a-doing* (London, 1644) , 8.
84 *Gods unusuall Answer* . . . (London, 1644) , 17.
85 W. Carter, *Light in Darknesse: Discovered* (London, 1648) , 3.
86 J. Ellis, *The Sole Path to a Sound Peace* (London, 1643) , 31.
87 *The Saints Hiding-place* (London, 1647) , 5.
88 *Ibid.*, 17.
89 *The Best Refuge* . . . (London, 1642) , 4.
90 *Ibid.*, 18.
91 *Israels Tears for Distressed Zion* (London, 1645) , 20, 24.

ally the preachers' teaching came to be dominated by the thesis that the covenant people might well provoke God, leading Him to take vengeance upon them, but that in the end He would not reject them.[92] "Gods people may be in the burning, but they shall certainly be rescued and perfectly delivered."[93] If the troubles they suffered were in fact God's judgment upon them and their cause, repentance and reform, the preachers proposed, were the proper and sure means to salvation. These remedies were available to the Long Parliament without further delay.

THE MEANS OF SALVATION

Edmund Calamy's sermon to the initial monthly humiliation of Commons has already been discussed. It was entitled *Gods Free Mercy to England*[94] and was something of a classic exposition of puritan doctrine for the times. In order to counter any Arminian construction of corporate piety, he formulated a doctrine to which most of his colleagues would have subscribed: "That Nationall mercies come from free grace, not from free will; Not from mans goodnes, but Gods goodnes."[95] If exaltation of free will threatened to deteriorate into Deuteronomic moralism, however, exaltation of free grace no less threatened to metamorphose into Antinomian irresponsibility toward the nation and its quest for regeneration and salvation. Calamy's subsequent doctrine allowed no such conclusion to be drawn: "The contemplation of Gods free mercy to Nations and persons ought to be a mighty incentive, and a most effectuall argument to make them ashamed, . . . ashamed for sin for the times past, and ashamed to sin for the time to come."[96] Repentance for the past and reform for the future, or change in attitude and change in action, were the available means of salvation. Sundered

[92] See H. Palmer, *The Glasse of Gods Providence* (London, 1644), and J. Strickland, *Mercy rejoycing against Judgment* (London, 1645).
[93] B. Pickering, *A Firebrand Pluckt* . . . (London, 1645), 4.
[94] (London, 1642).   [95] *Gods Free Mercy to England*, 17.
[96] *Ibid.*, 22.

from each other, both were ineffectual and potentially heretical. Conjoined, they defined the religious practices appropriate to a people or a nation in explicit covenant with God.

Appreciation for the theme of repentance is extraordinarily important to an understanding of the parliamentary sermons. Fundamentally the regular fast observances before Commons and the Lords *were* a mode of repentance: their correct title was "humiliation." The extraordinary fasts also were intended as expressions of abasement. In this collective behavior the brotherhood believed that the nation was engaging in a corporate repentance appropriate to this "people" in covenant with God. The people were represented through the houses, and—by intention at least—they participated in the ritual with the members of parliament. This operative assumption is all the more striking for remaining unarticulated in many of the sermons. An exhaustive analysis of the humiliations and thanksgivings would require an attempt to determine their significance as ritualized political behavior. Actually, little hard evidence bearing on this matter is available as far as the fast system of the Long Parliament is concerned. A theoretical framework for such an inquiry, which would necessarily be comparative in mode, is not readily available either (at least to my knowledge). In the present study, therefore, attention is directed only to the "framing up" or construction of formal doctrines regarding repentance. In broad terms the teaching may be summarized under two headings. The preachers identified the content of repentance as acknowledgment of sin and turning from it, and they believed that its expression should properly take the form of prayer, fasting, and associated acts of piety.

It was necessary that guilt be confessed, and England was not without its special sins. Cornelius Burges established the culpability of the people in his sermon on March 30, 1642.[97] He remarked that they had "provoked" the Lord, not only by their personal misdeeds but through "national

[97] *Two Sermons* (London, 1645), 7.

sins": the land was guilty of blood (Mary's reign), uncleanness and adultery abounded, Ireland's miseries continued, and there was a spiritual lukewarmness evident
both in the toleration of superstition and idolatry and in
the slack pace of church reform.[98] Subsequently, at a special fast in September 1644, Matthew Newcomen submitted
that "the violation of the Covenant of God"—twelve
months after its adoption—was a sin so terrible that it
might provoke the Lord into "striking" parliament.[99] This
was a theme that had already been suggested, though not
so baldly, by Thomas Case in April of the same year.[100] In
this as well as in other matters it was, of course, a duty for
each to face his own heart.[101] Richard Kentish observed,
however, that what began in the heart did not end there
but would necessarily go on to express itself in that reform
which will be discussed below.[102]

The special techniques prescribed for collective repentance were remarkably stylized and, not surprisingly, fundamentally analogous to those associated with personal
piety. Among the techniques prayer was dominant. Early
in the series Edward Reynolds commended the members of
parliament for providing the opportunity for days of
"united prayers,"[103] and he reminded them of its appropriateness in times of trouble. Robert Baillie, exercised
about Satan during his sermon on February 28, 1643-4,
advocated the posture of prayer for God's children whenever danger threatened.[104] Peter (or Brockett) Smith reassured Commons that God "hath put words into our mouthe,
wherewith we may come before him in all occasions and
occurences," thus making possible approach to Him in
view of "the diversity of his wayes and dealings with
us."[105] The way to victory for the saints was therefore

[98] *Ibid.*, 39ff. [99] *A Sermon . . .* (London, 1644), 32-35.
[100] *The Root of Apostacy* (London, 1644), 6ff.
[101] J. Lightfoot, *A Sermon Preached . . .* (London, 1647), 5.
[102] *A Sure Stay for a Sinking State* (London, 1648), 28f.
[103] *Israels Petition in Time of Trouble* (London, 1642), 7.
[104] *Satan The Leader in Chief* (London, 1643), 18.
[105] *A Sermon Preached . . .* (London, 1644), 5.

quite literally thought to be by means of "a power that comes out of the mouth."[106] Prayer, as one of the instrumental activities of piety, along with preaching, confession, covenanting, and associated acts, was highly regarded by God.[107] Saints must never yield in prayer until God's victory was achieved.[108] God's ministers, of course, had a special role in articulating the prayers of the people to God.[109]

Joined to prayer was the practice of fasting which, accompanied by weeping,[110] was alleged to please God.[111] Indeed, fasting was not to be entered into lightly and without warrant; Humphrey Chambers provided a full account of the danger of hypocrisy in this regard.[112] More generally, humiliation of soul[113] and abasement were cognate acts of piety.[114] Those who were themselves liberated from sin in this way would blush at the sin of other men.[115] Finally, the people had a duty to wait on the Lord in these practices. Patience and hope were requisite to corporate no less than to individual piety.[116] It was widely believed that God would strengthen those who waited on him.[117] Thus perseverance was the hallmark of collective piety just as it was of individual piety in the reformed tradition.

If repentance, or turning of the heart from sin to God, was central to the preachers' teachings, equally important was reform, or a conforming of agencies and acts to God's

---

[106] S. Marshall, *A Two-edged Sword out of the Mouth of Babes* (London, 1646), 18f.

[107] S. Marshall, *The Strong Helper* (London, 1645), 12ff.

[108] R. Harris, *A Sermon* (London, 1642), 3.

[109] M. Newcomen, *Jerusalems Watch-men* . . . (London, 1643), 3.

[110] W. Spurstowe, *Englands Patterne and Duty* . . . (London, 1643), 3ff.

[111] H. Palmer, *The Duty & Honour of Church-Restorers* (London, 1646), 4.

[112] *A Divine Ballance* . . . (London, 1643), *passim*, esp. 18ff.

[113] J. Caryl, *Heaven and Earth Embracing* (London, 1646), 11.

[114] J. Burroughs, *A Sermon Preached* . . . (London, 1646), *passim*.

[115] W. Price, *Mans Delinquencie* (London, 1646), 7.

[116] T. Valentine, *A Sermon* (London, 1643), *passim*.

[117] T. Young, *Hopes Incouragement* (London, 1644), 19ff.

will. For the puritans the two could not be dissociated: "The worke of God doth prosper best in such mens hands, whose sinnes are pardoned, and whose peace is made with him."[118] Gillespie, the Scottish Commissioner, carried this logic on to the conclusion that "acceptable service in the publike Reformation" was only open to those who were ashamed, confounded, and humbled.[119] The same preacher later argued that reformation without accompanying mortification was inadequate.[120] Ultimately those who were repentant owed obedience to God; so it was the duty of the saints to bring all under their jurisdiction "to be at Gods Command."[121] This was the way "to serve the Lord."[122] It was understood, of course, that God's "carpenters" could "pluck down" and "rear up" regardless of the opposition.[123] In this, as in so much theological dialectic, the ends justified the means.

It is not surprising that "church reformation" was a primary locus for puritan energies. Oliver Bowles affirmed that utmost zeal was called for in pursuit of this goal.[124] For another preacher, pacification of the church was the "much to bee desired" end.[125] A third made repair of "decayed Godlynesse" the means of saving the church and people from ruin.[126] "Times of deliverance" for the church were hard and difficult, and its friends must be active on her behalf.[127] Anthony Burges, echoing the contemporaneous Covenant, maintained that the Word of God provided the only rule for reform and that the people had a duty to remove all impediments to the dwelling of

---

118 W. Carter, *Israels Peace with God* (London, 1642), 6.

119 *A Sermon Preached . . .* (London, 1644), 10.

120 *A Sermon Preached . . .* (London, 1645), 28.

121 F. Cheynell, *A Plot for the good of Posterity* (London, 1646), 11.

122 See J. Greene, *The Churches Duty, for received Mercies* (London, 1647), *passim.*

123 H. Wilkinson, *Babylons Ruine . . .* (London, 1643), 4.

124 *Zeale for Gods House Quickened* (London, 1643), 7.

125 C. Tesdale, *Hierusalem: Or a Vision of Peace* (London, 1644), 4.

126 T. Manton, *Englands Spirituall Languishing* (London, 1648), 8.

127 H. Hardwick, *The Difficulty of Sions Deliverance and Reformation* (London, 1644), 7, 24.

Christ with them.[128] Herbert Palmer boldly summarized the teaching on church reform in anticipation of the Westminster Assembly's work. His sermon at the June fast in 1643, entitled *The Necessity and Encouragement, of Utmost Venturing for the Churches Help,*[129] was a half-plea, half-threat "that those who are extraordinarily raised up to a speciall opportunity of serviceablenesse of the Church, are intended by God to procure her help, if they will themselves, and be faithful."[130]

Although reformation of the church was of primary concern to the preachers, they made a point of stressing at the same time the indissoluble link between the health of the church and the stability of the commonwealth. The public good of both was best served by those who were "truly godly."[131] For the preachers, general reformation was the way to civil preservation.[132] In their minds, such diverse matters as church policy (=polity), the ministry, laws, and "selves" required thorough reform.[133] It was also evident to them that "people of all sorts" should yield themselves to the Lord in this reformation.[134] Thus saints might legitimately "separate" themselves from obstinate or obdurate uncleanness. At his one appearance during the series Ralph Cudworth asserted that the "will of Christ" was the standard of judgment in these matters.[135] In a similar vein Peter Sterry denominated Jesus Christ "the onely Master in Christianity."[136] Calamy expounded the instrumental connection between divine will and

---

[128] *The Difficulty of, and Encouragements to a Reformation* (London, 1643), 3ff., 19ff.

[129] (London, 1643).

[130] *The Necessity and Encouragement . . . ,* 64ff.

[131] W. Goode, *The Discoverie Of A Publique Spirit* (London, 1645), 3. Cf. S. Bolton, who linked civil and ecclesiastical reform, in *Harmartolos Hamartia: Or, The Sinfulnes of Sin* (London, 1646), *passim.*

[132] S. Simpson, *Reformation's Preservation* (London, 1643).

[133] *Ibid.,* 23ff.

[134] S. Ash, *Self-Surrender unto God* (London [1648]), 4.

[135] R. Cudworth, *A Sermon Preached . . .* (Cambridge, 1647), 7.

[136] *The Teachings of Christ in the Soule* (London, 1648), 5.

reform in his argument that the "Commandements of Gods Ministers . . . are Gods Commandements."[137]

On the assumption that Christ's standard was manifest (or at least articulated by the puritans in such a way as to be self-evident), the preachers insisted that a "neuter" or "waverer" or one "neutral in religion" was evil.[138] Reform must follow from repentance, as repentance had to follow from a true acknowledgment of sin. Thus the great condemning sin was refusing to "come to Christ."[139] As in so many other matters, Stephen Marshall expressed the spirit of this argument in his magnificent *Meroz Cursed*:[140] "All people are cursed or blessed according as they doe or doe not joyne their strength and give their best assistance to the Lords people against their enemies."[141]

Repentance and reform, then, were the means to salvation, distinct but interdependent. Thus, in the perspective of corporate piety, the regular as well as the extraordinary humiliations and the thanksgivings—and also the work of the Assembly of Divines—were the basic instrumentalities of the "puritan revolution."

COLLECTIVE ESCHATOLOGY

A final major series of doctrines framed within the parliamentary sermons requires attention since it represents additional teaching logically implied by the foregoing. This group comprises the symbols used by the preachers to portray the issue they anticipated from the events of their time. Religious imagery provided the terms in which they discussed the consequences to be expected from faithful performance of the piety they advocated before the members of the Long Parliament, who literally "stood for" the nation. Repentance and reform were believed to be pointing toward, and actually realizing, the end-state

---

137 *Englands Antidote* . . . (London, 1645), 4.
138 A. Salwey, *Halting Stigmatiz'd* . . . (London, 1644), 8.
139 T. Valentine, *Two Sermons Preached* . . . (London, 1647), 4.
140 (London, 1641).   141 *Meroz Cursed*, 9.

which was the goal of their enterprise. "Salvation" for the corporate entities of the "nation," "people," and "church" was construed in terms of the available Christian eschatological symbols. Just as within personal piety salvation was conceived under the eschatological symbols of bodily resurrection and life after death, so the collective piety enjoined upon England "framed up" their anticipations with the aid of appropriate symbols from the tradition.

One strikingly frequent figure was "Zion," synecdochically representing Jerusalem. Francis Cheynell constructed a sermon around this symbol for a monthly Commons fast in May 1643. *Sions Memento, and Gods Alarum*"[142] played upon the contrast between it and Babylon. The rise of one, according to the preacher, necessitated the downfall of the other. His second doctrine was that "Zion must take all faire opportunities, and use all lawfull meanes to deliver her self from Babylon."[143] For Cheynell, "Zion" designated essentially a reformed church "consisting of all nations."[144] Applying the same figure in a sermon two years later, Stephen Marshall took the stand that "the building of Zion is the Lords work, and the Lords onely."[145] For him no less than for Cheynell, however, Zion was the true church of God, and its appearance would be self-evident. This was the point made by Thomas Coleman as the Westminster Assembly began its work:

> If a stranger aske, what newes in England? what shall be our return, what shall we say? What? why, the best news that ever was, God hath established Sion, and the poore of his people are confident in her; Oh, here is a change of late, religion is here setled in purity, and peace; here is a ground work laid to erect the Kingdom of Jesus Christ upon, that the gates of hell shall never prevail against it; God hath established Sion, and as for his people, there is a new world with them. . . .[146]

[142] (London, 1643).
[143] *Sions Memento* . . . , 3f. Cf. 41ff.
[144] *Ibid.*, 3f.   [145] *Gods Master-piece* (London, 1645), 5.
[146] *The Christians Course and Complaint* (London, 1643), 70.

Intimately linked to the figure of "Zion" was the "Second Temple," which, in the return from Babylon and the rebuilding of Jerusalem, was the symbolic equivalent for the church of Jesus Christ in its anticipated purity. Thus Thomas Goodwin, in an early and notable sermon, *Zerubbabels Encouragement to Finish the Temple*,[147] reassured the Commons that the second temple was "built by degrees,"[148] and especially that it met with opposition.[149] No opposition, of course, could ultimately impede Jesus Christ in His work of completing the building.[150] Much the same idea was repeated two years later by John Greene in *Nehemiah's Teares and Prayers* where he discussed the deliberate pace of reform.[151] Nehemiah was, of course, a prototypical figure for the faithful magistrate in times of church reform. Indeed, he became a model for the well-affected parliament-man.[152] William Gouge did not shrink from offering an explicit and bluntly invidious comparison between Nehemiah as the "pattern of a good patriot" and the negligent members of the House of Commons to whom he preached.[153] Others voiced caution; "Temple-work," one preacher advised, "is not easily, not suddenly accomplished."[154]

The basic constellation of collective eschatological symbols was derived from the figure of the kingly ruler. Christ was explicitly identified as the "King of the Church," ruler and governor of his people:[155] "Christ the second person of the Trinitie is by designation of his Father, appointed to be King of his Church: a King to rule and governe all those whom hee hath redeemed to be a people for him-

---

[147] (London, 1642).

[148] *Zerubbabels Encouragement* . . . , 12.

[149] *Ibid.*, 21ff.   [150] *Ibid.*, 24ff.

[151] See *Nehemiah's Teares and Prayers* (London, 1644), 11ff.

[152] *Ibid.*, 23ff.

[153] *The Saints Support* (London, 1642), 14ff.

[154] T. Hill, *The Season for Englands Selfe-Reflection* (London, 1644), 25.

[155] See T. Temple, *Christ's Government In and over His People* (London, 1642).

self."[156] Throughout the preaching to the Long Parliament the same symbols remained prominent in the puritan analysis of collective eschatological expectations. For instance, George Hughes declared in May 1647 that "A Reformation-change of worldly Kingdoms to our Lord and his Christ, is a sure revelation from God" and "The Lord and his Christ shall (King it) or reigne over these reformed Kingdomes for ever and ever."[157] Some of the preachers anticipated a veritable *unio Christi*, a "soul-ravishing intimacy and bosome familiarity that passeth between Christ and his people."[158] Some propositions associated with the kingly theme appear to have been theologically conventional: for example, the assertion that "the Church and people of the New Testament, is the Kingdom of heaven."[159] The effect of such language needs to be recognized, however, in view of the revolutionary character of the period. Preaching in May 1644, Henry Hall went so far as to urge that "Those that would put in for a share in this Kingdome, they must not be dull and sluggish, but earnest and violent in pursuance of it."[160] A reader of this literature is forced to posit an inevitable, if indeterminate, relationship between the public expression of these expectations in the parliamentary pulpit and through the public press and the violent termination of an earthly reign in January 1648-9.

Christ as king over his people was a theme subject to various constructions. A number of preachers conceived of this development in essentially progressive terms. They identified continuing reformation as a means of realizing the divine rule. The patriarch Gouge, for example, delivered a sermon on *The Progresse of Divine Providence*[161] in September 1645 in which he contended that "The Lord hath provided his better things for the later times of his

---

[156] *Ibid.*, 4f.

[157] *Vae-Euge-tuba. Or, The Wo-joy-Trumpet* (London, 1647), 5.

[158] J. Langley, *Gemitus Columbae: The Mournfull Note of the Dove* (London, 1644), 5.

[159] *Heaven Ravished* (London, 1644), 10.

[160] *Ibid.*, 34.   [161] (London, 1645).

Church."[162] Stephen Marshall appears to have held a more advanced, though related, position: "That the greatest glory that ever the Lord sets upon any whom he useth is, that the Kingdom of Heaven is advanced by their Ministery or service."[163] Thus, to the saints, "Heaven there, and Heaven here . . . is all but one Kingdome."[164] By contrast an antiprogressive position was espoused by other preachers. William Bridge, one of this school, preached to Commons in May 1648 on *Christs Coming Opened in a Sermon*.[165] His argument was that Christ would come "at midnight," that is, unexpectedly and in "the darkest time."[166] Francis Woodcock was another who rejected a progressive view of the kingdom's arrival, stressing instead the violent exertions made by Antichrist prior to Christ's coming as a thief.[167] "Then when Antichrist being reduced to last exigents, sends abroad seducing spirits, to the Potentates of the earth, then is Christ a making ready for his second comming."[168]

All these constructions, however, whether weakly or rigorously progressive on the one hand, or dramatic and judgmental on the other, in common anticipated a period of earthly felicity. Woodcock explicitly espoused a millennial interpretation of this "period."[169] Bridge's view was less doctrinaire if no less a variation of the millenarian theme:

> I would not be mistaken here; for I do not thinke that Christ shall come and raigne, continue raigning upon earth a thousand years, I do not see how the Saints can spare him out of heaven so long. Neither do I thinke that this his coming is onely to be understood of a spirituall coming into the souls of his, so filling their soules with his spirit, that they shall have no need of Ordinances no more. . . .[170]

162 *The Progresse* . . . , 6.
163 *A Sermon Preached* . . . [Jan. 26, 1647-8] (London, 1647), 9.
164 *Ibid.*, 18.
165 (London, 1648).   166 *Christs Coming* . . . , 5.
167 *Christ's Warning-piece* (London, 1644), 8.
168 *Ibid.*, 6f.   169 *Ibid.*, 7-8.
170 *Christs Coming* . . . , 6.

So pervasive was this theme of a period of earthly felicity under the rule of Christ—though it appeared in a variety of specific forms—that it is plausible to cite it as that classical "heresy" which most threatened the orthodoxy of puritan piety during the civil war period. That many of the preachers actually perceived it in such a light is clear, and this negative evidence is exceedingly weighty.

As one example, William Gouge, whose espousal of a progressive view was candid, carefully distanced himself from, or passed by, "all conceits of our later Chiliasts or Millenaries, (whom in English we may call Thousandaries) who imagine, that Christ shall personally come down from heaven, in that nature in which after his resurrection he ascended into heaven, and raign here a thousand years with his Saints."[171] John Lightfoot devoted a complete sermon before the members of Commons in August 1645 to the errors of the "millenary" opinion.[172] He carefully analyzed his text—Revelation 20:1-2, a fountainhead of the opinion—and confuted the six groundless and mistaken principles in which, he alleged, it was rooted.[173] He then interpreted the text in the way he considered proper, effectively giving to it a "historical" reading in which human history represented a theatre for the struggle between good and evil.[174] Lightfoot took particular pains to discredit the doctrine that England was special to God as Israel had been; His way with her, he averred, was rather more like His dealings with Egypt and the Pharaohs![175]

A brace of sermons preached to the Lords during May 1645 most explicitly identified millenarian opinions and teachings as the perceived threat to (if also a plausible extension of) the collective piety enjoined upon England. Jeremy Whitaker, in the less noteworthy of the sermons (at least on this point), sought to rebut "atheism." His first doctrine was that "The foundation of all the comfort we

---

[171] *The Progresse of Divine Providence* (London, 1645), 29.
[172] *A Sermon Preached . . .* (London, 1645).
[173] *Ibid.*, 3ff.   [174] *Ibid.*, 7ff.   [175] *Ibid.*, 25.

doe enjoy, or can expect, [is] the Lord Jesus Christ."[176] From this assertion he moved on to affirm that the hope of a Christian could not be confined to this life: "If all the good that the soul expects from Christ should be limited to this life, then the best Christians should be the most miserable."[177] The more direct criticism of reigning confusion about Christ's kingdom, however, was provided by a Scottish Commissioner—Alexander Henderson. His doctrine makes this position clear: "That Christ Jesus the Sonne of God hath a Kingdome in this world, and that this Kingdome is a spirituall Kingdome, and not of this world."[178] His further explication of the point was a pure draught of reformed orthodoxy regarding the kingdom of Christ: "The quality then of the Kingdome of Christ, negatively is this, That his Kingdome is not of this world: it is not an earthly or worldly Kingdome, and therefore by consequence must be a spirituall and heavenly Kingdome."[179]

In certain respects emphasis upon the anticipated new "age"—explicitly millenarian or not—was the most striking and fundamental characteristic of the formal preaching before the Long Parliament, at least insofar as it is accessible through published sermons. The variety of specific opinions is remarkable and witnesses to the preachers' fascination with a new Jerusalem which they expected in that very time. Whatever else may be required to understand them, it is necessary to recognize in the sermons at the humiliations and thanksgivings an attempt on the part of the clerical puritans to establish a collective eschatological framework to confer historical meaning upon the exercise of their piety. In the next chapter this discussion will be continued. There consideration will be given to the contrast between prophetic and apocalyptic constructions of the time, a differentiation closely related to the

176 *The Christians Hope Triumphing* (London, 1645), 4.
177 *Ibid.*, 40.
178 *A Sermon Preached . . .* (London, 1645), 11.
179 *Ibid.*, 7.

progressive and anti-progressive interpretations of the kingdom of Christ.

In closing this analysis of the teaching regarding piety which was framed up by the members of the brotherhood, it may be appropriate simply to articulate the principle which has been implicit throughout the preceding pages. The political activity, or the revolutionary politics, of the civil war era which was evidently authorized by Puritanism, was clearly understood or comprehended by the puritan preachers in essentially religious terms. In advocating their doctrines, they were explaining their times. Thus their emphasis upon correct piety as the appropriate mode of response to the era was not accidental or incidental (or without parallel in other times). It was simply their manifest means of making intelligible the dreadful social and political (indeed, religious) crisis through which they were living. In this elementary observation a basic point is at issue. For the clerical puritans, religious language made possible a radical understanding of society. However inadequate to that purpose it seemed to some during the seventeenth century, or has appeared to future generations, it enabled them to come to grips with the civil strife of their time. But, if their theological conceptions did function to make social life comprehensible, then their religious language ought to have registered the civil stress. This observation has been made, at least in a partial way, by those who have commented upon the differentiation of the puritan movement as a consequence of its engagement in the turmoil of the decade. In this light the concluding chapter will analyze the sermons preached before the Long Parliament for what they may disclose about basic developments in Puritanism which were occasioned by the times of civil war.

VII

Puritanism in the Time of Civil War

THE FORMAL puritan response to the English civil wars of the 1640's was to enjoin upon the nation a corporate or collective piety. This religious perspective was believed to make the social crisis intelligible by setting it in a framework of national declension and anticipated regeneration. Of course, it was also believed that the exercise of piety on the basis of this insight would prove to be efficacious. Such was the explicit teaching in the "plain style" preaching before the Long Parliament. It was based upon texts, cast into "doctrines," defended with "reasons," and applied through "uses." Whatever different attitudes toward the civil strife individual puritans may have taken, whatever personal conceptions they may have developed concerning the reciprocal relationships between religious faith and political activity, or whatever special roles they may have played within the struggles, this doctrinal framework was the basic context offered by Puritanism for comprehending the times. The preceding review of puritan teaching about the times exhibited the construction placed by the brotherhood upon the decade of civil war. That has left, however, a further inquiry: what the preaching before parliament may disclose about changes within and developments on the part of Puritanism. The previous chapter examined the doctrinal content of the sermons to delineate the puritan understanding of the national crisis. The present chapter will consider the sermons before parliament with a view toward illuminating Puritanism itself during this epoch.

Most precisely put, the civil wars appear to have been the occasion for a differentiation within clerical puritan ranks which effectively brought to an end the movement which had been rendered relatively coherent up to that point through a common religious perspective. In recent years considerable interest has centered on the growth of sectarian movements out of the broadly puritan soil of the era—Baptists, Quakers, Fifth Monarchy Men, Levellers, Diggers, to name only those which have received the most attention. At least as important is the recognition that the brotherhood itself, the elite of divines who jointly defined Puritanism, experienced fissure and underwent division that in some sense made possible (if not necessary) the more striking and dramatic sectarianism on the periphery of (and probably derivative from) the central movement. The sermons before the Long Parliament exhibit this basic development not so much in their formal "doctrines" as through the less formal content and style of the exhortations. The preceding chapter took note of the divergence between progressive and anti-progressive conceptions of the kingdom or rule of Christ (or God) which may be found in the sermons. This is a useful starting point for discussion of the fundamental separation within Puritanism, which may best be understood in terms of the contrast between prophetic and apocalyptic eschatologies.

Prophetic and Apocalyptic Eschatologies

For some time a distinction between prophetic and apocalyptic sections of the scriptures has held currency within biblical studies. An obvious illustration would be the contrasting tempers of Hosea and Daniel. In its classical usage "prophecy" did not primarily signify "prediction" but rather the delivery of a "word" from the Lord. The "word" was usually one embodying both judgment and mercy. Israel was thought to be judged by the standards of her covenant relationship to Jahweh—and at once the "word" reminded her of this and offered her the opportunity for "turning" or "returning" to Him. The "word," then, was mainly directed toward the prophet's present. Insofar as a vision of the future was elaborated, it graphically portrayed those eventualities which would befall Israel should she fail to heed the "word" and refuse to return to His ways. Thus the essence of the prophetic message was a confidence in Jahweh's resources to bring good out of evil in his relationship to a covenanted people. The psychological focus of the prophet's declaration was Israel's responsibility in the present for a conditionally open future.

By contrast to classical prophetism, apocalypticism developed as a proclamation of hope in Israel's darkest hours. Here the emphasis lay not upon an open future but in the declaration that, appearances to the contrary notwithstanding, God ruled the course of historical events and *would* bring out of the ominous present a glorious future quite independently of human agency. The apocalypse was precisely a disclosure of this certain future, withheld from the worldly wise but delivered to the faithful (elite). Psychologically it offered reassurance; by definition the belief structure excluded the possibility of disconfirmation. In genesis the apocalyptic impulse was at least partly a development from prophecy, an extension of certain of its assumptions at the expense of other critical elements. The one at its core represented a scandalous confidence in the covenant relationship between Israel and Jahweh; the other, pressed to its logical conclusion, constituted a future claim upon God which might well father heresy within the present. In the one, human agency was invited to respond to divine purposes; in the other, the independence of the divine initiative from human agency was celebrated. This contrast offers a convenient vehicle for conveying the manner in which the exhortations to the Long Parliament reveal a deep division within the ranks of the puritan clergymen.

Those preachers whose interpretation of the times was prophetic fundamentally counseled a reformation. They exhorted the members of parliament to turn to God, and they implicitly elevated human ability to exercise agency. Thus they advocated a piety which joined divine will and human willing. By contrast the apocalyptic constructions of the civil war symbolized the contemporary events in terms of divine purposes thought to be in process of fulfillment apart from the knowledge of most subjects. Those who espoused this interpretation declared that divine intentions were reaching culmination in the events of the time, the true significance of which only the elite could properly recognize. On this authority they were able to exalt acts radically destructive of the social order; images of violence and revolutionary rhetoric permeated the language of their sermons. Both viewpoints might share a common understanding of the past, but their variant interpretations of the future led to rather distinctive attitudes toward the present.

This disjunction within Puritanism, which the civil strife of the 1640's first brought fully into the open, clearly had an earlier genesis. Its development and expression could only mark the end of the old Puritanism and make inevitable the religious settlement of the Restoration. Some of the puritan preachers died before that time. A certain few made their peace with that church. Others, of course, experienced the painful stigma of nonconformity. The present chapter will briefly review the sermons preached before the Long Parliament for the light they may cast on the basic differentiation within Stuart Puritanism exhibited during the 1640's.

THE PROPHETIC PROMISE

The prophetic construction of the times was presupposed in the preaching institution and "framed up" in the formal "doctrines." It provided context as well as content for the humiliations and thanksgivings that concern us here. This interpretation was boldly articulated in the first of the sermons to the Long Parliament. The ordinance which authorized the monthly fast program construed that routine as a proper expression of "repentance."[1] There-

[1] *An Ordinance . . . Exhorting . . . to . . . Repentance* (London, 1642).

after it served as a refrain throughout the exercises. In this respect it echoed the puritan preaching to earlier parliaments which was surveyed in Chapter II. Cornelius Burges offered this description of puritan hopes on November 17, 1640: "My businesse is, meerly to persuade you into a *Religious Covenant with God*, as himselfe hath prescribed and commanded; and, his people, in the best times of Reformation, have readily admitted: namely, every man to stirre up himself & to lift up his Soule to take hold of God, to be glued and united to him, in all faithfulnesse, sincerity, care, and diligence, to be onely his for ever."[2] Stephen Marshall emphasized the same point in his companion sermon: "Could I, as in a mirrour, set before your eyes, how infinitely farre off the body of this Kingdome is from *being with the Lord*, we should wonder that the Lord hath not wholly forsaken us long agone. . . ."[3] No less did it become the basic burden of the preaching to the monthly humiliations when that institution was inaugurated. In *Gods free Mercy to England*[4] Edmund Calamy employed the imagery of the "school" to this end:

> It is the duty of a Minister to follow God in his providence. When God sends judgments upon a Nation, then must we preach judgments to that Nation: But when he sends mercies, then must we preach mercy: Now God hath brought England into the *schoole of mercy*, and hath placed it *in the highest forme*, and hath made it Captaine of the schoole. And it is my duty to teach you what lessons you are to learne in this schoole. This Text [Ezekiel 36:32] holds forth one lesson, which is the proper lesson for this day, and that is, to be confounded and ashamed, that ever we should sinne against such a God.[5]

This was also the refrain of Stephen Marshall's *Meroz Cursed*,[6] which graced the same occasion: "Gods blessing

2 *The First Sermon* . . . (London, 1641), 57.
3 *A Sermon Preached* . . . *November 17. 1640* (London, 1641), 30.
4 (London, 1642).
5 *Gods free Mercy to England*, 2.   6 (London, 1641).

is upon them that come to helpe him: and . . . *Meroz*, and with *Meroz* all others are cursed, who come not out to the help of the Lord against the mighty."[7]

In a recent study of the sermons before the Long Parliament, James C. Spalding, clearly recognizing the significance of this motif, suggests that the preaching series constitutes "an excellent public parallel to the private puritan diary."[8] The exhortations expressed, he argues, a Deuteronomic interpretation of history, one basically similar to the moral framework within which the biblical books of Joshua, Judges, I and II Samuel, and I and II Kings construed the epochs of Israel's history which had preceded their composition. In these books the mundane failures and successes experienced by God's people were regarded as divine judgments and blessings. Certainly one must admit that major themes in the fast sermons constitute a Deuteronomic stratum. The preceding chapter took note of the prominence accorded the legend of England's Christian past, especially as shaped by John Foxe, as a mode in which to present the claims of Puritanism upon that generation of Englishmen. Still, even though Deuteronomic elements obviously were present throughout the preaching, it is doubly inappropriate to define the institution exclusively in these terms.

In the first place, it was the duty of the prophet in ancient Israel to address the present—making use, to be sure, of the legendary Deuteronomic past. The preachers to parliament, as messengers of God or vehicles of God's Word, were more strictly analogous to the prophets; so, too, John Foxe's work was more closely parallel to the Deuteronomic corpus. Thus, although the *Book of Martyrs* provided a context for puritan exhortation during the 1640's and contributed much of the material present in it, the preachers themselves were principally not legend-makers but sermon-deliverers. In the second place, the preach-

[7] *Meroz Cursed*, 54.
[8] "Sermons before Parliament (1640-1649)" *Church History*, xxxvi/1 (March 1967), 24-35. The specific quotation is from page 25.

ers understood themselves to be living under a new covenant established in Christ which situated them in a different
theological dispensation, however extensive the parallels
to ancient Israel may have been.[9] The preachers, then,
were not only God's chroniclers or diarists. More important,
they were reformists and potential revolutionaries primarily engaged with and responding to the present. They
availed themselves of a construction of England's past
which incorporated clear parallels to Deuteronomic ver-
sions of Israel's history, but as a means to immediate
rather than projected reforms.

Though not simply Deuteronomic, the prophetical cast
of the materials is nevertheless evident. Numerous citations
from the whole range of the sermons could be marshalled
to establish that this perspective represented the original,
and also the continuing, impulse underlying the preaching
before parliament. In this particular the institution faithfully reflected and developed the intention which had led
to the preaching before the earlier Stuart parliaments, a
subject which was reviewed in the second chapter of this
study. Thus the sermons pressed for a basic reformation

---

[9] See G. Walker's *A Sermon . . . before . . . Commons* (London,
1645), in which occurs this extended passage (13):
"I have been large in producing a multitude of examples, because I
would have you take notice, that wicked Rulers and Kings mentioned
in Scripture, never wanted pernicious Counsellors, nor Bands of cursed
instruments to spur and drive them on to destruction, and to bring a
curse on their Kingdomes. This is no new, nor strange thing to be
wondered at, and to dismay and astonish us. But that, in times
when Kings and Princes were Tyrants, oppressors, and back sliders
from true Religion to Idolatry, and had Bands of wicked instruments,
and of men of violence at command, God was so mercifull to his
Nation, and the people of old, as to reserve to himselfe a prevayling
party, and to put wisdome and courage into the great Counsell of the
Kingdome, to resist their violence, to preserve Religion from ruine,
the people from oppression, the Land from spoyling, to oppose the
bands of the wicked, to scatter them, and execute justice on them:
this we finde not in the Book of God, in all the Histories from the
first to the second *Adam*: this is a mercy proper to the times of the
Gospell, and to those Nations and Kingdomes in which Christ ruleth by
his holy Spirit, and his Church is surely established, by the word
of God faithfully preached, & true religion is planted in the hearts
of the people."

of life within the kingdom according to biblical inspiration and reformed Protestant norms.

One concern, therefore, was that the reformation be an authentic undertaking and not merely a stratagem founded on motives ulterior to acts which themselves might be appropriate: "Nothing is more fatall to a Nation, in Reforming times, than to oppose that Reformation within in their hearts, which outwardly they appear zealous to promote. This is to juggle with God, for base ends of their own, which never goes unpunished."[10] Another concern was that the reformation be expeditious and prompt: "If you will wisely enquire into a reason of Gods proceedings, reflect upon your selves, and charge the slownesse upon your owne soules."[11] Charles Herle was not above appealing to the chivalry of the Lords to win their support of Protestant reform: "Be pleased to imagine Religion (Protestant Religion) as an Orphan Virgin pursued by her so much the worse enemies, in that, . . . bath'd in her owne teares, and blood[,] throwing herselfe at your feet, sighing out some such sad complaint as this: Whether should a distressed Virgin flye, but to her guardians? You are they. . . ."[12] The international and historical significance of the reformation of English life was directly and repeatedly emphasized: "The eyes of all the *three Kingdomes,* yea of the *Protestant world* are now upon you, expecting much from your influence."[13] For these reasons the fasts ought to have been observed "with more obedience and solemnitie . . . then indeed of late they are."[14] This improvement was advisable simply because correct corporate piety was the proper path to the intended goal: "Now the rode [road] to this so desireable peace with the Lord

[10] C. Burges, *Two Sermons* (London, 1645), 2.
[11] R. Harris, *A Sermon* (London, 1642), 42. Cf. O. Sedgwick, *England's Preservation* (London, 1642), 43.
[12] *Davids Song of Three Parts* (London, 1643), 20.
[13] T. Hill, *The Trade of Truth Advanced* (London, 1642), 17-18.
[14] E. Reynolds, *Israels Petition In Time Of Trouble* (London, 1642), 7.

our God, lest any should mistake his way, lies through the fields of faith, prayer, and new obedience."[15]

The Solemn League and Covenant was predicated upon such a calculus, and it represented a direct expression of this prophetic premise. When it was adopted, Alexander Henderson pronounced a benediction over it to the effect that the "weight of this Covenant [would] cast the ballance, and make Religion and Righteousnesse to prevaile, to the glory of God, the honour of our King, the confusion of our common Enemies, and the comfort and safety of the people of God."[16] A year later, speaking after military reverses, Matthew Newcomen diagnosed the grounds of the defeat: "the violation of the Covenant of God is such a sinne as will make Israel turne their back before their Enemies."[17]

In this prophetic view those whose concerns were "publique" had a special responsibility. William Goode addressed the "honoured Senators" (Commons) in the following fashion in March 1645:

> Be you then exhorted, worthy Patriots, courageously, wisely, sincerely, and thoroughly to serve your owne generation. You have better opportunities then ever any Parliament of England had before you, to be effectuall means of the happinesse both of Church and Commonwealth. Remember that you must give a strict account unto the King of Kings, of that price that is put into your hands.[18]

Thus the figures of such biblical leaders as Nehemiah became archetypical (more than a Moses, for example) : "By this recollection of the principall acts of this Patriot, you see what remarkable matters he did. . . . Hereby also you may further see what becomes worthy Patriots to

15 J. Arrowsmith, *The Covenant-avenging Sword Brandished* (London, 1643), 27.

16 *The Covenant: with a Narrative of the Proceedings* (London, 1643), 34.

17 *A Sermon* . . . (London, 1644), 32.

18 *The Discoverie of a Publique Spirit* (London, 1645), 28.

doe. . . ."[19] Samuel Annesley, preaching to the monthly Commons humiliation in July 1648, gave voice to similar expectations where leaders were concerned:

> If godly Magistrates, under the greatest straits and un-paraleld sufferings from God, friends, and enemies, can clearly vindicate their former actions, and constantly maintain strong resolutions, never to justifie the wicked, nor swerve from their integrity; it will be graciously acceptable in the sight of God, highly commendable in the eyes of men, and singularly comfortable to their own souls.[20]

The prophetic perspective at bottom presupposed that God's providence was working in and through mundane events toward the realization of divine purposes. Toward this goal the faithful, and especially the faithful leaders, were summoned to contribute.[21] Thus the familiar theme of repentance echoed and re-echoed throughout the series: "Beloved, Repentance obtaineth audience and par-

---

[19] W. Gouge, *The Saints Support* (London, 1642), 29.

[20] *A Sermon Preached* . . . (London, 1648), 3f.

[21] An extended passage from J. Ward's *The Good-Will of him that Dwelt in the Bush* (London, 1645) gives expression to this prophetic and reforming perspective on the active role played by God on behalf of His people under the gospel dispensation (4f.):

"When a nation is not worthy to be beloved, and the rod of Gods displeasure is put into the hands of bloudthirsty and deceitfull men, and they help forward the affliction, and there be little or no proba-bility of better condition by men or means; if then the Lord will make offer and tender of his good will, and one may discerne in his workes, in his waies a gracious propensitie and purpose to redeem, though in the prosecution thereof there is such various and uneven dispensations of providence, as may give occasion to the enemy to be hardened and insolent, and the other side to be discouraged and dejected; yet if God so temper his judgements, as his own people shall feel the benigne and comfortable, and the Adversary the hurtfull and destructive effects thereof, he will step in, to restrain, or inhibit, or prevent the fraud or fury of the enemy, and take the advantage of their animositie and attempts, to glorifie himselfe, in shewing forth his wrath, and making his power known upon them; and the mean-while continue to protect, and repeate, and multiply wonders in favour of his people, to the confusion of the adversary, it must be confessed a very great mercy, transcending the good of peace and plenty."

don, that maketh every sin veniall, that saveth the soule, and that saveth a Nation from ruine and destruction; Repentance causeth God to repent, & maketh him better than his word, when he threateneth evill. . . ."[22] The title of William Gouge's sermon to the Lords humiliation in September 1648, which sought blessing upon negotiations with the King, illustrates the persistence of the basic prophetic temper until the end of the period under review: *The Right Way: or A direction for obtaining good Successe in a weighty Enterprise.*[23]

Fundamentally the prophetic interpretation of the civil war viewed it as an opportunity for God's faithful stewards to reform religious and civil practice according to the terms of the covenant and in conjunction with divine purposes. The much desired future was thought to be a possible development of forces at work in the present. The English social scene of the 1640's was in this way rendered intelligible, and the resulting perspective was recommended to a parliament which in some measure appears to have found such an interpretive framework informing, if not convincing. The humiliations and thanksgivings as corporate rituals presupposed this ideological position (that is, puritan teaching about the times), which was formally spelled out in the review of "doctrines" undertaken in the preceding chapter.

THE APOCALYPTIC FUTURE

Alongside and within this basically prophetic framework there was present in the preaching a related theme or pattern, an apocalyptic construction of the 1640's. This was represented by recourse to the imagery of Daniel and Revelation for symbols to decipher the civil struggles or for chronological speculation to establish the "times" according to the alleged biblical calendars. The fundamental meaning conveyed by the apocalyptic stratum was the as-

[22] S. Gibson, *The Ruine of the Authors and fomentors of civill warres* (London, 1645), 35.
[23] (London, 1648).

sumption that the future intended by God for the English was not to be the mundane and direct outgrowth of the civil strife but rather the result of intrusion upon the present. Implied further was the belief that God certainly did not require—and probably would not find it necessary to enlist—the agencies of those who aspired to be servants or stewards. Under the influence of the apocalyptic temper the future anticipated by the elite was judged to be discontinuous with the present. The apocalyptic mind discovered in the preaching before parliament an opportunity to make declarations about (if not revelations of) its esoteric knowledge. This was one way to make the times intelligible, of course, but it did so in an entirely different manner and according to a quite different set of expectations. Such "knowledge" of the civil wars, as of any revolutionary epoch, was primarily useful in legitimating thought and action destructive of constituted authority. It is intriguing to observe in some of the sermons preached before the Long Parliament the temptation to shift from the sober prophetic idiom to the dramatic and radical apocalyptic idiom. Indeed, prophetic doctrinal formulations regarding the times might be accompanied by introductions, passing comments, or concluding assertions which contradicted that framework of intelligibility. With these preliminary remarks out of the way, we can now pass on to a survey of evidence for the apocalyptic stratum in the preaching to parliament.

Apocalyptic tendencies were manifest in the formal institution of humiliations as early as the spring of 1642.[24] During that year and into the next, apocalyptic elements frequently found their way into the exhortations, although they were closely conjoined with and subordinated to expression of the prophetic perspective. For example, both sermons to the Commons fast on April 27, 1642, exhibited

[24] Expression of this "idiom," "temper," or "mind" was pronounced in certain of the sermons to sundry of the House of Commons during the preceding year. Reference to them is made in Chapter II, 43-52, and in Appendix Three, 275ff.

these characteristics in important respects. Thomas Goodwin's *Zerubbabels Encouragement to Finish the Temple*[25] offered technical "observations" or "doctrines" which might properly be construed as prophetic or reformative. The main burden of the sermon, though, was the typological application to England of Israel's effort to complete the second temple (the text was Zechariah 4:6-9). It followed from this position that existing patterns—that is, other reformed churches—retained corruptions which must be transcended: "Hence therefore the Churches comming out of the darknesse of Popery, must needs recover that fulnesse and perfection of light . . . by piece-meals and degrees."[26] For Goodwin, the apocalyptic visions were not "similitudinary examples" only but also "Prophetique Types of the like work of *finishing the Temple*, to fall out under the times of the Gospel, when the Church is come out of Popery."[27] The title of the companion sermon preached by Joseph Caryl, *The Workes of Ephesus Explained*,[28] suggests that, at least with reference to apocalypticism, it supplemented Goodwin's exercise. Explicitly calculated to "stirr up" Commons to remove the evils cloying the commonwealth and to "frame up" church discipline and government, Caryl's discourse nevertheless questioned all standards of reform other than "Christ" and the "Word of God":

> Whatsoever truth came from Heaven with Christ, shall never (in it selfe) feele decay. Whatsoever *moulds now*, though it be as old as the world, came but *from our borders, This World: Heaven is the farre country.* Therefore the tryall cannot be made by that which is usually called Antiquity: But by that which transcends all humane Antiquity, Customes, Councels and Traditions (though all those may contribute some help) *The Word of God.*[29]

25 (London, 1642).
26 *Zerubbabels Encouragement* . . . , 17.
27 *Ibid.*, 53-54.   28 (London, 1642).
29 *The Workes of Ephesus Explained*, 57.

The apocalyptic vein of imagery was worked by the fiery William Sedgwick in *Zions Deliverance and Her Friends Duty*,[30] which he delivered at the June fast in 1642: "The Tabernacle of God, is comming downe to dwell with men; whatever darke clouds appeare, let us continue praying, waiting, labouring, beleeving, God will at last *establish, and make Jerusalem a praise in the earth.*"[31] In similar fashion William Greenhill employed the language and symbolism of apocalypticism in addressing Commons in April 1643: "In the 17. *Rev.* when the Kings of the earth shall give their power to the Beast, and make warre with the Lamb, the victory is the Lambs, and they that are with him are *call'd, chosen* and *faithfull.*"[32] Stephen Marshall himself betrayed fascination with these materials in June 1643 in *The Song of Moses*.[33] He justified preaching on the text from Revelation (15:2-4) because, although it was hard to understand, "yet time . . . hath produced the events answering the types so full and clear."[34] His subject was the "behaviour of the Church during the time of the pouring out the vialls."[35] Thomas Hill undertook a parallel task in July of that year in *The Militant Church, Triumphant over the Dragon*[36]: "That which may embolden us to looke for more glorious victories hereafter, we finde in this 12. Chapter of the Revelation, even the infant Primitive Church becomming triumphant, when opposed by the fiercest of those heathenish Emperours."[37]

These sermons disclose not only that the apocalyptic idiom had attained a certain currency within the brotherhood but that frustration was already being acutely experienced by some who identified themselves in the terms of Puritanism, a frustration with the prophetic and reformist program for the era. From the summer of 1643 onward the preaching before parliament occasionally exhibited a fuller development of the apocalyptic approach to

---

[30] (London, 1642).   [31] *Zions Deliverance* . . . , 53-54.
[32] *The Axe at the Root* (London, 1643), 46.
[33] (London, 1643).   [34] *The Song of Moses*, 3.
[35] *Ibid.*, 4.   [36] (London, 1643).
[37] *The Militant Church* . . . , 3.

the age, along with continued incidental references to it. This was manifested in two basic and related ways: careful and laborious determination of the times according to symbolic chronologies discovered in scripture, and explicit espousal of millenarian symbols for the desired future. These characteristic elements were present throughout the preaching during the remainder of the decade.

Chronological interpretation of the period may be illustrated from a sermon entitled *Babylons Ruine, Jerusalems Rising*[38] preached to Commons in October 1643. Henry Wilkinson there took note of the "generall talk throughout the household among the domesticks . . . that Christ their king is comming to take possession of his Throne, they doe not onely whisper this, and tell it in the eare, but they speake it publikely. . . ."[39] Quite surprisingly, Wilkinson introduced this report not to belittle or mock it but to take it most seriously on the principle that "domesticks" usually know secrets before the general public learns of them![40] To this end he reviewed the prophetical calendars currently in vogue, especially the constructions proposed by Brightman and Mead (or Mede).[41] Stanley Gower gave even more detailed attention to these matters at the July fast in 1644. In *Things Now-a-doing*[42] he analyzed the text from Daniel (12:10) as a sacred calendar. According to Gower's calculations, the delivery and conversion of the Jews were to occur in 1650.[43] He thereby held out hope that numerous members of the Long Parliament would see this deliverance in their lifetimes and live to experience the subsequent era.[44] To buttress his optimistic predictions, Gower added an appendix to his sermon in which he took up the subject of the "four monarchies" and supported his designation of 1650 as the critical year by citing the same authorities—Broughton, Brightman, Mead, *et al.* At the monthly humiliation in October 1644, Francis

[38] (London, 1643).
[39] *Babylons Ruine . . .* , 21.
[40] *Ibid.*
[41] *Ibid.*, 22f.
[42] (London, 1644).
[43] *Things Now-a-doing*, A₃ *recto* and *verso*.
[44] *Ibid.*, 25.

Woodcock was no less certain that Christ's coming was at hand; his opinion especially rested on the "vials" of Revelation 16.[45] Thomas Goodwin was convinced, particularly by the vision of the ten horns in Revelation 17, that his time was the one in which the hope of all ages would be consummated.[46] John Maynard disclosed his similar belief: "For I conceive [that] we are under the seventh trumpet, to which all the seven vials full of the wrath of God, to be emptied upon the enemies of the Church, do belong. . . . Now is the time when Christ shall conquer Kingdoms, and subdue Nations to Himself, to reign over them for ever."[47] Others were not quite so sanguine. William Strong, for one, believed that the last and greatest calamity—the killing of the "Witnesses"—was yet to come.[48] Strong in no way drew back, however, from the enterprise of attempting to determine the "time."

Implicit in virtually all of this fascination with chronological speculation and determination of the "times" was the conviction that *the time* would usher in a millennial period. Brief reference was made in the preceding chapter to this expectation as it related to the structure of corporate piety "framed up" and advocated by the preachers. Not encumbered by doctrinaire distinctions between post- and pre-millenarianism—a theological dispute more pronounced during the nineteenth century than during the seventeenth—the Millennium anticipated by some of the preachers was basically understood to involve the direct reign of Christ. This symbol, of course, permitted a variety of actual interpretations.

Henry Hall, for instance, emphasized the rule of Christ in the church:

> The eyes of many thousands in the Land, and a great part of Christendome too, are now upon you; you are in the hearts of all the Saints in all the Churches, especially

---

[45] *Christ's Warning-piece* (London, 1644).
[46] *The Great Interest of States & Kingdomes* (London, 1646), 46ff.
[47] *A Shadow of the Victory of Christ* (London, 1646), 10.
[48] *The Way to the Highest Honour* (London, 1647), 48.

those at home, who are ready to live and dye with you, and what is their expectation and desire other then this, That Christ may raigne as an All-Commanding King, over his owne house; That Doctrin, Worship, Government, may be all exact, according to the Patterne in the Mount.[49]

Joseph Caryl, by contrast, intimated that the reign was not to be so exclusively embodied in or expressed through ecclesiastical structures:

> Christ is alwaies King, but it doth not alwaies appear how glorious a King he is, or what he shall be. Christ hath power, Kingdome, and glory, ... Christ will recover nations and new Kingdomes out of the hand of Satan, from Paganish and Turkish Tyranny. He will make such changes not only in AntiChristian but in Kingdomes truly called Christian, That even these shall be, as if they had not bin Christs, till then.[50]

John Maynard's portrait of Christ was, if anything, even more expansive.[51] Peter Sterry illustrates another form the interest in millenarianism took. Essentially he spiritized the symbol in terms of that "Divine Trinity, Light, Love, and Joy, which shall Unitedly & Universally reign in all hearts and eyes, at the Second Appearance of this Royall Spouse of Spirits."[52] He also believed that the second coming would be "Graduall" and would lead to universal paradise.[53]

The presence in the preaching before parliament of both pronounced apocalypticism and a frankly espoused millenarianism calls for attention to certain basic questions. What were the sources of this surprisingly prominent heresy within Puritanism, and how did it develop so rapidly as to be seemingly commonplace among at least some

49 *Heaven Ravished* (London, 1644) , 64.
50 *The Saints Thankfull Acclamation* . . . (London, 1644) , 25.
51 *Supra*, 212.
52 *The Clouds in which Christ Comes* (London, 1648) , 8.
53 *Ibid.*, 15-17.

members of the brotherhood early in the decade? Further-more, what did it mean, and how does it enable us to understand better the inner structure of Puritanism as a movement during the 1640's? Finally, what effects or consequences may be attributed to these apocalyptic and millenarian strains within the brotherhood during the civil wars? It will not be possible to offer more than basic observations about these matters here, however, since the present context is a monograph on the preaching to the Long Parliament and not a history or full-length study of the decline of Stuart Puritanism.

Apocalyptic Authorities

For the most part insufficient attention has been devoted to the speculation regarding the *eschaton* which developed in conjunction with late Elizabethan and early Stuart Puritanism. Obviously those puritans who were fascinated with apocalypticism and the Millennium during the 1640's had occasion to cite the work of contemporary as well as older continental divines—a good example being Alstedius the encyclopedist.[54] Primary references, however, were to English interpreters of the mysteries of history, since the ideas were generally placed in the service of nationalistic as well as Reformed Protestant purposes. In view of the paucity of available discussions of this tradition, it will be relevant to identify and characterize briefly the most prominent of the English apocalyptists to whom reference was repeatedly made by the generation of puritans who lived during, and responded to, the civil wars.[55]

[54] J. H. Alsted's views were published for the English populace in *The Worlds Proceeding Woes and Succeeding Joyes* (London, 1642) and, more important, in *The Beloved City Or, The Saints Reign On Earth A Thousand Yeares* (London, 1643).

[55] Joy B. Gilsdorf has given some attention to the English background in "The Puritan Apocalypse: New England Eschatology in the Seventeenth Century" (Ph.D. diss., Yale University, 1964). See brief comments by H. R. Trevor-Roper, "Three Foreigners," in *The Crisis of the Seventeenth Century* (New York, 1968), 246-249, where he discusses how the generation shaped by the events of the 1620's was influenced by apocalypticism.

Hugh Broughton (d. 1612) is perhaps the earliest apocalyptist whose name was consistently invoked by the preachers to the Long Parliament. Coming from a Shropshire family of some property, he entered Magdalene College, Cambridge, in 1569 and remained there at one or another college until he was installed in a London pulpit during the 1580's. Broughton became a Hebraist of repute, and a dispute with John Rainolds over his own work, *A Concent of Scripture* (1588), led to a period of exile on the continent. Curiously his relations with fellow Protestants there, especially Beza, were strained while, reputedly, he fraternized freely with Roman Catholic theologians. At the death of Elizabeth he returned to England for a brief period during which he suffered from keen disappointment over the omission of his name from the committee which produced the authorized translation of the Bible, a project which he had long promoted.[56] His later years were spent in Middelburg, Zeeland, which had a tradition of harboring puritan dissidents from England (like Thomas Cartwright and Robert Browne). Broughton's near obsession with biblical chronology, genealogical tables of the scriptures, and harmonization of divergent aspects of holy writ manifests the turn of his mind. His work was considered authoritative,[57] especially by those who were dissenters and expatriates located in the Netherlands during subsequent years.

Of more importance than Broughton was Thomas Brightman (d. 1607).[58] A native of Nottingham, Brightman entered Queens' College, Cambridge, in 1576. He received his BA in 1580-1, his MA and a fellowshp in 1584, and his BD in 1591, all from that college. He then became rector at Hawnes in Bedfordshire and remained there until his death. He was generally considered a puritan. All of his

[56] See his *Principall Positions for groundes of the holy Bible. A Short Oration of the Bibles Translation* (n.p.p., 1609).

[57] Especially his *A Revelation of the Holy Apocalyps* (n.p.p., 1610). The above remarks on Broughton are indebted to the article by Alexander Gordon in the *DNB*.

[58] See the article on Brightman by James Mew in the *DNB*.

publications were posthumous. *Apocalypsis Apocalypseous* first appeared in France in 1609, then at Heidelberg in 1612. Meanwhile a translation, *A Revelation of the Apocalyps*, was published in Amsterdam in 1611, followed by another edition in 1615.[59] A third edition, *The Revelation of S. John*, was issued at Leyden in 1616 and thereafter was reprinted at Amsterdam in 1644 and at London in the same year.[60] *Scholia in Canticorum* came out at Basel 1614, and *A Commentary on the Canticles* at London in 1644.[61] *A Most Comfortable Exposition of the Prophecie of Daniel* was printed at Amsterdam in 1635 and reprinted at London in 1644.[62] His *Workes*, published in London in 1644, included the above material on Revelation, Daniel, and Canticles.[63] Several popularizations of Brightman's works were issued as tracts during the early 1640's.[64]

Brightman's interpretation of Revelation consists of some nine hundred pages of sustained exposition of the bizarre symbolism of the book. Essentially his was an attempt to correlate "events" in ecclesiastical history with the symbols of the "trumpets" and the "vials." His own interpretation of Revelation he modestly thought to be the "fourth Vial" by which the "darkness of the mindes of men is enlightened."[65] Most notable was his conception that the thousand-year reign of Christ had been inaugurated in 1300 and had been increasingly manifest since that day: "This is the Kingdom of Christ, when he ruleth in the

[59] A. W. Pollard and G. R. Redgrave, *A Short-Title Catalogue of [English] Books . . . 1475-1640* (London, 1926), nos. 3754 and 3755.

[60] Pollard and Redgrave no. 3756; D. Wing, *Short-Title Catalogue . . .* (New York, 1945), B 4692, B 4693.

[61] Wing B 4681.

[62] Pollard and Redgrave no. 3753; see Wing B 4679.

[63] Wing B 4679. There were also other printed works by Brightman— e.g., *The Art of Self-Denial* (B 4680) —but they were not manifestly apocalyptic.

[64] Three examples are *Reverend Mr. Brightmans Judgment, or Prophecies . . .* (London, n.d.), *A Revelation Of Mr. Brightmans Revelation* (London, 1641), and *Brightmans Predictions And Prophesies* (n.p.p., 1641).

[65] *The Workes of . . .* (London, 1644), 536-538.

midst of any people, and swayeth them with the Scepter of his word. And this is indeed the most true Empire and kingdom of any nation, when it is subjected to Christs Empire alone, and when it is governed by his conduct and command alone."[66] Brightman's Millennium, then, was in the process of being realized, and he implied that it would exist in completeness after 1690, when the "Dragon" (the Turks) would be destroyed.[67] The new Jerusalem (described in Revelation 22) would be an "earthly paradise" where men would enjoy "a more cleare vision of God," though not that glorious vision reserved for the saints in heaven.[68] The dates proposed by Brightman are significant, for they underlay the explicit predictions in certain of the sermons to parliament. They should not distract attention, however, from his conception of a temporal Millennium in continuity with the preceding history and in part but direct fulfillment of events in the seventeenth century. In this regard Brightman was typical of most millenarians within the ranks of the brotherhood, few of whom (if any) expected a radical transformation of heaven and earth at the inauguration of the thousand-year reign of Christ.

Joseph Mead (or Mede), a contemporary of the preachers to the Long Parliament, was another major influential source of the apocalypticism and millenarianism within the Puritanism of the civil war years.[69] Mead belonged to a later generation than Brightman. The older man stood in the Elizabethan puritan tradition, although his work came to have its great currency only in the Stuart period. Born in 1586, Mead was admitted in 1602 to Christ's College, Cam-

[66] *Ibid.*, 824.

[67] *Ibid.*, 831. Cf. Daniel 12:12. In his analysis of Daniel 11:26ff. Brightman found the history of the Jews written under symbols. The end would come in 1650 (i.e., 3½ = 1290 + 360 [Julian] = 1650), which would signal the beginning of the overthrow of the Turks (*ibid.*, 967). This destruction would be completed by about 1695. This was an interpretation reinforced by the Song of Solomon 6 (cf. *ibid.*, 1050).

[68] *Ibid.*, 877ff. (quote from 883).

[69] See the *DNB*. Alexander Gordon, the author of the article, argues for "Mead," not "Mede."

bridge, where Daniel Rogers of that strongly puritan family was his tutor. Thus his mature life was set within the context of the Stuart church and dissent from it. By 1613 he was a Fellow of Christ's College, and from the next year until his death in 1638 he held the Greek lectureship at Cambridge which had been founded by Sir Walter Mildmay. He seems to have been without personal ambition, and he was not a supporter of any party. Suspected of Puritanism, in reality he appears to have been loyal to both doctrine and usage of the Church of England. His biographer maintains that he was sympathetic to Durie's irenic goals, if not to certain of his naive schemes. Mead's magnum opus, *Clavis Apocalyptica*, was published in 1627 and again in 1632, both times at Cambridge.[70] The rest of his writings were published posthumously. A translation of *Clavis* was printed in 1643 and again in 1650 under the title *The Key of the Revelation*.[71] The first portion of *Diatribae, Discourses* appeared in 1642, and a further part in 1652.[72] *Daniels Weeks* came out in 1643, *The Apostasy of the Latter Times* in 1641.[73] His *Works* appeared in several editions, the first in 1648.[74]

Mead's technical study of Revelation was meant to be just that. He resolutely declined to draw predictive inferences from it—at least in the course of the study itself.[75] Alexander Gordon summarizes the distinctiveness of Mead's approach to Revelation in this way: "He has the merit of perceiving that a thorough determination of the structural character of the Apocalypse must be a preliminary to any sound interpretation of it."[76] Mead's "key" was to analyze "the Synchronisme and order of the prophecies of the Revelation according as the things were to be accomplished, resting on no supposed interpretation, (as of a ground layed) or fore-judgeing of the falling out of ac-

---

[70] Pollard and Redgrave nos. 17766, 17767.
[71] Wing M 1600, M 1601.   [72] Wing M 1596, M 1598.
[73] Wing M 1595, M 1590-93.   [74] Wing M 1585-89.
[75] Some of Mead's comments in the *Diatribae* do not evidence this same judicious restraint and caution.
[76] *DNB.*

tions; but firmly demonstrated out of the very characters of the visions inserted by the Spirit of God of set purpose, and accordingly in a clear Scheme presented to view . . . ."[77] Mead noted that the simple chronological order of visions could not be accepted as the principle of interpretation because events must be narrated sequentially even if they occur contemporaneously.[78] It was therefore necessary to search out the structure of the book: "The order it self is not to be conformed to every aptnes of interpretation, according to the will of the interpreter; but according to the Idoea of this chronicall order framed before hand. . . ."[79] With the vision of the whore (Revelation 17:2ff.) as his basic starting point, and with the understanding that the "seals" and the "trumpets" together provided a chronology for Christian history, it simply remained for him to "synchronize" the remaining symbols with this structure.[80]

This insight constituted the substance of *The Key of the Revelation*. Mead took an important step in rejecting a sequential construction of the book, like Brightman's, which was basically arbitrary. In proposing to analyze the book according to its structure, Mead was pursuing an approach in principle close to literary criticism. Historical criticism, of course, has made the further assumption that apocalyptic books through their symbolism chiefly interpret the author's past and present, rather than the reader's or interpreter's. This additional perspective Mead had no reason to adopt, and his tightly argued "key" became the basis for a *Commentary on the Apocalypse*, presuming that what was revealed therein was the course of Christian history. Mead's rehearsal of this history, like Brightman's, is of interest primarily because of the uses made of the English Protestant conception of the decline of the

[77] *The Key of the Revelation* (London, 1643), 1. Cf. on the same page: "By a Synchronisme of prophecies I meane, when the things therein designed run along in the same time; as if thou shouldst call it an agreement in time or age: because prophecies of things falling out in the same time run on in time together, or Synchronize."
[78] *Ibid.*, 27ff.   [79] *Ibid.*, 27.   [80] *Ibid.*, 1f.

church and its anticipated delivery in Stuart England. The history itself was commonplace, but the sense of proportion, significance, and expectation it displays suggests the kind of insights that were derived from it within puritan circles.

Mead the scholar, irenically disposed toward all but the Papacy, pointedly restrained himself from offering predictions deduced from his scheme. As a proof of his integrity he included a discussion of the ancient traditions which rejected, as well as those which supported, belief in a Millennium.[81] He cited in support Justin and others as followers of the Apostles, but he placed primary emphasis on Daniel and Revelation. Mead noted the openness of "learned Hebrews" toward a kingdom of Christ and a day of judgment as a strong instrumental argument in favor of the belief.[82] He thought such doctrines useful as apologetics toward them since the reign of Christ would fulfill Jewish hopes and since accepting them removed a decisive stumbling block: wresting out of context prophecies which clearly referred to a second coming in order to apply them to His first.[83]

The rigor and ingenuity with which Mead analyzed Revelation are of some interest in their own right and deserve attention. But Mead's studies, however detached he may have been in pursuing them, had importance of another sort among his contemporaries. Under pressure from the Laudian church, the Stuart puritans found their own particular struggles explained within this eschatological framework. For most clerical puritans the chronological speculation provided one method of weighing the significance of the issues they judged important. Religious imagination—a phenomenon foreign in its traditional form to the educated of our day—enabled them to take this symbolism with great seriousness. Obviously they derived inspiration and comfort from it without requiring it to yield exact predictions according to scientific criteria. The

81 *Ibid.*, Part 2, 121 ff.   82 *Ibid.*, 129-135.
83 *Ibid.*, 134-135.

preface to Mead's *Apostasy* supports this contention. There William Twisse wrote that he frankly expected Mead's insight to be bettered. He also made reference to discussions about the tract involving the patriarch Richard Sibbes, who had died in the 1630's. Apparently Stephen Marshall had also commended the discourse.[84] Arthur Jackson expressed one kind of interest in Mead's work which was widespread among his clerical contemporaries:

> The book it selfe gives much light for the understanding of many obscure Passages in that sweet and comfortable Prophecie, and though Master Medes opinion concerning the thousand years of the seventh Trumpet be singular from that which hath beene most generally received by Expositors of best esteem, and I conceive he hath no just ground, yet he therein delivers his judgment with such modestie and moderation that I think the Printing of it will not be perillous. . . .[85]

Speculation of the kind undertaken by Brightman and Mead nourished a sense of impending momentous events. It also hardened into apocalyptic convictions. In this way millenarianism melded with mythologies of English history, taking on nationalistic overtones. At the same time it appears to have become more programmatic. Mead's work —and very likely Brightman's, too—was certainly not intended to be a trumpet call to action of a revolutionary sort within Stuart society. But with relatively little change of emphasis such explorations in apocalyptic imagery could become instruments and symbols serving activist purposes in very immediate ways.

Several points must be made absolutely clear about Brightman and Mead insofar as their publications are viewed as sources for the metamorphosis within Stuart Puritanism during the civil war era which is disclosed in the sermons preached to parliament. First of all, their sustained

[84] J. Mead, *The Apostasy of the Latter Times* (London, 1641), "Preface."
[85] J. Mead, *The Key of the Revelation,* page opposite the title-page.

interpretations and applications of Daniel and Revelation derived relevance from the already corporate consciousness of England as it had been shaped in the secular and religious life of the nation. Foxe's *Book of Martyrs* was ordained in Revelation according to Brightman. It was no less present, if more subtly so, in the *Clavis* as Mead applied it. Brightman and Mead were part of this earlier but still existing tradition, although they marked a further development of it.

In the second place, there developed under the early Stuarts a broad consensus regarding the Millennium which, for all the varied forms it took, was rooted in certain common assumptions. Both Brightman and Mead anticipated temporal spans of a thousand years, that is, millennia in strict continuity with preceding historical epochs. They were conceived of as more than a reform of the present and less than a completion of time itself. This was so much the way Brightman viewed the matter, at least in his reading of the Apocalypse, that he declared the reign of Christ to have already existed for some three hundred years. History would not end but would continue in a purified condition, with the "principle of evil" in bondage to Christ until the final judgment. Furthermore, Christ's reign would be "spiritual" and therefore direct. Rule by Christ was seldom construed to require His immediate personal presence. On this point the Millennium anticipated within Stuart puritan ranks did not conform to either of the later and mutually exclusive options typical of the nineteenth century—pre- and post-millenarianism. Within this general climate of expectancy various particular constructions were espoused and different series of symbols utilized. The important point, however, is that serious apocalyptic interpretation of Daniel and Revelation, emphasizing an imminent Millennium, was very much alive in seventeenth-century England within the universities and among the divines who were inclined toward Puritanism. This tradition was the source for the apocalyptic and millenarian sentiments disclosed in the preaching to the Long Parliament. It consisted basically in a belief that Christ's temporal reign, become imminent, would represent a transformation of the order in which believers lived, rather than a simple extension of the morally ambiguous past and present into the future. Since it was agreed that Christ would soon manifest himself in a return and rule, the precise form of his appearance did not need to be—indeed, could not be—fully delineated.

THE INDEPENDENCY OF THE INDEPENDENTS

The ready availability within puritan culture of these immediate sources for apocalypticism and millenarianism helps to explain why it was possible for this speculation to become so prominent within the preaching to the Long Parliament as early as 1642. To ask about its significance for understanding the development of Puritanism during this decade, however, entails other considerations. Most frequently these opinions seem to have been held by those preachers to the Long Parliament who were denominated "Independents." As a hypothesis it may be proposed that through the Independents this speculative and apocalyptic exegesis of the scriptures, with the derivative millenarianism, moved from the background to the foreground of Puritanism as the differentia of a party within the movement. Evidence for substantiating this thesis was already implicit in the preceding discussion of the millenarianism present in the parliamentary sermons. Of the dozen examples cited in that section, seven preachers were without question commonly thought to be Independents, including such prominent figures as Thomas Goodwin, Joseph Caryl, and William Strong. Reference was also made to Stephen Marshall, whose equivocal role in the brotherhood has been discussed. Others, like Stanley Gower, were probably drawn toward Independency, if not wholly identified with it. In any case, the present study does not argue that *only* those who were to *become* Independents were apocalyptically oriented and millenarian in their convictions or that *only* millenarians would later become associated with this party within the brotherhood. Rather, the point is that the puritan divines were responding in basically different ways to the stresses of civil conflict. Although prophetic assumptions and imagery continued to be valid for many, others came to be convinced that apocalyptic language and symbolism were alone adequate to the task of making the times comprehensible. On this view English Independency, conceived in terms of the language its adherents used to make intelligible their experience of turmoil, was coming into being out of Puritanism during the 1640's. The broader puritan movement was simply proving to be incapable of retaining the allegiance of all its clerical members for that reformist program of national regeneration which had been its rallying standard.[86]

There are additional kinds of evidence that may be marshalled in support of this thesis. Outside the preaching to the Long Parliament one may discover tantalizing references and some surviving materials which only make sense if one views consistent millenarianism as a theological expression of emerging Independency. Within the limits of the present inquiry these must be taken merely as corroborative citations and not as the fruits of a full historical survey.

One kind of evidence is provided by the prominence of apocalypticism and millenarianism among the expatriates in the Low Countries during the later 1630's who became Independents upon their return to England early in the next decade. The important tract *A Glimpse Of Sions Glory*[87] appears to have originated at a fast of humilia-

---

[86] Such an understanding of how the clerical Independents discovered themselves and were brought together by their need to comprehend the times is important in two respects: (1) it makes necessary a dynamic conception of the relationship between the preachers and the revolutionary context in which Independency coalesced, and (2) it suggests both the manner in which religious labels developed political currency (especially after the first civil war) and the reason why these labels must be used with great caution when applied to political groupings (cf. *supra*, n. 3, 106).

[87] (London, 1641).

tion in Holland at the gathering of a church.[88] Its author was probably Thomas Goodwin,[89] whose contribution to the exhortation of the Long Parliament has been carefully noted. *The Personall Raigne of Christ Upon Earth*[90] was penned by John Archer, an associate of Goodwin's with the same English expatriates at Arnheim.[91] Apparently he died before recrossing the Channel, although other writings of his were also published in England. In some respects the ubiquitous John Canne should be understood in this light as a contributor to the development of Independency.[92]

A second type of evidence is to be found in the manifest dependence of English Independency on John Cotton of New England.[93] Of all the New England divines, he was accounted the closest to the English party; he was a father in Christ to many and corresponded with them regularly. Although his rivals—Thomas Hooker, for instance, or Thomas Shepard—were not without admirers, it was John Cotton who was considered soul-brother to the English Independents. Cotton's own apocalyptic and millenarian streak has often been overlooked. Several of his works published during the early 1640's—works which have no parallel among the writings of men like Thomas Hooker —display a considerable fascination with these questions. *The Powring out of the Seven vials: or, An Exposition of the Sixteenth Chapter of the Revelation, with an Application of it to our Times,* originally a series of expository sermons delivered in the colonial Boston, prominently touches upon themes such as those which have received attention

[88] *A Glimpse of Sions Glory*, 3, 7, 33.
[89] I have argued this point fully in *Church History*, xxxi/1 (March 1962), 66-73.
[90] (London, 1641).
[91] See Thomas Edwards, *Antapologia* (London, 1644), 23, 187.
[92] See my article "Another Look at John Canne," *Church History*, xxxiii/1 (March 1964), 34-48.
[93] See G. F. Nuttall, *Visible Saints, The Congregational Way, 1640-1660* (Oxford, 1957), 14-17; also R. Baillie, *A Dissuasive from the Errours of the Time* (London, 1645).

in this chapter.[94] *The Churches Resurrection, or the Opening of the Fift and sixt verses of the 20 Chapter of the Revelation* applies many of these same themes more directly.[95] It is not too much to claim that within these writings Cotton portrayed the Bay Colony experiment as a proleptical participation in the millennial reign or kingdom.[96]

Other evidence for the hypothesis exists in materials which had their source in the developing Independency of the civil war years and the Interregnum. For example, three sermons allegedly preached by Thomas Goodwin (probably during the 1640's) were published—undoubtedly without his authorization—in 1654 and 1655 "for Truths sake," that is, to make it clear that the distinguished Independents then sitting at Cromwell's right hand and holding important university positions had indeed been the immediate inspiration for the millenarianism which had since manifested itself in the Fifth Monarchy Movement. The first of these tracts was *A Sermon Of The Fifth Monarchy* ("Proving by Invincible Arguments, That the Saints shall have a Kingdom here on Earth, Which is yet to come, after the Fourth Monarchy is destroy'd by the Sword of the Saints, the followers of the Lamb").[97] Two other previous lectures by Goodwin were brought out together as *The World to Come* ("Or, The Kingdome of Christ asserted. In two Expository Lectures on Ephes. 1.21, 22, verses. Prooving That between the state of this World as now it is, and the state of things after the day of Judgment, when God shall be all in all: There is a world to come which is of purpose, and in a more especiall manner appointed for Jesus Christ to be King, and wherein he shall more eminently Reign").[98] Apparently they had been preached at St. Antholin's in London in years past.

It is possible to give a plausible account of how these sermons or lectures by Goodwin reached print since they strongly suggest that he had been publicly engaged in ex-

[94] (London, 1645).   [95] (London, 1642).
[96] *The Churches Resurrection* . . . , 9ff., 23ff.
[97] (London, 1654).   [98] (London, 1655).

plicit millenarian preaching during the early years of the civil war. Undoubtedly they had been copied into the numerous "commonplace books" of the day by eager listeners. Probably they circulated in this form among the sectarians and radical millenarians of the late 1640's and the early 1650's, for both groups wished to make clear that they looked for their initial inspiration to the distinguished Independents, men since become respectable. Just as *A Glimpse of Sions Glory* had probably been printed without Goodwin's permission, or possibly against his wishes, so it is likely that these pieces were in no fashion authorized for circulation by him. They do represent excellent evidence, however, that Thomas Goodwin, the chief English Independent divine of the 1640's, had been preaching the imminent reign of Christ that would be inaugurated in the gathered covenant churches. In this light we should read John Rogers's plaintive reproach of the distinguished Independents who had abandoned that cause by the 1650's when it had become an embarrassment. The point is that they were responsible for the millenarianism even if they were not directly to blame for the crass form it assumed in the Fifth Monarchy Movement.[99]

Jeremiah Burroughs (d. 1646), a close associate of Goodwin's and a prominent preacher to the Long Parliament, was also implicated in these activities. A tract published in 1675 supports this allegation. There is no reason to doubt its attribution to Burroughs, although it must have been preserved in "commonplace books" throughout the intervening years. The title was *Jerusalems Glory Breaking forth into the World* ("Being a Scripture-Discovery Of the New Testament Church, In the Latter Days Immediately before the Second Coming of Christ").[100] Others like William Bridge, Joseph Symonds, Nathaniel Homes, and Henry Burton disclosed similar convictions before "sundry of the

[99] See John Canne, *The Time of the End* (London, 1657), "An Epistolary Perambulation to Everyone by John Rogers." On this theme, see my "Comment on 'Two Roads to the Puritan Millennium,'" *Church History*, xxxii/3 (Sept. 1963), 339-343.

[100] (London, 1675).

House of Commons," in sermons which in temper, tone, and intent were closely related to these extra-parliamentary tracts of Goodwin's and Burrough's and which suggest that these items were not simply the products of personal idiosyncrasy.[101]

A final kind of evidence for the apocalyptic form and millenarian content of Independency is preserved in the writings of contemporary critics. Robert Baillie, for example, in *A Dissuasive from the Errours of the Time*,[102] devoted an entire chapter to the proposition that "The Thousand Yeares of Christ his visible Raigne upon Earth is against Scripture."[103] He termed the Independents "Chiliasts," and prominently included the belief among "all the Sparckles of new light wherewith our Brethren doe intertaine their owne and the peoples fancie."[104] *The Revelation Unrevealed*[105] also illustrates the response of contemporaries to Stuart millenarianism. Generally attributed to Bishop Joseph Hall, it was an eminently sane discussion. Its author, not as dogmatically hostile a critic as Baillie, actually looked for a "more flourishing state" of the church on earth before the final return of Christ—which he expected soon—but he dared not presume to read the times.[106] Thus his criticism of the millennialists was that "they put a meerly-literall construction upon the prophesies and promises of Scripture, which the holy Ghost intended onely to be spiritually understood."[107] Although Hall did not make it his purpose to identify the leading figures who were involved, he appears to have regarded Alsted and Mead as immediate authorities for the heresy, Archer as author of its most characteristic exposition, and Cotton and Burroughs as prominent advocates.[108] Thus during the decade of the 1640's Independents seem clearly to have been regarded as proponents of the belief in an imminent Millennium within an England torn by civil war.

[101] See Ch. II, 43-52, and Appendix Three, 275ff.
[102] (London, 1645).   [103] *A Dissuasive* . . . , Ch. 11, 224-252.
[104] *Ibid.*, 224.
[105] (London, 1650).   [106] *The Revelation Unrevealed*, 10-12.
[107] *Ibid.*, 102.   [108] See *ibid.*, 57ff. and 71ff.

In these terms it is possible to defend the thesis that Stuart Puritanism underwent differentiation during the 1640's in response to the relaxation of the Laudian repression and the experience of civil struggles. The poles of the division were basically different readings of history: one continuing the prophetic and reformist emphasis of the earlier movement; the other, apocalyptic and transformist in its language and symbolism, frequently leading to espousal of a naked millenarianism. This latter, more radical principle of intelligibility for the times was expressed politically and ecclesiologically as an option—Independency—which was as vague and inclusive a designation as its theological expression suggests it might have been. For this reason the Independents have always seemed an anomalous grouping, and they have consequently constituted a stumbling block to satisfactory religious and political interpretation of the decade of the 1640's.[109]

Implied in this thesis about the relationship of Independency to Puritanism is an observation about the conventional explanation for the origin of the group. Generally it is held that Independency primarily grew out of disputes over specific issues essentially involving church polity and practice; it seems likely that these particular issues should be seen as derived from and sustained by convictions concerning the character of that historical epoch and its significance within sacred history. The thesis also makes it plausible to argue that the founding of "gathered churches" by the Independents, whether in the Low Countries or London, must be understood fundamentally as specific anticipation of a broader reign of Christ. Additionally it locates very precisely continuities between one prominent wing of Puritanism and the sectarian ferment

[109] G. P. Gooch is one of the very few interpreters who have candidly recognized the prominence of millenarianism within the English social scene of the early as well as late 1640's: "At the basis of the creed of every religious body of the time, except the Presbyterians, lay the Millenarian idea." *English Democratic Ideas* (New York, 1959), 108.

229

swirling around it in the general population.[110] Finally, it provides an explanation for the Independents' lack of interest in constructing a national church. In these ways this thesis significantly revises and clarifies perception of the internal ideological structure of Puritanism during the civil war period.

CONCLUSION

The present chapter has attempted to put the preaching before the Long Parliament to advantage in gauging the development of Puritanism that was occasioned by the civil struggles of the decade. The conclusion is simply that during the period under review a fundamental differentiation occurred within Puritanism (that is, among the puritan divines) which is incidentally recorded in and displayed through the sermons. This change was manifested in at least two ways. On one level the brotherhood of preachers experienced inner divisiveness, which, within parliamentary preaching, was expressed through the contrast between prophetic-reformist and apocalyptic-transformist conceptions of the times. These alternative convictions led to extensive debates over such matters as church polity, which have usually been interpreted as the substantial issues on which the movement foundered. At another level—the domain of social policy—there no longer existed a shared consensus on the expressed goal of a reformed nation, the achievement of which would have required concerted, if not united, action from the brotherhood if its aims were to be achieved. Some divines asserted, indeed, that a more radical transformation—a subordination of the realm to Christ—was to be expected. Such revolutionary claims at least potentially legitimated the destruction of all established order. Put simply, in substantially disagreeing about the program Puritanism might offer to the times, the preachers further found themselves no longer in control

[110] The preceding quotation from Gooch attests to the importance of the millenarian substratum for the sectarianism of the civil war era.

of the implications to be drawn from their rhetoric. These two levels of consequences require additional attention.

Almost without exception students of Puritanism have failed to recognize or take sufficiently seriously the differentiation of the movement prior to and during the early years of the first civil war. It is a common, though unspoken, assumption that the brotherhood was internally coherent with regard to all but relatively trivial issues until challenged both by events following the first civil war and by the intransigence of the sectarians on the periphery of the movement. Apocalypticism and millenarianism have been discerned in the New Model Army and later among the Fifth Monarchists, but these ideas have been treated as if they came from hidden sources or were spontaneously generated. In either case they have been interpreted as if they were late and peripheral heresies. This study provides proof that such a construction is manifestly inadequate. Radical religious ideas were promulgated from the parliamentary pulpit by university-trained preachers beginning early in the decade. Although a formal doctrinal structure of piety might continue to make the brotherhood *seem* to be united, the voices espousing apocalypticism and millenarianism within the movement indicate that in fact divergent parties were forming and claiming allegiance from the divines. These parties were not so much oriented toward immediate political action as they were determined by types of response to the stresses of civil struggle. These responses are registered in the religious language the preachers employed. Thus the differentiation within the clerical brotherhood was signaled by the public expression of the apocalyptic and millenarian elements latent in English Puritanism. When subsequently preached to the soldiers in the army, or expounded by tub-preachers, or worked into pamphlets for the booksellers, these elements were liberated from the theological structure which had imposed restraints upon them and served to veil their radical implications. By the early 1640's at least, the brotherhood had already begun to split decisively and to explain that break with those very ideas which, when rendered commonplace in the public forum, would scandalize the original authors of them.

The second level of consequences concerns the impetus toward revolutionary activity which became inevitable once it was clear that the brotherhood could not sustain the common and unifying goal of a reformed nation. In broad terms, the anticipation of the apocalyptic kingdom was the basis for a rhetoric which must be judged to have been wholly destructive of authority within Stuart society.[111] Although manifest references might be made, for example, to Christ as "king" or "ruler," the effective result was a denigration first of Charles I as the accepted king or ruler within the realm and then of a parliament composed of other than the saints. This was precisely the revolutionary import of this language, which in its effect went far beyond its explicit meaning. To work out this point in terms of the actual rhetoric used and to illustrate it adequately would require a separate monograph. In the present study it should suffice to reproduce a passage of some length from Stephen Marshall's *A Sacred Panegyrick*,[112] preached to an extraordinary thanksgiving on January 18, 1643-4, which celebrated the unity of the parliamentary coalition. Marshall's text was I Chronicles 12:38-40—the assembly at the accession of David—a text suited to the event since it was occasioned by delivery of the common cause from numerous designs and plots against it.

> But it may bee you will say, We want a David, to make the paralell full; we want a David to bee with us, a King who might concurre with us, and we with him in the same business; I confesse indeed, that in the *literall* sense God hath not *yet* made us so blessed, the Sonnes of Belial have stollen away both his Majesties Person, and affection from us, but even that is the thing which we contend for, that we might recover him out of their hands;

[111] G. F. Nuttall has commented upon the connection between revolutionary rhetoric and biblical apocalypticism in *The Welsh Saints, 1640-1660* (Oxford, 1957), 46ff.

[112] (London, 1644).

the expence of all our treasure, and all our blood hath bin to that end that he might have the wicked removed from his throne. . . . (2 Samuel 23:3-4.) And as we have in our Covenant solemnly sworne (so much as in us lies) to preserve and maintain his person and authority, in the defense of Libertie and Religion, so if God have any delight in him, and to doe us good by him, hee will in the end incline his heart unto such Counsels, that hee shall come home, and make this paralell full, and even bee the light of our Israel, and the breath of our Nostrills: But in the meane time, wee do not want a David to suit this David in the Text, we have here the true David, of whom that David was in this very thing a Type, that is, the Lord Jesus Christ, whom wee are endeavouring to set upon his throne, that hee might be Lord and King in his Israel, over his Church, amongst us: And as Davids person, and Kingdome, were but types of our Lord Christ and his Kingdome; so this great joy and unanimity of heart, which met in all these at Davids Coronation in Hebron, was but a type of that rejoycing and gladnesse of heart, which should be among the Nations, when there should bee the like concurrence of the Nobles, and Commons, and Princes, and Ministers, and Citizens, with one heart, to set up the Lord Christ, to be Lord and King over them.[113]

In one sense no exception could be taken to this as a measured interpretation of the occasion in terms of conventional biblical symbolism. But the tendency or inner logic of the rhetoric was to qualify radically the status of Charles as King and thus to undermine his authority in a decisive manner. Implied in Marshall's rhetoric was a further question: what need for an earthly monarch if a heavenly king be at hand? In this way even such relatively moderate sentiments as those articulated by the equivocal Marshall testify that the apocalypticism and millenarianism which were clearly present in some of the preaching to the Long

---

[113] *A Sacred Panegyrick*, 5-6.

Parliament worked toward revolutionary ends, whether or not they were directly intended to do so. Stated very simply, whereas prophetic and reformist puritans sought merely to make the times intelligible, another strain within Puritanism labored to interpret the times according to a calculus which required their basic transformation. That latter rhetoric, in effect if not intent, was basically disruptive of all acknowledged authority.[114] Thus rendered ineffective, Puritanism could play no constructive role in the return to a durable and stable order because the most radical and revolutionary assumptions remained unqualified and unchecked. The spilled blood of Charles, no less than the creation of a "nominated parliament" and a "Protector," were implied in the sponsorship of such rhetoric before the members of the Long Parliament. This phenomenon in its broader aspect is, of course, what astonished Thomas Hobbes.

In the present monograph on the pulpit in the Long Parliament, such broader interpretations of Puritanism have only been suggested. It would be inappropriate to devote more attention to these larger issues in the context of this restricted study. It is evident, however, that the perspective on Puritanism here commended does stand as a corrective to some common approaches to, and interpretations of, the movement. It calls into question those descriptions of Puritanism which have presumed that the movement was essentially static and did not undergo any basic changes during the decade of the 1640's. The sermons exhibit strains and tensions in the language used by the brotherhood that direct the student to manifold materials

[114] In these pages it will be evident that the author is indebted to the writings of Michael Walzer, especially *The Revolution of the Saints* (Cambridge, Mass., 1965) but also "Puritanism as a Revolutionary Ideology," *History and Theory*, III/1 (1963), 59-90. Walzer, in my view, devotes too little attention to the manifest content of puritan rhetoric and inordinate attention to the latent consequences, and his selection of evidence may be termed arbitrary. At the same time, his studies are enormously suggestive and help to focus analysis of the relationship between English Puritanism and the public realm, especially during the 1640's.

(not here under review) which corroborate that judgment. The perspective likewise calls into question those religious interpretations of Puritanism which have placed excessive emphasis upon technical issues of church polity as the fundamental source of division within the movement. Such constructions appear to have been derived from those "whiggish," denominationally oriented church historians who have failed to recognize the radical engagement of the divines in the turmoil of the nation. The perspective offered here also undercuts those interpretations of Puritanism which have played up continuities between that movement and the assumptions undergirding liberal society. A mediate and long-term legacy there may have been; certainly there was no immediate infusion of ideals or concepts taken over without remainder. Finally, this perspective requires acknowledgment of the latent revolutionary impetus within Puritanism. Without doubt, however, puritan literature—for all of the direct as well as indirect political influence it may have exerted during the civil wars—requires interpretation as first and foremost the expression of a manifest religious movement.

Thus the program of humiliations and thanksgivings in the Long Parliament permits a demonstration that reference may properly and correctly be made to Caroline Puritanism. It was a social movement with principles of intelligibility derived from theological conceptions and expressed in religious language. At the same time, it is necessary to recognize that precisely during the civil wars Stuart Puritanism experienced a differentiation and decline which effectively marked the end of it as a significant, influential, and coherent social movement. That broader story is writ small in the preaching to representative England sitting at Westminster.

APPENDIX ONE

Calendar and Checklist of Humiliations, Thanksgivings, and Preachers in the Long Parliament

THIS WORKING list represents an attempt to establish the dates of the humiliations and thanksgivings explicitly authorized and held by the two houses of the Long Parliament between November 1640 and the expulsion of the Rump on April 20, 1653. A further purpose is to identify the men who preached at them. The terminal date for study of the sermons in the preceding chapters is February 1648-9. That terminus is chosen on the basis of major and concurrent changes both in the realm and in this particular institution. Together these changes fundamentally affected preaching to the Long Parliament: Commons was purged during December 1648; Charles was put to death on January 30, 1648-9; the Lords did not meet after early February, 1648-9; the program of monthly humiliations was ended in April 1649; a significantly different generation of clerics had become prominent in the preaching to parliament; the printing of the exhortations virtually ceased after the beginning of 1649, rendering them inaccessible for study of content.

The primary sources for this calendar and checklist are the *Journals of the House of Commons* and the *Journals of the House of Lords*, as well as the actual sermons identified in print, a list of which constitutes Appendix Two. Certain booksellers obligingly issued summary calendars covering particular periods. The celebrations through April 24, 1644, are compiled in Thomas Case's *Gods Rising, His Enemies Scattering* (London, 1644), 53ff., and John Strickland's *Gods Work of Mercy* (London, 1644), 34ff. These lists are identical, and both were printed for Luke Fawne. Regular fasts between January 29, 1644-5, and December 31, 1645, and thanksgivings between September 7, 1641, and

March 12, 1645-6, may be found listed in John Whincop's *Gods Call to Weeping and Mourning* (London, 1646), 51-52. This was published for Nathanael Web(b) and William Grantham. The celebrations through December 30, 1646, are enumerated in William Goode's *Jacob Raised* (London, 1647) following page 29 and in Thomas Horton's *Sinne's Discovery and Revenge* (London, 1646) at the end of the sermon on page 40. The former was printed for Nathanael Web(b) and William Grantham, the latter for Samuel Gellibrand.

The official *Journals* are not wholly satisfactory for establishing precise dates and particular preachers. The proposal for a fast, for instance, may not be followed by an entry to indicate whether the initial motion was implemented. Moreover, preachers were nominated irregularly; indeed, there seem to have been occasions, perhaps increasingly frequent, on which last minute substitutions took place.[1] On some few other occasions, apparently out of displeasure with a sermon, a house would refuse to acknowledge it and fail to call for its publication.[2] Generally the *Journals of the House of Commons* is more consistent than the *Journals of the House of Lords* in reporting these matters. In the pages of the latter it is not made clear whether in particular months the fast program was abridged or ignored altogether; in some months only one preacher seems to have exhorted the house. Finally, during the latter years of the decade the Lords fasts were often moved from Westminster Abbey and most frequently held at St. Martin-in-the-Fields.

One purpose of this calendar and checklist is to establish the approximate number of formal fasts within the Long Parliament—that is, a reasonably accurate overview

[1] See e.g., Stephen Marshall, *The Sinne of Hardnesse of Heart* (London, 1648), 1.

[2] See, e.g., Nathaniel Ward, *A Sermon Preached . . . Commons . . . June 30, 1647* (London, 1647), "Epistle." A more dramatic instance was the reception of William Dell's sermon *Right Reformation* (London, 1646). Both incidents have been mentioned in the text of this study (*supra*, 88 and 92).

of the preaching institution—as background to study of the published exhortations which originated in them. Appendix Two is a calendar of the sermons which have been identified in print.

Each entry in this calendar takes the following form:[3]

Date — Occasion
preacher (s) to

Commons   Joint Affairs   Lords

Nov. 17, 1640 — Initial Fast
Burges, C.
Marshall, S.

Nov. 29, 1640 — Receiving of the Sacrament
Gauden, J.
[Morley, G.]

Sept. 7, 1641—Thanksgiving for Union between England and Scotland
Burroughs, J.
Marshall, S.

Nov. 5, 1641 — Powder Plot Anniversary
Burges, C.

Dec. 22, 1641 — Fast for the Irish Crisis
Calamy, E.   Ussher, J.
Marshall, S.

Feb. 23, 1641-2 — Initial Monthly Fast
Calamy, E.
Marshall, S.

March 30, 1642 — Monthly Fast
Ash, S.
Burges, C.

April 27 1642 — Monthly Fast
Caryl, J.
Goodwin, T.

[3] Brackets around the name of a preacher signify that the sermon has not been identified and probably was not published. A question mark signifies that the entry is uncertain.

Commons	Joint Affairs	Lords

May 25, 1642 — *Monthly Fast*
Harris, R.
Sedgwick, O.

June 29, 1642 — *Monthly Fast*
Gouge, W.
Sedgwick, W.

July 27, 1642 — *Monthly Fast*
Hill, T.
Reynolds, E.

Aug. 31, 1642 — *Monthly Fast*
Carter, W.
[Downing]

Sept. 28, 1642 — *Monthly Fast*
Hodges, T.
Wilson, T.

Oct. 26, 1642 — *Monthly Fast*
Case, T.
Temple, T.

Nov. 5, 1642 — *Powder Plot Anniversary*
Newcomen, M.

Nov. 30, 1642 — *Monthly Fast*
Herle, C.
Vines, R.

Dec. 28, 1642 — *Monthly Fast*
Corbett, E.
Valentine, T.

Jan. 25, 1642-3 — *Monthly Fast*
Arrowsmith, J.
Whitaker, J.

Feb. 22, 1642-3 — *Monthly Fast*
Bridges, W.
Ellis, J.

Commons	Joint Affairs	Lords

March 29, 1643 — Monthly Fast
[Gibbons]
Lightfoot, J.

April 26, 1643 — Monthly Fast
Greenhill, W.
Ley, J.

May 31, 1643 — Monthly Fast
Cheynell, F.
Pe(a)rne, A.

June 15, 1643 — Thanksgiving for Discovery of Plot against Parliament and the City

Marshall, S.		Calamy, E.
Sedgwick, O.		Herle, C.

June 28, 1643 — Monthly Fast
Carter, T.
Palmer, H.

July 7, 1643 — Special Fast, Parliament and the Assembly
Bowles, O.
Newcomen, M.
[Twisse (?)]

July 21, 1643 — Fast for the Reformation of the Church
Hill, T.
Spurstowe, W.
[Vines]

July 26, 1643 — Monthly Fast
Conant, J.
Simpson, S.

Aug. 30, 1643 — Monthly Fast
Coleman, T.
Tuckney, A.

Sept. 25, 1643 — Covenant Convention
Henderson, A.
Nye, P.

Appendices

Commons	Joint Affairs	Lords

Sept. 27, 1643 — Monthly Fast
Burges, A.
Chambers, H.

Sept. 29, 1643 — Covenant-taking Ceremony
Coleman, T.

Oct. 6, 1643 — Covenant-taking Ceremony
Caryl, J.

Oct. 25, 1643 — Monthly Fast
Salwey, A.
Wilkinson, H.

Nov. 29, 1643 — Monthly Fast
Bridge, W.
Mewe, W.

Dec. 15, 1643 — Funeral for John Pym
Marshall, S.

Dec. 27, 1643 — Monthly Fast
Henderson, A.
Strickland, J.

Jan. 18, 1643-4 — Extraordinary Thanksgiving, Parliament, Assembly, etc.
Marshall, S.

Jan. 31, 1643-4 — Monthly Fast
Cawdrey, D.
Rutherford, S.

Feb. 28, 1643-4 — Monthly Fast
Baillie, R.
Young, T.

March 27, 1644 — Monthly Fast
Bond, J.
Gillespie, G.

April 9, 1644 — Thanksgiving for Waller's Victory
Case, T.
Sedgwick, O.

Appendices

Commons	Joint Affairs	Lords

April 23, 1644 — Thanksgiving for Fairfax's Victory
Caryl, J.
[Perne, A.]

April 24, 1644 — Monthly Fast
Greene, J.
Staunton, E.

May 29, 1644 — Monthly Fast
Hall, H.
Smith, P.

June 26, 1644 — Monthly Fast
Hardwick, H.
Hickes, G.

July 18, 1644 — Thanksgiving for Marston Moor, York
Henderson, A.
Vines, R.

July 31, 1644 — Monthly Fast
Gower, S.
[Rathband, W.]

Aug. 13, 1644 — Day of Humiliation for both Houses
Hill, T.
Palmer, H.

Aug. 28, 1644 — Monthly Fast
Reyner, W.
Tesdale, C.

Sept. 12, 1644 — Fast for Lines of Communication
Coleman, T.
Newcomen, M.

Sept. 25, 1644 — Monthly Fast
Proffet, N.
Seaman, L.

Oct. 22, 1644 — Extraordinary Solemn Fast

Commons	Lords
Calamy, E.	[Chambers, H.]
Sedgwick, O.	[Palmer, H.]
Vines, R.	[Temple, T.]

Appendices

Commons	Joint Affairs	Lords

Oct. 30, 1644 — Monthly Fast

| Scudder, H. | | [Smith, P.] |
| Woodcock, F. | | Staunton, E. |

Nov. 5, 1644 — Thanksgiving for Deliverance of New-castle and Tinmuth Castle; Powder Plot Anniversary

| Burges, A. | | Spurstowe, W. |
| Herle, C. | | Strickland, J. |

Nov. 27, 1644 — Monthly Fast

| Gipps, G. | | Hill, T. |
| Pickering, B. | | Wilkinson, H. |

Dec. 18, 1644 — Special Fast

	[Hill]	
	[Marshall]	
	[Sedgwick, O.]	

Dec. 25, 1644 — Monthly Fast

| Langley, J. | | Calamy, E. |
| Thorowgood, T. | | [Sedgwick, O.] |

Jan. 29, 1644-5 — Monthly Fast

| Walker, G. | | [Newcomen, M.] |
| Whincop, J. | | [Vines, R.] |

Feb. 26, 1644-5 — Monthly Fast

| Maynard, J. | | Ash, S. |
| [Nye, P.] | | [Perne, A.] |

March 12, 1644-5 — Thanksgiving for Victories

| | Arrowsmith, J. | |
| | Vines, R. | |

March 26, 1645 — Monthly Fast

| Goode, W. | | Cheynell, F. |
| Ward, J. | | Marshall, S. |

April 30, 1645 — Monthly Fast

| Burges, C. | | [Valentine, T.] |
| Marshall, S. | | [Ward (?)] |

244

Appendices

Commons	Joint Affairs	Lords

May 28, 1645 — Monthly Fast
Caryl, J.
[Ford, T.]

Henderson, A.
Whitaker, J.

June 19, 1645 — Thanksgiving for Naseby, Leicester
               Marshall, S.
               [Vines, R.]

June 25, 1645 — Monthly Fast
Byfield, R.
[Hodges, T.]

[Cawdrey, D.]
Rutherford, S.

July 22, 1645 — Thanksgiving for Rout of Goring, etc.
[Chambers, H.]
[Hickes, G.]

[Sedgwick, O.]
Ward, J.

July 30, 1645 — Monthly Fast
Coleman, T.
Woodcock, F.

Baillie, R.
[Hodges, T.]

Aug. 22, 1645 — Thanksgiving for Victories in the West
Bond, J.
Case, T.

Aug. 27, 1645 — Monthly Fast
[Caryl, J.]
Lightfoot, J.

Burges, A.
Gillespie, G.

Sept. 5, 1645 — Humiliation for Miseries of Scotland
[Cawdrey, D.]
[Gillespie, G.]
[Ward]

[Henderson, A.]
[Seaman, L.]

Sept. 22, 1645 — Funeral for William Strode
               Hickes, G.

Sept. 24, 1645 — Monthly Fast
Gibson, S.
[Temple, T.]

Gouge, W.
Whincop, J.

Oct. 2, 1645 — Thanksgiving for Victories
[Coleman, T.]
[Ley, J.]

[Ash, S.]
[Hicks (?)]

Appendices

Commons	Joint Affairs	Lords

Oct. 29, 1645 — Monthly Fast

Strickland, J.   Burges, C.
Taylor, F.   [Wilson, T.]

Nov. 5, 1645 — Powder Plot Anniversary

[Calamy, E. (?)]
[Newcomen, M. (?)]

Nov. 26, 1645 — Monthly Fast

Dury, J.   Burroughs, J.
Sterry, P.   White, J.

Dec. 31, 1645 — Monthly Fast

Foxcroft, J.   [Gower, S.]
Strong, W.   [Greenhill, W.]

*Jan. 14, 1645-6 — Humiliation for Settlement of Church
    by Parliament, Assembly, etc.*

[Marshall, S.]
Whitaker, J.

Jan. 28, 1645-6 — Monthly Fast

Caryl, J.   Evance, D.
Vines, R.   Hickes, G.

Feb. 5, 1645-6 — Thanksgiving for taking Dartmouth

[Bond, J.]   [Ley, J.]
[Harford, A.]   [Strong, W.]

Feb. 19, 1645-6 — Thanksgiving for taking Chester

Case, T.   Caryl, J.
Woodcock, F.   [Cawdrey, D.]

Feb. 25, 1645-6 — Monthly Fast

Burges, A.   Jenkyn, W.
Goodwin, T.   [Perne, A.]

*March 12, 1645-6 — Thanksgiving for Victory at
    Torrington*

[Hickes, G.]   [Bond, J.]
[Strong, W.]   [Sedgwick, O.]

Commons	Joint Affairs	Lords

March 25, 1646 — Monthly Fast
Bolton, S.   Case, T.
Cheynell, F.   [Harris, R.]

April 2, 1646 — Thanksgiving for Successes in Cornwall
Caryl, J.
Peter, H.

April 29, 1646 — Monthly Fast
Nalton, J.   [Esthorp]
Owen, J.   [Ford, T.]

May 12, 1646 — Thanksgiving for Regaining Garrisons
[Herle, C.]   [Cawdrey, D.]
Torshell, S.   [Ley, J.]

May 27, 1646 — Monthly Fast
Heyricke, R.   Taylor, F.
[Ward, J.]   [Proffett]

June 24, 1646 — Monthly Fast
[Smith, P.]   [Herle, C.]
[Spurstowe, W.]   [Johnson, R.]

July 21, 1646 — Thanksgiving for Surrender of Oxford
Cradock, W.
Wilkinson, H.

July 29, 1646 — Monthly Fast
[Caryl, J.]   Bolton, S.
[Whitaker, J.]

July 29, 1646 — Burial of Dr. Twisse
[Harris, R.]

Aug. 26, 1646 — Monthly Fast
Burroughs, J.
[Cawdrey, D.]

Sept. 8, 1646 — Humiliation for the Blessings of God
[Goodwin, T.]
[Sedgwick, O.]

Commons	Joint Affairs	Lords

Sept. 30, 1646 — Monthly Fast
Palmer, H.
[Symonds, J. (?)]

Oct. 22, 1646 — Funeral for Essex
Vines, R.

Oct. 28, 1646 — Monthly Fast
Lockyer, N.   Bridge, W.
Maynard, J.   Marshall, S.

Nov. 5, 1646 — Powder Plot Anniversary
Strong, W.   [Sedgwick, O.]

Nov. 25, 1646 — Monthly Fast
Dell, W.   Price, W.
[Love, C.]   [Ward]

Dec. 9, 1646 — Fast over Rain
[Ward, J.]   [Herle, C.]
[Whitaker, J.]   Roberts, F.

Dec. 30, 1646 — Monthly Fast
Marshall, S.   Goode, W.
Newcomen, M.   Horton, T.

Jan. 27, 1646-7 — Monthly Fast
Arrowsmith, J.   Jenkyn, W.
Sedgwick, O.   Seaman, L.

Feb. 24, 1646-7 — Monthly Fast
Greene, J.   Hardy, N.
Lightfoot, J.   Strong, W.

March 10, 1646-7 — Humiliation for Growth of Heresy
Hodges, T.   [(?)]
Vines, R.   [(?)]

March 31, 1647 — Monthly Fast
Cudworth, R.   [Hickes, G.]
Johnson, R.   [Hodges, T.]

Commons	Joint Affairs	Lords

April 28, 1647 — Monthly Fast
  Ash, S.   [Cawdrey, D.]
  Strong, W.   [Tuckney, A.]

May 26, 1647 — Monthly Fast
  Case, T.   Hussey, W.
  Hughes, G.   Valentine, T.

June 30, 1647 — Monthly Fast
  Manton, T.   [Rainbow (?)]
  Ward, N.   [Smith]

July 30, 1647 — Monthly Fast
  [Jaggard]   [Langley]
  [Whitcott]   [Love (?)]

*Aug. 12, 1647 — Thanksgiving for Restoring Parliament
                  to Honor and Freedom*
                    Marshall, S.
                    [Nye, P.]

Aug. 25, 1647 — Monthly Fast
  [Fowler]   [Caryl (?)]
  [Robinson]   [Spurstowe, W.]

Aug. 31, 1647 — Thanksgiving for Victory against Rebels
                    [Simpson, S.]
                    [Temple, T.]

Sept. 29, 1647 — Monthly Fast
  [Horton, T.]
  Valentine, T.

Oct. 27, 1647 — Monthly Fast
  [Herle, C.]
  Sterry, P.

Nov. 5, 1647 — Powder Plot Anniversary
  Bridge, W.

Nov. 24, 1647 — Monthly Fast
  Carter, W.   [Burges, A.]
  Kentish, R.   [Simpson (?)]

Commons	Joint Affairs	Lords

Dec. 29, 1647 — Monthly Fast
[Caryl, J.]
[Seaman, L.]

[Bolton, S.]
[Whitaker, J.]

Jan. 26, 1647-8 — Monthly Fast
Marshall, S.
[Wilson, T.]

[Goodwin, T.]
[Wilkinson, H.]

Feb. 23, 1647-8 — Monthly Fast
Ash, S.
[Nye, P.]

[Cawdrey, D.]
[Simpson, S.]

March 29, 1648——Monthly Fast
[Goodwin, T.]
[Whitaker, J.]

[Sedgwick, O.]
Sterry, P.

April 26, 1648 — Monthly Fast
[Gower, S.]
[Symonds (?)]

[Cawdrey, D.]
[Heyricke, R.]

May 17, 1648 — Thanksgiving for Victory in South Wales
Bridge, W.
Marshall, S.

May 31, 1648 — Monthly Fast
[Burges (?)]
[Caryl, J.]

[Strong, W.]

June 28, 1648 — Monthly Fast
Manton, T.
[Vines, R.]

July 19, 1648 — Thanksgiving
Bond, J.
[Sedgwick, O.]

July 26, 1648 — Monthly Fast
Annesley, S.
Marshall, S.

Aug. 30, 1648 — Monthly Fast
[Bolton, S.]
[Strong, W.]

[Yates (?)]

Commons	Joint Affairs	Lords

Sept. 7, 1648 — Thanksgiving for Victories
  [Bond]   [Sedgwick, O.]
  [Caryl]

Sept. 12, 1648 — Humiliation for Blessing on Treaty
                   with King
  [Marshall]   [Burges (?)]
                                           Gouge, W.

Sept. 27, 1648 — Monthly Fast
  [Arthur (?)]   [Cawdrey, D.]
  [Reyner, W.]   [Greene]

Oct. 25, 1648 — Monthly Fast
  Barker, M.   [Carter (?)]
  [Fuller (?)]   [Cawdrey, D.]

Nov. 29, 1648 — Monthly Fast
  Cokayn, G.   [Salwey, A.]
  [Sedgwick (?)]   [Ward (?)]

Dec. 8, 1648 — Humiliation
  [Caryl]
  [Marshall]
  [Peter]

Dec. 22, 1648 — Humiliation for both Houses
                   [Cokayn and/or
                       Rawlinson (?)]
                   [Peter]

Dec. 27, 1648 — Monthly Fast
  Brooks, T.   [Seaman (?)]
  Watson, T.   [Temple, T.]

Jan. 31, 1648-9 — Monthly Fast
  Cardell, J.   [Ley (?)]
  Owen, J.   [Marshall, S.]

Feb. 28, 1648-9 — Monthly Fast
  [Carter]

Commons	Joint Affairs	Lords

April 19, 1649 — Humiliation
[Caryl]
Owen, J.
Warren, J.

May 3, 1649 — Humiliation
[Goodwin]
[Knight]
[Vening]

June 7, 1649 — Thanksgiving
[Goodwin]
[Owen]

July 11, 1649 — Humiliation for Ireland
[Bond]
[Caryl]
[Strong]

Aug. 29, 1649 — Thanksgiving for Victories
Cooper, W.
[Greenhill]

Nov. 1, 1649 — Thanksgiving for Victory
[Marshall]
Sterry, P.

Nov. 5, 1649 — Powder Plot Anniversary
[Bond]

Feb. 28, 1649-50 — Humiliation
Owen, J.
Powell, V.

June 13, 1650 — Humiliation
[Caryl]
[Owen]
[Strong]

July 26, 1650 — Thanksgiving
[Bond]
[Bridge]

Appendices

Commons	Joint Affairs	Lords

Oct. 8, 1650 — Thanksgiving
  [Brooks]
  [Strong]

Nov. 5, 1650 — Powder Plot Anniversary
  [Nye]

March 13, 1650-1 — Humiliation
  [Ley (?)]
  [Owen (?)]
  [Simpson (?)]

June 4, 1651 — Humiliation
  [Caryl (?)]
  [Owen (?)]

Aug. 26, 1651 — Humiliation
  [Bond]
  [Caryl]

Sept. 23, 1651 — Humiliation
  [Caryl]
  [Lockyer]

Oct. 24, 1651 — Thanksgiving
  [Goodwin]
  Owen, J.

Nov. 5, 1651 — Powder Plot Anniversary and
                 Thanksgiving
  Sterry, P.

June 9, 1652 — Humiliation
  [Caryl]
  [Strong]

Sept. 3, 1652 — Thanksgiving
  [Strong (?)]

Oct. 13, 1652 — Humiliation
  [Feake (?)]
  [Goodwin (?)]
  Owen, J.

253

Commons	Joint Affairs	Lords

Nov. 5, 1652 — Powder Plot Anniversary
  [Barker (?)]

Jan. 31, 1652-3 — Humiliation
  [Caryl]
  [Nye]
  [Peter]   }"Prayed and Preached"
  [Strong]

March 3, 1652-3 — Humiliation
  [Ames]
  [Lockyer] }"Prayed and Preached"
  [Marshall]

April 12, 1653 (?) — Thanksgiving
  [Knight (?)]
  [Nye (?)]

APPENDIX TWO

Calendar of Printed Sermons Preached to Members of the Long Parliament

THE following list of short-titles includes all sermons which have been identified as preached before members of the Long Parliament when assembled for humiliations and thanksgivings. A few additional sermons, preached to members on other occasions, are included. The predominant number were arranged by formal request and printed by authority either of the Lords or Commons. Unless otherwise noted, individual sermons on the list were preached to Commons.

Dr. Williams's Library, Gordon Square, London, possesses a very extensive collection of sermons preached before the Long Parliament. It was assembled (in chronological order) by Dr. S. W. Carruthers, and he included notations concerning different editions and variant printings of the sermons. Research for this monograph benefited greatly from access to that collection. Virtually all of the sermons preached to members of the Long Parliament are also in the McAlpin Collection at Union Theological Seminary in New York. Some of Dr. Carruthers's notations are also available there.

The Wing reference numbers are taken from D. Wing, *Short-Title Catalogue of Books Printed in England, . . . 1641-1700*, 3 vols. (New York, 1945).

Nov. 17, 1640
Burges, Cornelius, The first sermon . . . (London, 1641). Wing B 5671. (See also B 5682-5684, 5687.)
Marshall, Stephen, A sermon (London, 1641). Wing M 776.

Nov. 29, 1640
Gauden, John, The love of truth and peace (London, 1641). Wing G 362, 363.

[*April 4, 1641*]
  [Fairclough, Samuel, The troublers troubled (London, 1641). Wing F 109.][1]
  [Wilson, Thomas, David's zeale for Zion (London, 1641). Wing W 2947.][1]
[*undetermined date(s)*]
  [Bridge, William, Babylons downfall (London, 1641). Wing B 4448.][1]
  [Case, Thomas, Two sermons (London, 1641, 1642). Wing C 845, 846.][1]
[*May 30, 1641*]
  [Symonds, Joseph, A sermon (London, 1641). Wing S 6358.][1]
  [Ho (l) mes, Nathaniel, The new world . . . (London, 1641). Wing H 2570.][1]
[*June 15, 1641*]
  [F., T. (Ford, Thomas ?), Reformation sure and stedfast (London, 1641). Wing F 1515.][1]
[*June 20, 1641*]
  [Burton, Henry, Englands bondage and hope of deliverance (London, 1641). Wing B 6162.][1]
[*undetermined date*]
  [Sedgwick, William, Scripture a perfect rule for church government (London [1643]). Wing S 2388.][1]
[*undetermined date*]
  [Simpson, Sidrach, A sermon . . . (London, 1643). Wing S 3826.][2]
Sept. 7, 1641
  Burroughs, Jeremiah, Sions joy (London, 1641). Wing B 6119.
  Marshall, Stephen, A peace-offering to God (London, 1641). Wing M 766.
Nov. 5, 1641
  Burges, Cornelius, Another sermon (London, 1641). Wing B 5668.

[1] These were exhortations not formally authorized by Commons or the Lords. They are discussed in Appendix Three, "Sermons Preached to Sundry of the House of Commons, 1641."
[2] See Ch. I, 13.

Dec. 22, 1641

Calamy, Edmund, Englands looking-glasse (London, 1641, 1642). Wing C 235-239.

Marshall, Stephen, Reformation and desolation (London, 1642). Wing M 770.

[Ussher, James, Vox Hibernae (London, 1642). Wing U 228. To the Lords.][3]

[Feb. 6, 1641-2]

[Marston, John, A sermon preached . . . (London, 1642). Wing M 817. Sunday sermon.][4]

Feb. 23, 1641-2

Calamy, Edmund, Gods free mercy to England (London, 1642). Wing C 253.

Marshall, Stephen, Meroz cursed (London, 1641, 1642, 1645). Wing M 762-764.

March 30, 1642

Burges, Cornelius, Two sermons . . . (London, 1645). Wing B 5688, 5689.

Ash, Simeon, The best refuge for the most oppressed (London, 1642). Wing A 3949.

April 27, 1642

Goodwin, Thomas, Zerubbabels encouragement to finish the temple (London, 1642). Wing G 1267, 1268.

Caryl (l), Joseph, The workes of Ephesus explained (London, 1642). Wing C 790.

May 25, 1642

Harris, Robert, A sermon (London, 1642). Wing H 875.

Sedgwick, Obadiah, England's preservation (London, 1642). Wing S 2372.

June 29, 1642

Gouge, William, The saints support (London, 1642, 1645). Wing G 1397, 1398.

Sedgwick, William, Zions deliverance and her friends duty (London, 1642, 1643). Wing S 2392, 2393.

[Cheshire, Thomas, A sermon preached . . . (London, 1642). Wing C 3781. To the Lords and Judges.][5]

3 Pirated sermon. See Ch. II, 55, n. 150.
4 See reference to this sermon, Ch. I, 13.
5 See reference to this sermon, Ch. I, 11.

July 27, 1642

Hill, Thomas, The trade of truth advanced (London, 1642). Wing H 2031.

Reynolds, Edward, Israels petition in time of trouble (London, 1642). Wing R 1256.

Aug. 31, 1642

Carter, William, Israels peace with God (London, 1642). Wing C 679A.

Sept. 28, 1642

Hodges, Thomas, A glimpse of Gods glory (London, 1642). Wing H 2314.

Wilson, Thomas, Jerichoes down-fall (London, 1643). Wing W 2948.

Oct. 26, 1642

Case, Thomas, Gods rising, his enemies scattering (London, 1644). Wing C 830.

Temple, Thomas, Christ's government in and over his people (London, 1642). Wing T 634.

Nov. 5, 1642

Newcomen, Matthew, The craft and cruelty of the churches adversaries (London, 1643). Wing N 907-908B.

Nov. 30, 1642

Herle, Charles, A payre of compasses for church and state (London, 1642). Wing H 1561.

Vines, Richard, Calebs integrity in following the Lord fully (London, 1642, 1646). Wing V 546, 547.

Dec. 28, 1642

Corbett, Edward, Gods providence (London, 1642). Wing C 6241, 6242.

Valentine, Thomas, A sermon (London, 1643). Wing V 26.

Jan. 25, 1642-3

Arrowsmith, John, The covenant-avenging sword brandished (London, 1643). Wing A 3773.

Whitaker, Jeremiah, Ejrenopojos, Christ the settlement of unsettled times (London, 1642). Wing W. 1712, 1712A.

Feb. 22, 1642-3
Bridges, W (alter), Joabs counsell, the King Davids seasonable hearing it (London, 1643). Wing B 4483A.
Ellis, John, The sole path to a sound peace (London, 1643). Wing E 592.

March 29, 1643
Lightfoot, John, Elias redivivus (London, 1643). Wing L 2053.

April 26, 1643
Ley, John, The a. fury of warre, and the b. folly of sinne (London, 1643). Wing L 1879.
Greenhill, William, The axe at the root (London, 1643). Wing G 1848.

May 31, 1643
Cheynell, Francis, Sions memento, and Gods alarum (London, 1643). Wing C 3816.
Perne, Andrew, Gospell courage (London, 1643). Wing P 1577.

June 15, 1643
Marshall, Stephen, The song of Moses (London, 1643). Wing M 789.
Sedgwick, Obadiah, Haman's vanity (London, 1643). Wing S 2374.
Calamy, Edmund, The noble-mans patterne (London, 1643). Wing C 260, 261. To the Lords.
Herle, Charles, Davids song of three parts (London, 1643). Wing H 1556. To the Lords.

June 28, 1643
Carter, Thomas, Prayers prevalencie for Israels safety (London, 1643). Wing C 668.
Palmer, Herbert, The necessity and encouragement, of utmost venturing (London, 1643). Wing P 242, 243.

July 7, 1643
Bowles, Oliver, Zeale for Gods house quickened (London, 1643). Wing B 3884. To parliament and the Assembly.

Newcomen, Matthew, Jerusalems watch-men, the Lords remembrancers (London, 1643). Wing N 911. To parliament and the Assembly.

July 21, 1643

Hill, Thomas, The militant church, triumphant over the dragon and his angels (London, 1643). Wing H 2024. To the Lords and Commons.

Spurstowe, William, Englands patterne and duty in it's monthly fasts (London, 1643). Wing S 5094. To the Lords and Commons.

July 26, 1643

Simpson, Sidrach, Reformation's preservation (London, 1643). Wing S 3825.

Conant, John, The woe and weale of Gods people (London, 1643). Wing C 5689.

Aug. 30, 1643

Coleman, Thomas, The christians course and complaint (London, 1643). Wing C 5050.

Tuckney, Anthony, The balme of Gilead (London, 1643). Wing T 3210.

Sept. 25, 1643

Nye, Philip, in [Coven, Stephen], The covenant: with a narrative of the proceedings [pp. 11ff.] (London, 1643). Wing C 6621. Covenant convention.[6]

Henderson, Alexander, in [Coven, Stephen], The covenant: with a narrative of the proceedings [pp. 26ff.] (London, 1643). Wing C 6621. Covenant convention.[6]

Sept. 27, 1643

Burges, Anthony, The difficulty of, and encouragements to a reformation (London, 1643). Wing B 5643.

Chambers, Humfry, A divine ballance to weigh religious fasts in (London, 1643). Wing C 1915.

Sept. 29, 1643

Coleman, Thomas, The hearts ingagement (London, 1643). Wing C 5052. Covenant subscription.

---

[6] These sermons were not separately published and have generally been excluded from analysis in this study.

Oct. 6, 1643
Caryl (l) , Joseph, The nature, solemnity, grounds, property, and benefits, of a sacred covenant (London, 1643) .
Wing C 782. Covenant subscription.

Oct. 25, 1643
Salwey, Arthur, Halting stigmatiz'd in a sermon (London, 1644) . Wing S 522.
Wilkinson, Henry, Babylons ruine, Jerusalems rising (London, 1643, 1644) . Wing W 2220, 2221.

Nov. 29, 1643
Bridge, William, A sermon preached . . . (London, 1643) .
Wing B 4465.
Mewe, William, The robbing and spoiling of Jacob and Israel (London, 1643) . Wing M 1950.

Dec. 15, 1643
Marshall, Stephen, Threnodia, the churches lamentation for the good man his losse (London, 1644) . Wing M 793. Funeral for John Pym.

Dec. 27, 1643
Henderson, Alexander, A sermon preached . . . (London, 1644) . Wing H 1439, 1440.
Strickland, John, Gods work of mercy, in Sions misery (London, 1644) . Wing S 5970.

Jan. 18, 1643-4
Marshall, Stephen, A sacred panegyrick (London, 1644) .
Wing M 772. To parliament, etc.

Jan. 31, 1643-4
Cawdrey, Daniel, The good man a publick good (London, 1643) . Wing C 1628.
Rutherfurd, Samuel, A sermon preached . . . (London, 1644) . Wing R 2391, 2392.

Feb. 28, 1643-4
Baillie, Robert, Satan the leader in chief . . . (London, 1643) . Wing B 468.
Young, Thomas, Hopes incouragement pointed at (London, 1644) . Wing Y 92.

March 27, 1644

Bond, John, Salvation in a mystery (London, 1644).
Wing B 3574.

Gillespie, George, A sermon preached . . . (London,
1644). Wing G 756, 757.

April 9, 1644

Case, Thomas, The root of apostacy (London, 1644).
Wing C 839.

Sedgwick, Obadiah, A thanksgiving sermon (London,
1644). Wing S 2381.

April 23, 1644

Caryl (l), Joseph, The saints thankfull acclamation at
Christs resumption of his great power and the initials
of his kingdome (London, 1644). Wing C 787.

April 24, 1644

Greene, John, Nehemiah's teares and prayers for Judah's
affliction, and the ruines and repaire of Jerusalem
(London, 1644). Wing G 1822.

Staunton, Edmund, Rupes Israelis, the rock of Israel
(London, 1644). Wing S 5342.

May 29, 1644

Hall, Henry, Heaven ravished (London, 1644). Wing
H 340.

Smith, Peter, A sermon preached . . . (London, 1644).
Wing S 4142.

June 26, 1644

Hardwick, Humphrey, The difficulty of Sions deliverance
and reformation (London, 1644). Wing H 704.

Hickes, Gaspar, The glory and beauty of Gods portion
(London, 1644). Wing H 1838.

July 18, 1644

Henderson, Alexander, A sermon preachd . . . (London, 1644). Wing H 1441, 1442. To parliament.

Vines, Richard, Magnalia Dei ab aquilone; set forth
(London, 1644, 1646). Wing V 559, 560. To parliament.

July 31, 1644
Gower, Stanley, Things now-a-doing (London, 1644).
Wing G 1462.

Aug. 13, 1644
Hill, Thomas, The season for Englands selfe-reflection
(London, 1644). Wing H 2027. To parliament.
Palmer, Herbert, The glasse of Gods providence (London, 1644). Wing P 235. To parliament.

Aug. 28, 1644
Reyner, William, Babylons ruining-earthquake (London, 1644). Wing R 1324.
Tesdale, Christopher, Hierusalem: or a vision of peace (London, 1644). Wing T 792.

Sept. 12, 1644
Coleman, Thomas, Gods unusuall answer to a solemne fast (London, 1644). Wing C 5051. To parliament.
Newcomen, Matthew, A sermon, tending to set forth (London, 1644). Wing N 913. To parliament.

Sept. 25, 1644
Proffet, Nicholas, Englands impenitencie under smiting (London, 1645). Wing P 3647.
Seaman, Lazarus, Solomons choice (London, 1644). Wing S 2177.

Oct. 22, 1644
Calamy, Edmund, Englands antidote, against the plague of civil ware (London, 1645, 1652). Wing C 233, 234.
Sedgwick, Obadiah, An arke against a deluge (London, 1644). Wing S 2364.
Vines, Richard, The posture of Davids spirit (London, 1644, 1656). Wing V 563, 564.

Oct. 30, 1644
Scudder, Henry, Gods warning to England (London, 1644). Wing S 2139.
Woodcock, Francis, Christ's warning-piece (London, 1644). Wing W 3429.
Staunton, Edmund, Phinehas's zeal in execution of judgment (London, 1645). Wing S 5341. To the Lords.

Nov. 5, 1644

Burges, Anthony, Romes cruelty & apostacie (London, 1645). Wing B 5655.[7]

Herle, Charles, Davids reserve and rescue (London, 1645, 1646). Wing H 1554, 1555.[7]

Spurstowe, William, Englands eminent judgments (London, 1644). Wing S 5093. To the Lords.[7]

Strickland, John, Immanuel (London, 1644). Wing S 5971. To the Lords.[7]

Nov. 27, 1644

Gipps, George, A sermon preached . . . (London, 1645). Wing G 779.

Pickering, Benjamin, A firebrand pluckt out of the burning (London, 1645). Wing P 2150.

Hill, Thomas, The right separation incouraged (London, 1645). Wing H 2026. To the Lords.

Wilkinson, Henry, The gainefull cost (London, 1644). Wing W 2222. To the Lords.

Dec. 25, 1644

Langley, John, Gemitus columbae: the mournfull note of the dove (London, 1644). Wing L 404.

Thorowgood, Thomas, Moderation iustified (London, 1645). Wing T 1069.

Calamy, Edmund, An indictment against England (London, 1645). Wing C 256. To the Lords.

Jan. 29, 1644-5

Walker, George, A sermon preached . . . (London, 1645). Wing W 364.

Whincop, John, Gods call to weeping and mourning (London, 1645, 1646). Wing W 1662, 1663.

Feb. 26, 1644-5

Maynard, John, A sermon preached . . . (London, 1645). Wing M 1452.

---

[7] These sermons celebrated the delivery of Newcastle and Tinmuth Castle in addition to commemorating the anniversary of the Powder Plot. Thus they represent two classes of preaching: the minor class of Powder Plot anniversary sermons and the major class of sermons preached on extraordinary occasions. (See Ch. I, 7-9.)

Ashe, Simeon, The church sinking, saved by Christ (London, 1645). Wing A 3951. To the Lords.

March 12, 1644-5

Arrowsmith, John, Englands Eben-ezer or, stone of help (London, 1645). Wing A 3775. To parliament, etc.

Vines, Richard, The happinesse of Israel (London, 1645, 1656). Wing V 551, 552. To parliament.

March 26, 1645

Goode, William, The discoverie of a publique spirit (London, 1645). Wing G 1093.

Ward, John, God judging among the gods (London, 1645). Wing W 773.

Cheynell, Francis, The man of honour, described (London, 1645). Wing C 3812. To the Lords.

Marshall, Stephen, Gods master-piece (London, 1645). Wing M 756. To the Lords.

April 30, 1645

Marshall, Stephen, The strong helper (London, 1645). Wing M 790.

Burges, Cornelius, Two sermons (London, 1645). Wing B 5688. (See also B 5680, 5681.)

May 28, 1645

Caryl(l), Joseph, The arraignment of unbelief (London, 1645). Wing C 749.

Henderson, Alexander, A sermon preached . . . (London, 1645). Wing H 1443. To the Lords.

Whitaker, Jeremiah, The christians hope triumphing (London, 1645). Wing W 1710. To the Lords.

June 19, 1645

Marshall, Stephen, A sacred record (London [1645]). Wing M 773. To parliament, etc.

June 25, 1645

Byfield, Richard, Zion's answer to the nations ambassadors (London, 1645). Wing B 6395.

Rutherfurd, Samuel, A sermon preached . . . (London, 1645). Wing R 2393. To the Lords.

Appendices

July 22, 1645

Ward, John, The good-will of him that dwelt in the bush (London, 1645). Wing W 774. To the Lords.

July 30, 1645

Coleman, Thomas, Hopes deferred and dashed (London, 1645). Wing C 5053, 5054.

Woodcock, Francis, Lex talionis: or, God paying every man (London, 1646). Wing W 3431, 3432.

Baillie, Robert, Errours and induration (London, 1645). Wing B 459. To the Lords.

Aug. 22, 1645

Bond, John, Ortus occidentalis: or, a dawning in the west (London, 1645). Wing B 3573.

Case, Thomas, A sermon preached . . . (London, 1645). Wing C 842.

Aug. 27, 1645

Lightfoot, John, A sermon preached . . . (London, 1645). Wing L 2068.

Burges, Anthony, The reformation of the church (London, 1645). Wing B 5654. To the Lords.

Gillespie, George, A sermon preached . . . (London, 1645, 1646). Wing G 758, 759. To the Lords.

[*Sept. 22, 1645*]

[Hickes, Gaspar, The life and death of David (London, 1645). Wing H 1839. Funeral for William Strode.][8]

Sept. 24, 1645

Gibson, Samuel. The ruine of the authors and fomentors of civill warres (London, 1645). Wing G 671.

Gouge, William, The progresse of divine providence (London, 1645). Wing G 1393. To the Lords.

Whincop, John, Israels tears for distressed Zion (London, 1645). Wing W 1664. To the Lords.

Oct. 29, 1645

Strickland, John, Mercy rejoycing against judgment (London, 1645). Wing S 5973.

---

8 Technically this funeral sermon does not belong to the series of sermons officially delivered to parliament; circumstantially, however, it resembles other funeral sermons which must be considered part of the pulpit in parliament.

Taylor, Francis, Gods covenant the churches plea (London, 1645). Wing T 278.

Burges, Cornelius, The necessity of agreement with God (London, 1645). Wing B 5673. To the Lords.

Nov. 26, 1645

Durye, John, Israels call to march out of Babylon unto Jerusalem (London, 1646). Wing D 2867.

Sterry, Peter, The spirit convincing of sinne (London, 1645, 1646). Wing S 5483, 5484.

Burroughs, Jeremiah, A sermon preached . . . (London, 1646). Wing B 6117. To the Lords.

White, John, The troubles of Jerusalems restauration (London, 1645, 1646). Wing W 1783, 1784. To the Lords.

Dec. 31, 1645

Foxcroft, John, The good of a good government (London, 1645). Wing F 2034.

Strong, William, Humera apokalupseus. The day of revelation (London, 1645). Wing S 6003.

Jan. 14, 1645-6

Whitaker, Jeremiah, The danger of greatnesse (London, 1646). Wing W 1711. To parliament and the Assembly.

Jan. 28, 1645-6

Caryl (l), Joseph, Heaven and earth embracing (London, 1646). Wing C 779.

Vines, Richard, The purifying of unclean hearts and hands (London, 1646). Wing V 565, 566.

Evance, Daniel, The noble order (London, 1646). Wing E 3443. To the Lords.

Hickes, Gaspar, The advantage of afflictions (London, 1645). Wing H 1837. To the Lords.

Feb. 19, 1645-6

Case, Thomas, A model of true spiritual thankfulnesse (London, 1646). Wing C 833.

Woodcock, Francis, Joseph paralled by the present parliament (London, 1646). Wing W 3430.

Caryl (l), Joseph, Joy out-joyed (London, 1646). Wing C 780. To the Lords.

Feb. 25, 1645-6

Burges, Anthony, Publick affections, pressed in a sermon (London, 1646). Wing B 5653.

Goodwin, Thomas, The great interest of states & kingdomes (London, 1646). Wing G 1246.

Jenkyn, William, Reformation's remora (London, 1646). Wing J 650. To the Lords.

March 25, 1646

Bolton, Samuel, Hamartolos hamartia: or, the sinfulnes of sin (London, 1646). Wing B 3516.

Cheynell, Francis, A plot for the good of posterity (London, 1646). Wing C 3814.

Case, Thomas, Deliverance-obstruction: or, the set-backs of reformation (London, 1646). Wing C 827. To the Lords.

April 2, 1646

Caryl (l), Joseph, Englands plus ultra (London, 1646). Wing C 751, 752. To parliament, etc.

Peter(s), Hugh, Gods doings, and mans duty (London, 1646). Wing P 1703-1705. To parliament, etc.

April 29, 1646

Nalton, James, Delay of reformation provoking Gods further indignation (London, 1646). Wing N 122.

Owen, John, A vision of unchangeable free mercy (London, 1646). Wing O 825.

May 12, 1646

Torshel (l), Sam (uel), The palace of justice opened and set to view (London, 1646). Wing T 1940.

May 27, 1646

Heyricke, Richard, Queen Esthers resolves (London, 1646). Wing H 1748, 1749.

Taylor, Francis, The danger of vowes neglected (London, 1646). Wing T 272. To the Lords.

July 21, 1646

Cradock, Walter, The saints fulnesse of joy in their fellowship with God (London, 1646). Wing C 6764, 6765.

Wilkinson, Henry, Miranda, stupenda. Or, the wonderfull and astonishing mercies (London, 1646). Wing W 2224.

July 29, 1646

Bolton, Samuel, Deliverance in the birth (London, 1647). Wing B 3519. To the Lords.

Aug. 26, 1646

Burroughs, Jeremiah, A sermon preached . . . (London, 1646). Wing B 6118.

Sept. 30, 1646

Palmer, Herbert, The duty & honour of church-restorers (London, 1646). Wing P 230.

Oct. 22, 1646

Vines, Richard, The hearse of the . . . Earle of Essex (London, 1646). Wing V 553-554A. Funeral for Essex.

Oct. 28, 1646

Lockyer, Nicholas, A sermon preached . . . (London, 1646). Wing L 2800.

Maynard, John, A shadow of the victory of Christ (London, 1646). Wing M 1453.

Bridge, William, The saints hiding-place (London, 1647). Wing B 4461. To the Lords.

Marshall, Stephen, A two-edged sword out of the mouth of babes (London, 1646). Wing M 797. To the Lords.

Nov. 5, 1646

Strong, William, [Hebrew] The commemoration and exaltation of mercy (London, 1646). Wing S 6000.

Nov. 25, 1646

Dell, William, Right reformation (London, 1646, 1650). Wing D 926-928.[9]

---

[9] The printing of this item was unsolicited, and it moved Commons to rebuke both Dell and the printer.

Price, William, Mans delinquencie (London, 1646). Wing P 3401. To the Lords.

Dec. 9, 1646

Roberts, Francis, A broken spirit, God's sacrifices (London, 1647). Wing R 1580. To the Lords.

Dec. 30, 1646

Marshall, Stephen, The right understanding of the times (London, 1647). Wing M 771.

Newcomen, Matthew, The all-seeing unseen eye of God (London, 1647). Wing N 904.

Goode, William, Jacob raised (London, 1647). Wing G 1094. To the Lords.

Horton, Thomas, Sinne's discovery and revenge (London, 1646). Wing H 2882. To the Lords.

Jan. 27, 1646-7

Arrowsmith, John, A great wonder in heaven (London, 1647). Wing A 3776.

Sedgwick, Obadiah, The nature and danger of heresies, opened (London, 1647). Wing S 2377.

Jenkyn, William, A sleeping sicknes the distemper of the times (London, 1647). Wing J 654. To the Lords.

Seaman, Lazarus, The head of the church, the judge of the world (London, 1647). Wing S 2176. To the Lords.

Feb. 24, 1646-7

Greene, John, The churches duty, for received mercies (London, 1647). Wing G 1820.

Lightfoot, John, A sermon preached . . . (London, 1647). Wing L 2069.

Hardy, Nathaniel, The arraignment of licentious liberty, and oppressing tyrannie (London, 1647, 1657). Wing H 709-711. To the Lords.

Strong, William, The way to the highest honour (London, 1647). Wing S 6013. To the Lords.

March 10, 1646-7

Hodges, Thomas, The growth and spreading of haeresie (London, 1647). Wing H 2315.

Vines, Richard, The authours, nature, and danger of haeresie (London, 1647, 1662). Wing V 545, 545A.

March 31, 1647
   Cudworth, Ralph, A sermon preached . . . (Cambridge, 1647) . Wing C 7469.
   Johnson, Robert, Lux & lex, or the light and law of Jacobs house (London, 1647) . Wing J 818.
April 28, 1647
   Ash, Simeon, Gods incomparable goodnesse unto Israel (London, 1647) . Wing A 3955.
   Strong, William, The trust and the account of a steward (London, 1647) . Wing S 6009.
May 26, 1647
   Case, Thomas, Spirituall whoredome discovered in a sermon (London, 1647) . Wing C 843.
   Hughes, George, Vae-euge-tuba. Or, the wo-joy-trumpet (London, 1647) . Wing H 3310.
   Hussey, William, The magistrates charge, for the peoples safetie (London, 1647) . Wing H 3818. To the Lords.
   Valentine, Thomas, A charge against the Jews, and the christian world (London, 1647) . Wing V 24. To the Lords. (See also V 27.)
June 30, 1647
   Manton, Thomas, Meate out of the eater (London, 1647) . Wing M 525.
   Ward, Nathaniel, A sermon preached . . . (London, 1647, 1649) . Wing W 784, 785.
Aug. 12, 1647
   Marshall, Stephen, A sermon preached . . . (London, 1647) . Wing M 779. To parliament.
Sept. 29, 1647
   Valentine, Thomas, Christs counsell to poore and naked souls (London, 1647) . Wing V 25. (See also V 27.)
Oct. 27, 1647
   Sterry, Peter, The clouds in which Christ comes (London, 1648) . Wing S 5475.
Nov. 5, 1647
   Bridge, William, England saved with a notwithstanding (London, 1648) . Wing B 4452.

Appendices

Nov. 24, 1647

Carter, William, Light in darknesse: discovered (London, 1648). Wing C 680.

Kentish, Richard, A sure stay for a sinking state (London, 1648). Wing K 320.

Jan. 26, 1647-8

Marshall, Stephen, A sermon preached . . . (London, 1647). Wing M 780.

Feb. 23, 1647-8

Ash, Simeon, Self-surrender unto God (London, 1648). Wing A 3966.

March 29, 1648

Sterry, Peter, The teachings of Christ in the soule (London, 1648). Wing S 5486. To the Lords.

May 17, 1648

Bridge, William, Christs coming opened in a sermon (London, 1648). Wing B 4451.

Marshall, Stephen, Emmanuel: a thanksgiving-sermon (London, 1648). Wing M 753.

June 28, 1648

Manton, Thomas, Englands spirituall languishing (London, 1648). Wing M 523.

July 19, 1648

Bond, John, Eshcol, or grapes (among) thorns (London, 1648). Wing B 3570.

July 26, 1648

Anne (s) ley, Samuel, A sermon preached . . . (London, 1648). Wing A 3236.

Marshall, Stephen, The sinne of hardnesse of heart (London, 1648). Wing M 783.

Sept. 12, 1648

Gouge, William, The right way (London, 1648). Wing G 1394. To the Lords.

Oct. 25, 1648

Barker, Matthew, A christian standing . . . (London, 1648). Wing B 772.

Nov. 29, 1648

Cokayn, George, Flesh expiring, and the spirit inspiring
in the new earth (London, 1648). Wing C 4902.

Dec. 27, 1648

Brooks, Thomas, Gods delight in the progresse of the
upright (London, 1649). Wing B 4941.

Watson, Thomas, Gods anatomy upon mans heart (London, 1649, 1657). Wing W 1125, 1126.

Jan. 31, 1648-9

Cardell, John, Gods wisdom justified, and mans folly
condemned (London, 1649). Wing C 492.

Owen, John, A sermon preached . . . (London, 1649).
Wing O 805.

April 19, 1649

Owen, John, Ouranon ourania. The shaking and translating of heaven and earth (London, 1649). Wing O
789.[10]

Warren, John, The potent potter (London, 1649).
Wing W 976.[10]

Aug. 29, 1649

Cooper, William, Hebrew Ierusalem fatall to her assailants (London, 1649). Wing C 6064.[10]

Nov. 1, 1649

Sterry, Peter, The comings forth of Christ in the power
of his death (London, 1650). Wing S 5476.[10]

Feb. 28, 1649-50

Owen, John, The stedfastness of promises, and the sinfulness of staggering (London, 1650). Wing O 808.[10]

Powell, Vavasor, Christ exalted above all creatures by
God his father (London, 1651). Wing P 3081. (See
also Part 2 of 3092.) [10]

---

[10] These sermons fall outside the limits of the present study. They
do indicate that only a very few of the sermons preached to the Long
Parliament between 1649 and 1653 actually reached print. (Cf. Appendix One.) The practice of preaching to parliament continued until
adjournment of the Long Parliament, but at a greatly reduced rate
and on an extraordinary rather than a regular basis.

Oct. 24, 1651

Owen, John, The advantage of the kingdome of Christ in the shaking of the kingdoms of the world (Oxford, 1651, 1652). Wing O 711, 712.[10]

Nov. 5, 1651

Sterry, Peter, England's deliverance from the northern presbytery, compared with its deliverance from the Roman papacy (London, 1652). Wing S 5478, 5479.[10]

Oct. 13, 1652

Owen, John, A sermon preached to the parliament (Oxford, 1652). Wing O 806.[10]

[10] These sermons fall outside the limits of the present study. They do indicate that only a very few of the sermons preached to the Long Parliament between 1649 and 1653 actually reached print. (Cf. Appendix One.) The practice of preaching to parliament continued until adjournment of the Long Parliament, but at a greatly reduced rate and on an extraordinary rather than a regular basis.

APPENDIX THREE

Sermons Preached to Sundry of the House of Commons, 1641

IN Chapter II mention was made of nine or ten published sermons delivered to members of the Long Parliament during the spring (and possibly early summer) of 1641. They were not part of the formal preaching before the parliament. As a group, however, they clearly anticipated, and probably helped to create support for, the system of monthly fast days (supplemented irregularly with additional humiliations and thanksgivings) which was fully operative by the spring of the following year (1642). In two of the three studies of preaching to the Long Parliament this phenomenon is basically ignored. James C. Spalding makes only passing reference to it in his recent article.[1] Hugh Trevor-Roper, on the other hand, whether intentionally or not, isolates Samuel Fairclough's sermon from others of the class and construes it as a paradigm for the pulpit in the Long Parliament.[2] Ethyn W. Kirby, while giving significant attention to them in a review of the "Sermons before the Commons, 1640-42," fundamentally fails to discriminate between these exhortations to "sundry of the house" and the broader monthly program implemented in February 1641-2.[3] Some of the critical issues raised by study of these items, especially their dates of delivery, will be discussed in this appendix.

Mrs. E. W. Kirby discovered many of the extant sermons which were originally preached to "sundry of the House of Commons." She characterizes them as "examples par excellence of propagandist literature" and remarks that the "tone of authority which the Puritan divines used seems

1 "Sermons before Parliament (1640-1649)," *Church History*, xxxvi/1 (March 1967), 29.
2 "Fast Sermons," 302-303.
3 *American Historical Review*, xliv/3 (April 1939), 534-538.

the more impressive because of their relative obscurity."[4] Her analysis is fundamentally flawed, however, because she does not recognize that the developed fast program was an institution distinct from the initial fast and test communion. At the same time, Mrs. Kirby does not generally make distinctions between the classes or types of sermons which were preached under different conditions and auspices noted in this study but, instead, assimilates these informal exhortations to the later monthly fasts.[5] Furthermore, her determination of the chronological order of the sermons is inaccurate at major points.

I. Dates of delivery for the following sermons are clearly established in each of the respective documents:

> *April 4, 1641*   Samuel Fairclough, *The Troublers Troubled* (London, 1641). Thomas Wilson, *David's Zeale for Zion* (London, 1641).
>
> *May 30, 1641*   Joseph Symonds, *A Sermon Lately Preached* (London, 1641). Nathaniel Ho[l]mes, *The New World, or the New Reformed Church* (London 1641).

Mrs. Kirby proposes July 20 as the date for Symonds's sermon, attempting to conform these sermons to the later and regular monthly sequence.[6] She appears not to have known of Homes's sermon.

> *June 15, 1641*   T. F., *Reformation Sure and Stedfast* (London, 1641).

Mrs. Kirby identifies "T. F." as Thomas Fuller, subsequently an Anglican royalist. Fuller's later loyalties do not bear on this matter, since deep divisions had not yet become so manifest as to exclude others from the pulpit who subsequently remained loyal to Charles—for example, John Gauden and George Morley.[7] Others who did preach, like Samuel Fairclough, refused to participate in deliberations about the reconstruction of the Church of England in

---

[4] *Ibid.*, 528, 529.   [5] *Ibid.*, 535.   [6] *Ibid.*, 537.
[7] *Supra*, Ch. II, 41-43.

the Westminster Assembly. It is more significant that Fuller's biographer does not claim this sermon as one of his.[8] Nor is it attributed to him in a modern critical bibliography of his works.[9] Donald Wing, following the *Catalogue of the McAlpin Collection,* assigns it to Thomas Ford, who was made a member of the Assembly on the death of Oliver Bowles and who preached in the fast program— probably not publishing the sermon(s).[10]

> *June 20, 1641*   Henry Burton, *Englands Bondage and Hope of Deliverance* (London, 1641).

Mrs. Kirby judges that "T. F." and Henry Burton might have been paired on the twentieth of June. Clearly they were not, and these sermons *may* have been sponsored under quite different auspices.

II. The dates of delivery of the additional sermons in this class have not been established with precision. Each must be considered individually.

> William Bridge, *Babylons Downfall* (London, 1641).

Mrs. Kirby alleges that this sermon was preached on May 5 on the evidence of the following entry in the *Commons Journals* under April 28, 1641: "Mr. Rouse reports for the Committee for a Fast, the Motives, conceived by that Committee, for a Fast."[11] It is clear that Commons decided to approach the Lords on this subject, but it is equally certain that the project came to nought. Without any warrant Mrs. Kirby appears to have identified Bridge's sermon with this reference.[12] The document carries the notice that Dering's committee authorized its publication on April 6, 1641.[13] It was subsequently registered with the Stationer's Company on April 28. In sum, Bridge's *Babylons Downfall* was

---

8 John E. Bailey, *The Life of Thomas Fuller, D.D. with notices of his books* (London, 1874).

9 S. Gibson, *A Bibliography of the Works of Thomas Fuller, D.D.* (Oxford, 1936).

10 *Short-Title Catalogue . . . 1641-1700* (New York, 1945).

11 II, 129.

12 *Op.cit.,* 535.   13 *Babylons Downfall,* 34.

certainly preached, and quite possibly published, before the date Mrs. Kirby proposes for its delivery. One might argue that, like the sermons of Fairclough and Wilson, this one was preached on April 4, a Sunday, at Westminster. This solution would explain the date of the action in Dering's committee. If this was indeed the date, it further calls into question the emphasis Trevor-Roper places on Fairclough's sermon as by itself distinctly ennunciating a decisive shift in Pym's tactics toward Strafford, apart from the more general context of puritan struggle for reform of "church and commonwealth." If this sermon was preached *before* April 4, its fundamental similarity to the sermons delivered on that date suggests that Fairclough's exhortation did not intentionally herald such a basic shift in tactics. This observation is equally damaging to Trevor-Roper's exclusive interpretation of the sermons before parliament as vehicles for declaring changes in policy.

Thomas Case, *Two Sermons Lately Preached at Westminster* (London, 1641).

Mrs. Kirby postulates an August date for this item apparently as a way of filling out the monthly sequence which she thinks already existed.[14] Since the first edition of these two separate sermons was entered in the Stationer's *Register* on May 24, 1641, her deduction is certainly wrong. The entry in the *Register* may be used to argue for the latest possible date of preaching, since the time between delivery and publication might vary considerably: Wilson's, for example, was entered on May 28 and Fairclough's on July 15 —both having been preached on April 4. Many of Mrs. Kirby's errors result from her attempt to assimilate the sermons under consideration to the monthly pattern of fasts adopted at the end of the year. This document actually contains two separate sermons, without obvious connection or continuity, each of which appears to belong in this class. The subject of the first, church reform, might argue

14 *Op.cit.*, 535, 537-538.

for its delivery during April and May, when the Root and Branch agitation was a primary interest of parliament. The second, an exhortation to national and personal convenanting, explicitly echoed the theme Marshall and Burges had presented at the initial fast in the Long Parliament.[15] No precise dating of these sermons has been possible.

William Sedgwick, *Scripture a Perfect Rule For Church Government* (London [1643?]).

This item is not identified by Mrs. Kirby. Since it does not have a date of publication, it may have actually originated outside the limits (April through June 1641) during which the preceding sermons appear to have been preached and often printed. In theory the Thomason *Catalogue* ought to be helpful at this point.[16] Apparently George Thomason did not manage to purchase this particular item, however, and so it is not included. In her attempt to reconstruct the order in which these sermons were preached, Mrs. Kirby generally takes the dating of the *Catalogue* too much at face value. Without exception she follows the sequence in which the above items are listed in the *Catalogue*. It certainly is possible, as was suggested above, that the sermon by Bridge and also one or both by Case were in fact preached prior to those by Fairclough and Wilson on April 4. Unfortunately, the dates given in the Thomason *Catalogue* for these early months of his collection are not based upon Thomason's own notations of the day on which he purchased the item —a practice he soon adopted as he sensed the scope of his project in the mounting volume of publications. In sum, the dates—and therefore the order—attributed to items in the early sections of this *Catalogue* are expressions of editorial opinion, not Thomason's notations regarding date of purchase. The *Catalogue of the McAlpin Collection* as-

15 T. Case, *Two Sermons* . . . (London, 1641), 17 (second series of pages).

16 *Catalogue of the Pamphlets* . . . *collected by George Thomason, 1640-1661*, 2 vols. (London, 1908).

signs the date 1643 to this sermon by William Sedgwick, possibly because that is the date suggested in the *Dictionary of National Biography*. No direct evidence for this date has been discovered, though.

The existence of this class of quasi-official exhortations to the Long Parliament during the spring months of 1641 does pose a series of interesting questions. Were the individual patrons of the particular preachers chiefly responsible for this effort, arranging both opportunities and locations? Did this, on the other hand, in any sense represent a coherent program of puritan preaching to the members of Commons? If actually a program, was it far more extensive than is suggested by the available materials presently identified with it? Further, was the preaching generally radical (especially if the sermon "T. F." preached was not fully part of this group)? And, if concentrated in April and May, how directly was it correlated with the specific agitation over reform of the church which mounted during this period? A general search for answers to these and similar questions has not been successful. Conceivably an exhaustive review of manuscript diaries and private letter collections might produce some clues.[17] In the present monograph these exhortations assume importance as anticipations of the extensive preaching in the fast program developed during the following months. That is the setting within which they have been considered in the text of this study.

[17] Mrs. Kirby does note in passing some contemporary comments about the significance of preaching before parliament. Similarly, Trevor-Roper mentions notices which he has discovered. Unfortunately, these fragmentary and biased secondary references do not constitute a bank of floodlights on the phenomenon.

Index

Allen, Francis, 105, 107
Allen, Matthew, 105
Alstedius (J. H. Alsted), 214, 228
Annesley, Samuel, 128n, 129, 250, 272; quoted, 206
apocalypticism: dependence on continental sources, 214; English authorities, 214ff; fascination with calendrical speculation, 211f; manifesting breakdown of puritan brotherhood, 231f; prophetic eschatology contrasted, 198-214. *See also* millenarianism
Apologeticall Narration, 77
Archer, John, 225, 228
Arrowsmith, John, 68, 91, 124, 175n, 181n, 240, 244, 248, 258, 265, 270; quoted, 204f
Ash, Simeon, 113-115, 156n, 157, 169, 182, 188n, 239, 244, 245, 249, 250, 257, 265, 271, 272; discussion of sermon by, 160f; sermon quoted, 173f
Ashurst (Ashenhurst), William, 104

Baillie, Robert, 76, 84, 85, 121, 153n, 177, 185, 225n, 228, 242, 245, 261, 266
Balcanquhall, Walter, preacher to 1628 fast, 33
Bargrave, Isaac, analysis of sermon by, 27f
Barker, Matthew, 128f, 251, 254, 272
Barnardiston, Sir Nathaniel, 44
Barrington, Sir Thomas, 41n, 101n, 104, 106n
Bastwick, John, 50
Bell, Mr., 16
Blakiston, John, 103f
Blench, J. W., 138
Bolton, Samuel, 114, 188n, 247, 250, 268, 269; discussion of sermon by, 164
Bond, John, 77, 93, 117-119, 242, 245, 246, 250, 251, 252, 253, 262, 266, 272

Bowles, Oliver, 71, 126, 187, 241, 259, 277
Bray, William, 15
Bridge, William, 46f, 52, 68n, 75, 89, 92f, 101n, 107, 117f, 122f, 179, 182, 242, 248, 249, 250, 252, 256, 261, 269, 271, 272, 277ff; sermon quoted, 193
Bridges, Walter, 68f, 128n, 129, 175, 240, 259
Brightman, Thomas, 211, 215-217, 221-223
Brooks, Thomas, 94, 101n, 128f, 251, 253, 273
Broughton, Hugh, 211, 215
Brounrick, Dr., to preach at test sacrament (1640), 36
Brown, J., 6n
Brown, Louise F., 28n
Burges, Anthony, 74, 81, 113, 116n, 172n, 187f, 242, 244, 245, 246, 249, 250, 251, 260, 264, 266, 268
Burges, Cornelius, 12-13, 86n, 106, 115f, 154, 169n, 184f, 239, 244, 246, 255, 256, 257, 265, 267, 279; probable preacher to fast (1628), 34; sermon at fast opening Long Parliament, 37, 39ff, 43; sermon on Nov. 5, 1641, 54; sermon at second monthly fast, 64; sermon quoted, 37f, 40f, 144, 201, 204
Burroughs, Jeremiah, 86, 89, 122, 186n, 227f, 239, 246, 247, 256, 267, 269; sermon at thanksgiving (1641), 52f
Burton, Henry, 49ff, 227, 256, 277
Byfield, Richard, 127n, 245, 265

Calamy, Edmund, 14, 70, 79f, 82, 88f, 103, 114n, 115f, 153n, 168f, 177, 188f, 239, 241, 243, 244, 246, 257, 259, 263, 264; discussion of sermon by, 158f, 183f; preaches at 1641 humiliation, 55f; sermon at first monthly fast, 63; sermon quoted, 56, 201
Calder, I. M., 28n

Index

Cambridge (University):
Emmanuel College, significance
of, 134; wide representation of
colleges through preachers, 134
Canne, John, 225, 227n
Cardell, John, 95, 128n, 129, 251,
273
Carruthers, S. W., 255
Carter, Thomas, 126, 241, 259
Carter, William, 66, 117-119, 152n,
182n, 187n, 240, 249, 251, 258,
272
Caryl(l), Joseph, 15, 64n, 73, 78,
84, 85f, 94, 106, 107, 110-113,
153n, 154, 155, 168n, 170n, 171,
180, 186n, 223, 239, 242, 243, 245,
246, 247, 249, 250, 251, 252, 253,
254, 257, 261, 262, 265, 267, 268;
sermon quoted, 83, 209, 213
Case, Thomas, 16, 47f, 77f, 113f,
155, 169, 178, 181, 185, 237, 240,
242, 245, 246, 247, 249, 256, 258,
262, 266, 267, 268, 271, 278f
Cawdrey, Daniel, 77, 92, 117-120,
242, 245, 246, 247, 249, 250, 251,
261
Cecil, Sir Edward, proposes fast,
26
Chambers, Humphrey, 74, 79, 124,
164, 186, 242, 243, 245, 260
Charles I: agreement to fast (1628),
33; alleged relations with Irish
Catholics, 54; assent to fast
(1640), 36; authorizes monthly
fast program, 60f; comments on
power of pulpit, 96; death of,
10; duplicity revealed, 70; flight
to Scots (1646), 87; Hugh
Peter's role at death of, 133;
link between puritan rhetoric
and death of, 192; negotiations
with Army (1648), 94; personal
celebration of fast (1625), 32;
puritan denigration of authority
of, 232ff; puritan suspicion of
perfidy of, 63; relations with
Scots (1641), 52; sermons at
death of, 163; supporters rally
at York, 65; tactical advantage
(1644), 79; tactics (1642), 67;
trial and execution, 95

Cheshire, Thomas, 80n, 257
Cheynell, Francis, 70n, 82, 124,
175, 187n, 190, 241, 244, 247,
259, 265, 268
Clarendon, 70n; quoted, 12-13
Cokayn, George, 94, 128n, 129,
251, 273
Coleman, Thomas, 73, 79, 85, 115,
152n, 154, 169, 171, 182, 241,
242, 243, 245, 260, 263, 266;
sermon quoted, 190
Comenius, 42
Conant, John, 127n, 179, 241, 260
Cooper, William, 252, 273
Corbett, Edward, 68, 101n, 127n,
168, 240, 258
Corbett, M., 101n
Corbett, Sir John, 101n
Cotton, John, 255f, 228
Covenant, theological as applied
to England, 168ff
Cradock, Walter, 87f, 132, 247,
269
Cromwell, Oliver, 81, 87, 90, 98,
106, 119; John Owen, favorite
of, 133
Cross, Claire, 20n
Cudworth, Ralph, 131, 188, 248,
271

Davies, Godfrey, 6
Davies, Horton M., 6n
Dell, William, 88, 89, 92n, 105,
131f, 167n, 238n, 248, 269
Dering's committee, 44n, 278
Dering, Sir Edward, 45
D'Ewes, Sir Simonds, 105
"dissenting brothers" of the
Westminster Assembly, 52, 117f;
as preachers, 89
Downing, Calibut, 130n, 131, 240
Dury, John, 42, 86, 131, 246, 267
Dyke, Jeremiah, 33, 37; discussion
of sermon to fast (1628), 34f

Edwards, Thomas, 225n
Elizabeth I, response to puritan
proposals, 22f
Ellis, John, 128n, 129, 182n, 240,
259

English history as interpreted by preachers, 173f

Essex, Earl of, 8

Esthorpe, Reuben, 130n, 247

Evance (Evans), Daniel, 128n, 152n, 246, 267

Fairclough, Samuel, 44f, 51, 256, 276, 278f

Fawne, Luke, 237

Feoffees scheme, 28

Fitz-Jeoffrey, Mr., preacher to fast (1628-9), 35

Ford, Thomas, 130n, 245, 247, 277. *See also* F., T.

Fowler, Matthew or Richard, 130n, 249

Foxcroft, John, 86n, 127n, 246, 267

Foxe, John, *Book of Martyrs* presupposed, 173, 202, 222

F., T. (Ford, Thomas?), 48f, 256, 276f, 280

Fuller, Thomas, 276f

Gardiner, Samuel R., 14n, 32n, 41n, 54n, 64n, 67n, 70n, 73n, 81n, 86n, 87n

Gauden, John, 239, 255, 276; sermon at test sacrament for Long Parliament, 41f; sermon compared with Marshall's and Burges's, 43

Gellibrand, Samuel, 238

Gerard, Sir Gilbert, 105, 106n

Gibbons, Dr. or John, 130n, 241

Gibson, Samuel, 127n, 181n, 245, 266; sermon quoted, 206f

Gillespie, George, 76, 78, 85, 121f, 187, 242, 245, 262, 266

Gipp(e)s, George, 81n, 127n, 175, 244, 264

Glow, Lotte, 107n

Gooch, G. P., 229n, 230n

Goode, William, 124n, 188n, 238, 244, 248, 265, 270; sermon quoted, 205

Goodwin, A., 101n

Goodwin, Thomas, 64n, 89, 101n, 117f, 122, 170n, 191, 212, 223, 225, 239, 246, 247, 250, 252, 253,

257, 268; discussion of sermon by, 209; tracts attributed to, 226ff

Gordon, Alexander, 215n, 217n, 218

Gouge, William, 65, 72, 93, 123, 191, 192f, 194, 207, 240, 245, 251, 257, 266, 272; discussion of sermon by, 162f; sermon quoted, 205f

Gower, Stanley, 125, 223, 243, 246, 250, 263; apocalyptic calculations, 211

Grantham, William, 238

Greene, John, 78, 125, 187n, 191, 243, 248, 251, 262, 270

Greenhill, William, 69f, 127n, 176, 241, 246, 252, 259; sermon quoted, 210

Guy Fawkes Day, *see* Powder Plot

Hall, Henry, 127n, 151, 173n, 192, 243, 262; sermon quoted, 212f

Hall, Joseph, 228

Haller, William, 4, 5, 50n, 110, 114n, 173n

Hardy, Nathaniel, 128n, 167n, 248, 270

Hardwick, Humphrey, 127n, 187n, 243, 262

Harford, A., 130n, 246

Harley, Sir Robert, 102f, 107

Harris, John, D.D., 119

Harris, Robert, 65, 123, 186n, 240, 247, 357; preacher to fast (1628-9), 35; proposed as preacher to fast (1628), 33; sermon quoted, 204

Hartlib, Samuel, 42

Heimert, Alan, 64

Henderson, Alexander, 72f, 76, 78, 84, 121f, 170, 195, 241, 242, 243, 245, 260, 261, 262, 265; sermon quoted, 205

Herle, Charles, 16, 67, 70, 81, 113, 240, 241, 244, 247, 248, 249, 258, 259, 264; sermon quoted, 204

Hexter, J. H., 107n

Heylyn, P., 32n, 33n

Heyrick(e), Richard, 127n, 247, 250, 268

Hickes, Gasper, 114, 172n, 243, 245, 246, 248, 262, 266, 267

Hill, Christopher, 5, 30n

Hill, Thomas, 16, 66, 71, 79, 81, 82, 115f, 173, 191n, 240, 241, 243, 244, 258, 260, 263, 264; sermon quoted, 204, 210

Hobbes, Thomas, 3-4, 5, 6, 234

Hodges, Thomas, 91, 114, 154, 178, 240, 245, 248, 258, 270

Holdsworth, Richard, 29; chosen to preach at fast (1640), 36

Holles, Denzil, 105

Homes (Holmes), Nathaniel, 48, 51, 227, 256, 276

Hooker, Thomas, 225

Horton, Thomas, 128, 177n, 238, 248, 249, 270

Howell, W. S., 139n

Hughes, George, 128n, 129, 153n, 192, 249, 271

Hussey, William, 128n, 172n, 249, 271

Hyde, Edward, 64. *See also* Clarendon

Independency, as religious party, 110, 120, 122, 133

Independent, as political label, 106n; clerics come to prominence, 90

Independent preachers: characterized by millenarianism, 223-30; frequency of preaching to Commons, 134f; issue *The Apologeticall Narration*, 77; relations with Bay Colony puritans, 92

Ireby, Sir Anthony, 104

Jackson, Arthur, quoted, 221

Jaggard, Richard, 130n, 249

Jenkyn, William, 128, 181n, 246, 248, 268, 270

Johnson (Johnston), Robert, 126, 247, 248, 271

Kentish, Richard, 128n, 129, 185, 249, 272

Kirby, Ethyn W., 41n, 44n, 50n, 135f, 275-280

Knightley, Richard, 104f

Langley, John, 127n, 152n, 192n, 244, 249, 264

Laud, William: destruction of begun, 80f; discussion of sermon, 32f; preaches at opening of Parliament (1625-6), 32f, (1627-8), 33; preaches at Whitehall (1625), 32

Ley (Leigh), John, 69, 114, 241, 245, 246, 247, 251, 253, 259

Lightfoot, John, 130f, 163, 185n, 194, 241, 245, 248, 259, 266, 270

Lincoln's Inn, location of thanksgiving (Sept. 1641), 52

Lockyer, Nicholas, 128f, 168n, 248, 253, 254, 269

London, Lord Mayor of, participation in fasts and thanksgivings, 9

Long Parliament: calendar of humiliations, thanksgivings, and preachers, 237ff; classes of preaching to, 7-9, 137f; House of Lords abolished, 95; humiliations (monthly) authorized by (Dec. 1641), 54ff, (Oct. 1644), 80; purge by Colonel Pride, 15, 94; Rump continues sitting, 94ff; Rump preached to, 117, 120, 133; Solemn League and Covenant, 8, 72ff; test sacrament at opening of, 41f

Fasts: arranged *ad hoc* by Commons, 15; as ritual humiliations, 184; discipline of members on fast days, 17; private (Dec. 1645), 82, (Dec. 1648), 94; proposed, 36f; routine of sitting, 98f; with Westminster Assembly (1643), 71

Monthly fast program: adopted by Lords (1644), 62, 80, 99; as national institution, 60f; authorized by Charles I,

60; clerical participants,
108-136; decisive changes in, 95f;
end of institution, 96; first of
Commons monthly fasts, 63f,
last of, 96; generalizations
about preachers, 108f, 116f,
120, 121f, 125, 126-128, 129,
133-136; less useful for study
after 1646, 90; occasionally
preachers denied invitation to
print sermons, 88, 92, 95, 131f,
167n; originally proposed by
Commons, 57; prayer added to
preaching, 85; pulpit restricted
to Westminster divines, 65;
specific arrangements for, 61f;
sponsors in Commons, 99-107
    Preaching to, 7ff; abridged,
10; daily service sponsored by
Commons, 16; reaches plateau
(1645-1646), 82f; sermons to
sundry members (1641), 43ff,
51f, 275ff; Sunday preaching
sponsored by Commons, 16;
Wednesday exhortations
sponsored by Commons, 16-17
Love, Christopher, 130n, 248, 249
Low Countries: cited as precedent
for fast, 26; expatriates in, 48,
52, 122, 132

Maclear, James F., 34n
Manton, Thomas, 93, 128, 187n,
249, 250, 271, 272
Marshall, Stephen, 12-13, 15, 16,
72, 82, 84, 86, 87, 88, 90f, 92,
93, 94, 95, 100, 101n, 103, 105,
109-113, 114n, 115, 116, 118,
151, 153f, 155, 167, 169, 170n,
177, 179, 181, 186n, 189, 190,
193, 210, 221, 223, 238n, 239,
241, 242, 244, 245, 246, 248, 249,
250, 251, 252, 254, 255, 256, 257,
259, 261, 265, 269, 270, 271, 272,
279; preacher at funeral for
Pym, 75f; sermon at fast
opening Long Parliament, 37ff,
43; sermon at first monthly
fast, 63f, 71; sermon at
humiliation (1641), 56f;

sermon at thanksgiving
(1641), 52f; sermon at
thanksgiving (1643-4), 77; to
preach at fast (1640), 36;
sermon(s) quoted, 53, 56f, 201f,
232f
Marston, John, 13, 257
Masham, Sir William, 100, 102n,
103
Massachusetts Bay Company, 28
May, Thomas, 70n
Maynard, John, 124, 151f, 168n,
213, 244, 248, 264, 269; sermon
quoted, 212
Mead (Mede), Joseph, 211,
217-223, 228
Melton, Sir John, 103
Mew, James, 215n
Mewe, William, 127n, 179, 242,
261
millenarianism, as manifestation
of breakdown of puritan
brotherhood, 231f
Millennium: conception of
within Puritanism, 222f; critical
to Independency, 223ff;
important place of in
Puritanism during 1640's, 212f
Miller, Perry, 30n, 138, 139n, 142n,
156n, 180n
Mitchell, W. F., 138
Morgan, I., 30n
Morley, George, 41, 239, 276

Nalton, James, 87, 128n, 171n, 247,
268
Neale, J. E., 37n
Newcomen, Matthew, 66, 67, 71,
79, 91, 114n, 115f, 152n, 177n,
178n, 185, 186n, 205, 240, 241,
243, 244, 246, 248, 258, 260, 263,
270
New Model Army, success
acknowledged, 84
Nicholas, Anthony, 105
Nuttall, Geoffrey F., 47n, 132n,
225n, 232n
Nye, Philip, 16, 72f, 89, 117f, 121,
122, 170f, 241, 244, 249, 250,
253, 254, 260

Owen, John, 87, 89, 95, 96, 108, 133, 168n, 247, 251, 252, 253, 268, 273, 274; discussion of sermon by, 163

Oxford (University), wide representation of colleges among preachers, 134

Palmer, Herbert, 16, 79, 115, 183n, 186n, 188, 241, 243, 248, 259, 263, 269

parliament (1625-6), preaching on opening day, 32f

parliament (1627-8), fast at first session, 33ff; fast at second session, 35; preaching on opening day, 33; test sacrament at, 33

parliament (1640) [Short Parliament], fast scheduled, re-scheduled, 35f; test sacrament scheduled, re-scheduled, 36

parliamentary fast days, proposed by Commons under Elizabeth I, 22f; proposed by Commons under James I (1614), 23ff, (1620-1), 25f, (1623-4), 26ff; proposed under Charles I (1625), 29ff, (1627-8), 33f, (1628-9), 35, (1640), 35f

parliamentary preaching as means of interpreting Puritanism during civil wars, 197ff

parliamentary sermons: authorized *ad hoc* in Long Parliament, 14; classes of in Long Parliament, 7-12; percentage published, 11; preached to sundry members of the Long Parliament, 227f, 275-280. *See also* Long Parliament

Pearl, Valerie, 107n

Perkins, William, 139

Perne (Pearne), Andrew, 70n, 115f, 241, 243, 244, 246, 259

Peter, Hugh, 15, 86f, 89, 94, 95, 132f, 152n, 167, 247, 251, 254, 268

Pickering, Benjamin, 81n, 127n, 153n, 183, 244, 264

plain style preaching: general structure of, 141-143; method deemphasized, 164f

Porter, H. C., 139n

Powder Plot: annual commemoration (1641), 54, (1642), 66, (1645), 81; background to Jacobean proposals, 24; sermons in Long Parliament, 178

Powell, Vavasor, 96, 252, 273

preachers to parliament, authority of, 136, 167. *See also* Long Parliament

Presbyterian: as political label, 106n; clerics lose position, 89; strain of Erastianism among English, 85

Presbyterianism, as religious party, 110, 119f

Preston, John, 37; analysis of fast sermon (1625), 29-31

Price, William, 127n, 186n, 248, 270

Prideaux, Sir Edmund, 105, 106n

Proffett, Nicholas, 79n, 127n, 179, 243, 247, 263

Prynne, William, 50

puritan doctrine: collective eschatology, 189-196; collective piety, 185-187; divine judgment, 180-183; kingship of Christ, 191-194; Millennium, 192-195; reformation of the church, 187-189; salvation of the nation, 183-189; troubles of the time, 174-183

Puritanism: biblicism of, 18-20; construction of English history associated with, 20; constructive phase ended, 97; convictions of movement articulated in preaching, 135f; development of, 31n; differentiation of during civil war, 229ff; doctrines of render times intelligible, 165, 166-196; interpreted through preaching, 198ff; perspective upon adopted in study, 234f

puritan preachers, presuppositions of, 202f

puritan preaching in plain style, 139-146

puritan sermons, Deuteronomic interpretation of inadequate, 202ff

puritans return from New England, 132f

puritan teaching regarding collective entities, 168-174

puritan use of apocalyptic and prophetic materials, 200-214; contrast between, 198-200

Putney debates (1647), 91

Pym, John, 8, 41, 44, 67, 68, 69, 70, 75f, 87, 98, 102, 104, 105, 106, 107, 109, 278

Ramist logic, 140f

Ramus, Petrus, 139f

Rathband, William (?), 130n, 243

Reyner, William, 127n, 153n, 175, 243, 251, 263

Reynolds, Edward, 66, 126, 185, 204n, 240, 258

Richardson, Carolyn F., 6n

Roberts, Francis, 90, 128n, 129, 248, 270

Robinson, Ralph, 130n, 249

Rogers, John, 227

Rolle, John, 101n

Rous, Francis, 102, 103, 105, 277

Rutherford, Samuel, 76, 121, 242, 245, 261, 265; discussion of sermon by, 164f

sacrament as test communion, 23-25, 26-28, 36

St. John, Oliver, 41, 105, 106n

St. Margaret's, Westminster, 52; location of Commons monthly fast program, 61f; location of test communion (1614), 24, (1640), 36; regular preaching sponsored in by Commons, 16

St. Martin-in-the-Fields, Lords fasts moved to, 238

Salwey, Arthur, 74f, 127n, 189n, 242, 251, 261

Salwey, Humphrey, 102n, 103

Scots: Charles I's flight to, 87; negotiations with English Commissioners (1643), 72

Scottish Commissioners to Westminster Assembly, 72, 121f; invited to preach before Commons fasts, 76f; before Lords fasts, 83ff

scriptural interpretation, 143, 145f

scripture: choice of texts in preaching, 146-155; viewed as precedential, 143ff

Scudder, Henry, 127n, 172, 244, 263

Seaman, Lazarus, 79n, 114f, 153n, 243, 245, 248, 250, 251, 263, 270; discussion of sermon by, 162

Sedgwick, Obadiah, 51, 65, 71, 79f, 82, 91, 94, 110-113, 155, 162n, 169, 178, 181, 240, 241, 242, 243, 244, 245, 246, 247, 248, 250, 251, 257, 259, 262, 263, 270; discussion of sermon by, 157f

Sedgwick, William ("Doomsday"), 51, 65, 128n, 129, 152n, 175, 240, 256, 257, 279f; sermon quoted, 210

Shaw, W. A., 65n, 68n, 71n, 72n, 74n, 81n, 125n, 130n, 132n

Shepard, Thomas, 225

Shute, Josias, 29

Sibbes, Richard, 221

Simpson, Alan, 18n

Simpson, Sidrach, 13, 72n, 124, 188n, 241, 249, 250, 253, 256, 260

Smith, Peter (or Brockett), 88, 123, 185, 243, 244, 247, 249, 262; discussion of sermon by, 161

Solemn League and Covenant, 170f, 205; drafting of, 72; parallel to parliamentary test sacrament, 74; ratified by Scotland, 72; relationship to fast program, 62f; subscribed to at Westminster, 72f

Index

Solt, Leo, 6, 13n, 77n
Spalding, James, 147n, 202f, 275
Spurstowe, W., 101n
Spurstowe, William, 71f, 81, 88,
    101n, 114f, 186n, 241, 244, 247,
    249, 260, 264
Stationer's Company, 277f
Staunton, Edmund, 16, 78, 80,
    124, 179, 181n, 243, 244, 262,
    263; discussion of sermon by,
    159f
Stearns, R. P., 86n, 87n, 95n, 133n
Sterry, Peter, 89, 92, 96, 117-119,
    177n, 188, 246, 249, 250, 252,
    253, 267, 271, 272, 273, 274;
    sermon quoted, 213
Stoughton, John, 131
Strickland, John, 76, 81, 124, 179,
    183n, 237, 242, 244, 246, 261,
    264, 266
Strong, William, 89, 107, 117f,
    152n, 172n, 177n, 212, 223, 246,
    248, 249, 250, 252, 253, 254, 267,
    269, 270, 271
Stuart policy toward puritans,
    contrasted with Elizabeth's, 57f
Symonds, Joseph, 48, 51, 130n,
    227, 248, 250, 256, 276

Talon, Omer, *see* Ramus, Petrus
Taylor, Francis, 86n, 123, 152n,
    171n, 246, 267, 268
Temple Church, location of
    parliamentary services, 24f
Temple, Sir John, 101n
Temple, Thomas, 66, 79, 101n,
    124n, 191n, 240, 243, 245, 249,
    251, 258
Tesdale, Christopher, 127n, 187n,
    243, 263
thanksgiving celebrations: for
    reconciliation of England and
    Scotland, 52; for Marston Moor
    and York, 78
Thomason, George, 279
Thurgood (Thoroughgood),
    Thomas, 82, 127n, 244, 264
Torshel(l), Samuel, 128n, 247, 268
Trevor-Roper, Hugh R., 5, 13n,
    15, 34n, 36n, 41n, 42, 43n, 44,

45, 51, 61, 63, 68, 69n, 70n, 76n,
    80, 81n, 82n, 83n, 85, 87, 92n, 94,
    95n, 96n, 98, 101n, 105f, 110,
    131, 133n, 214n, 275, 278, 280n
Tuckney, Anthony, 72n, 127n,
    154, 241, 249, 260
Twisse, William, 130n, 221, 241

Underdown, D., 107n
Ussher, James, Archbishop of
    Armagh, 55n, 148n, 239, 257;
    preacher in 1620-1, 25f

Valentine, Thomas, 68, 114, 186n,
    189n, 240, 244, 249, 258, 271
Vane, Sir Henry, 41, 81, 82, 106
Vines, Richard, 67, 78, 79, 91,
    110-113, 122, 154, 155, 168, 169,
    177, 178, 240, 241, 243, 244, 245,
    246, 248, 250, 258, 262, 263, 265,
    267, 269, 270

Walker, George, 127n, 177, 244,
    264; sermon quoted, 203n
Waller's Plot, 70
Walzer, Michael, 5, 234n
Ward, John, 84n, 117f, 244, 245,
    248, 251, 265, 266; sermon
    quoted, 206n
Ward, Nathaniel, 92, 118n, 132,
    167n, 238n, 249, 271
Warren, John, 96, 252, 273
Warwick, Earl of, 104
Watson, Thomas, 95, 101n, 128n,
    129, 131n, 167n, 251, 273;
    discussion of sermon, 155f
Web(b), Nathanael, 238
Wentworth, Sir Peter, 104
Westfield, Dr., 29
Westlake, H. F., 25n
Westminster Abbey: location of
    Lords fast program, 62; Lords
    fasts moved from, 238; regular
    services in sponsored by
    Commons, 16; rejected as
    location of test communion
    (1614), 23f
Westminster Assembly: *Directory*,
    141f; "dissenting brethren" of,
    117f, 122, 124; early work of, 72;

failure to shape national church,
89; members of preach less
frequently after 1646, 88;
preachers to parliament reflect
geographical representation of,
134; preaching basically by
members of, 7, 11; preaching
reflects failure to resolve issues
in, 176f; thanksgivings and fasts
joined in by members of, 9
Wheler (Wheeler), William, 16,
104, 107
Whichcote (Whitcott), Benjamin,
130n, 131, 249
Whincop, John, 123, 182, 238,
244, 245, 264, 266
Whitaker, Jeremy, 16, 68, 84, 86,
113, 152n, 175, 194f, 240, 245,
246, 247, 248, 250, 258, 265, 267
White, John, 72, 126, 246, 267;
sermon quoted, 144
Wilkinson, Henry, 75, 81, 114,
180, 187n, 242, 244, 250, 261,
264, 269; sermon quoted, 211
Wilson, John F., 225n, 227n
Wilson, Thomas, 45ff, 66, 124, 240,
246, 250, 256, 258, 276, 278f
Woodcock, Francis, 124f, 180, 193,
211f, 244, 245, 246, 263, 266, 267
Woodhouse, A.S.P., 4f, 91n

Yelverton, Sir Christopher, 105
Young, Thomas, 77, 114n, 127n,
152n, 186n, 242, 261
Yule, George, 107, 111n